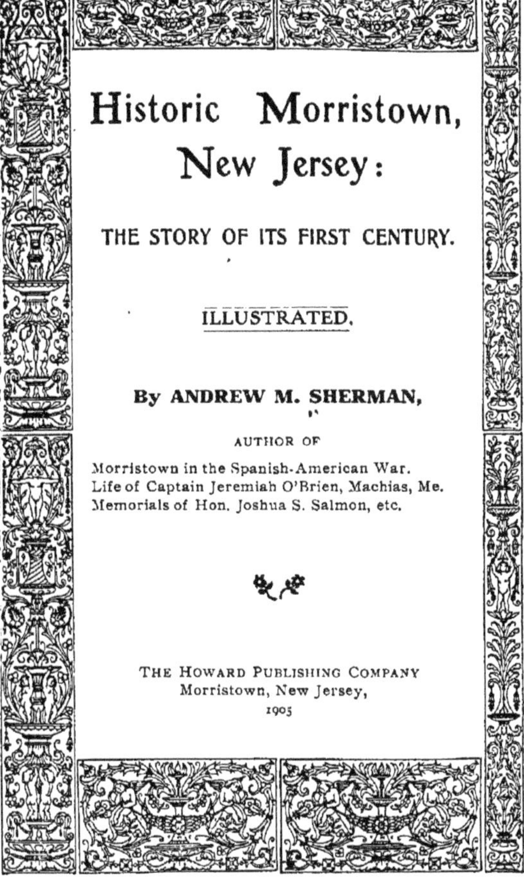

Historic Morristown, New Jersey:

THE STORY OF ITS FIRST CENTURY.

ILLUSTRATED.

By ANDREW M. SHERMAN,

AUTHOR OF

Morristown in the Spanish-American War.
Life of Captain Jeremiah O'Brien, Machias, Me.
Memorials of Hon. Joshua S. Salmon, etc.

THE HOWARD PUBLISHING COMPANY
Morristown, New Jersey,
1905

PREFACE.

A decade and more has elapsed since the author of this volume delivered, before a large Sunday morning congregation, an historical sermon in commemoration of the sixty-fourth anniversary of the dedication of the church edifice in Morris County, New Jersey, in which there worshiped the religious organization of which he was then the regularly installed pastor. The preparation of this sermon, which was subsequently published in pamphlet form, necessitated careful research of township and county annals, which were found to be of rare interest; so far, particularly, as concerned their relation to the seven years struggle for national independence.

Later and more thorough research of the annals of the county seat of Morris, the story of which, as the author was impressed, had never been consecutively nor adequately related, fruited in the purpose to attempt, in the not distant future, the writing of a history of Morristown which should aid at least in giving it the prominent place in the annals of our great country to which it is rightfully entitled. In accordance, therefore, with this purpose, the author has for several years past been gathering material for the contemplated work; meanwhile he has consulted every known and available source of information concerning his subject. Not alone from printed page and musty document, however, but from not a few living repositories of local history and tradition, has material been procured by the author for the present volume.

For the verification of the locale and present appearance of the various camping grounds of Washington's army in Morristown and vicinity, during the winters of 1777, and 1779-80, as described by several local historians, the author has, either alone or in company with rseidents of the county seat, more or less acquainted with these grounds, gone over them nearly a score of times during the year now nearing its close. Kodak and camera have been kept busy during the year past transferring to practically imperishable paper the accurate and indisputable representations of historic grounds and buildings and monuments and ruins, the sight of which in photographic form, cannot fail to quicken the heart action of even this distinctively commercial age and people.

As the author has again and again, in the deep quietude of the woods and hill-slopes tramped over the grounds once alive with the armed participants in the War of the Revolution, and looked, not always with dry eyes, upon the countless heaps of stones once composing the fire-places and chimneys of the rude log huts which sheltered their occupants in the awful winter of

1779-80, it has occurred to him that no finer thing in the way of an exhibition of patriotism could be done, than to gather these stones, bring them to the beautiful county seat of Morris, and there, in some central location, construct of them a suitable memorial building, the presence of which would furnish inspiration to coming generations, and aid in keeping alive the sentiment of our beloved Whittier, enunciated in the words:

"Freedom's soil hath only place
For a free and fearless race!"

The author gratefully acknowledges his indebtedness for several photographs for illustrations for this volume, and for interesting data, to the following named individuals: Mrs. Mary D. Halsey, widow of the late Hon Edmund D. Halsey, of Rockaway; Maltby G. Pierson, William A. Dunn, Hon. Charles F. Axtell, Isaac N. Pierson, J. Frank Holloway, Harrie A. Freeman, Mrs. Julia R. Cutler, widow of the late Hon. Augustus W. Cutler, Emory McClintock, LL.D., George W. Fleury, John W. Melick, Philip H. Hoffman, Henry B. Hoffman, Clifford A. Fairchild, Frank H. Fairchild, Francis E. Woodruff, John D. Guerin, Mrs. Charlotte C. Lee, Frederick F. Curtis, Mrs. Anna W. Little, widow of the late Theodore Little, Esq., Mrs. M. G. Twining, Secretary of the Morristown and Madison Chapter, D. A. R., Amidee Boisaubin (deceased), Gustav A. Kissell, John S. Green, Edward Howell, Heyward G. Emmell, of Morristown. To these names should be added those of Henry V. Condict, Esq., of Jersey City; Samuel A. Farrand, one of the headmasters of the famous Newark Academy, of Newark; Mrs. Adrain Dickerson, of Montclair, whose maiden name was Elizabeth Anna Lewis, daughter of Major William Johnes Lewis, formerly of Morristown (now deceased); Rev. James A. Ferguson, D. D., pastor for considerably more than a quarter centnry, of the Hanover Presbyterian Church; Amos L. Shangle, of Oskaloosa, Iowa, a native of Morris County; Edwin A. Ely, of Livingstone; R. Heber Breintnall, Adjutant-General of the State of New Jersey; Dr. M. S. Simpson, of Middle Valley; Aaron K. Fairchild, of Hanover; Frederick A. Canfield, of Dover; Mrs. James B. Bowman, of Mendham; Miss Eleanor A. Hunter, of Montclair; Joseph M. Sayre, of Newark; Mrs. Charlotte Sayre Boorman, of Fort Washington, New York City; Alfred B. Johnson, of South Orange; Dr. B. L. Dodd, of Newark; John M. Lindley, Ph.G., of Winfield, Iowa, and John S. McMaster, Esq., of Jersey City.

Andrew M. Sherman.

Morristown, New Jersey, October 25, 1905.

SYNOPSIS OF CONTENTS

CHAPTER I

CHAPTER II

CHAPTER III.

CHAPTER IV

CHAPTER V

CHAPTER VIII

SYNOPSIS OF CONTENTS

CHAPTER X

CHAPTER XI

CHAPTER XII

CHAPTER XIV

SYNOPSIS OF CONTENTS

CHAPTER XVI

Exorbitant prices of necessities—Reward is offered for a runaway negro....................302-326

CHAPTER XVII

An important gathering in Dickerson's tavern—The court-martial of Benedict Arnold—Sketch of his career—Resumé of his services—Composition of the court—The room in which the trial occurred —The charges against Arnold—He demands an investigation—Active hostilities prevent—An opportune time arrives—Arnold's personal appearance at the trial—He offers evidence—He addresses the court—The court is adjourned—Arnold's acquittal was expected—The court reassembles—Arnold is convicted—The sentence is a reprimand from Washington—The reprimand—Arnold is disappointed and indignant—He resolves to quit the service—He is dissuaded by Washington—He is assigned to West Point—He requests leave of absence—He is still brooding over the verdict of the court-martial—He betrays his country—Dies in obscurity in England—On whom rests the responsibility for Arnold's rash act?—The celebration in Morristown of the festival of St. John, by the Military Union Lodge of Free and Accepted Masons—A fruitless expedition to Staten Island—Half-humorous letter of Quartermaster General Lewis—A specimen of newspaper patriotism—The soldiers return to camp, many with frozen feet—The British retaliate on Elizabethtown—Washington orders an investigation—An assembly opened at Morristown—Subscriptions to the series of balls—A bit of word painting—How "Tempe" Wick saved her favorite saddle horse

—The popular version given—The foot-prints of "Tempe's" horse were seen for many years—"Leddell's mill" still in operation..............327-354

CHAPTER XVIII

Washington's customary seriousness—An occasional laugh is indulged in—A braggart's attempt to break a young horse—Washington laughs heartily—Sketch of General John Doughty—He settles in Morristown—Two distinguished foreigners visit Morristown—They attend a military parade—A grand ball in the "Continental House"—Tallow candles are the only light—Death of Don Juan de Miralles—An imposing funeral—Soldiers guard his grave—The history of the "Continental House"—Officers quartered in the building—Captured British cannon stored there—Courtship of Alexander Hamilton—Hamilton and the sentinel as related to Lossing—Captain "Jack" Steele's letter from Headquarters—The main portion of the American army leaves Morristown—The second battle at Springfield—Colonel Benoni Hathaway is wounded—He prefers charges against General Heard—Pennsylvania troops are left in Morristown—Misunderstanding over the soldiers' term of enlistment—The soldiers resolve to mutiny—They procure arms, ammunition and provisions—Accidental shooting of Captain Adam Bettin—General Wayne hastens from his quarters to camp—He addresses the mutineers—A shot is fired over his head—"Shoot me, if you will"—Wayne returns to his quarters—The mutineers start for Philadelphia—They seek justice—General Wayne vainly endeavors to dis-

CHAPTER XX

SYNOPSIS OF CONTENTS

Jacob Mann is the new editor—The first postmaster in Morristown—A fire association is organized at the county seat—Names of the officers—The "Morris Aqueduct" is incorporated—Names of the proprietors—A description of the "Morris Aqueduct"—The inauguration of the first stage route between Morristown and Powles Hook—A rival stage is put on—Flaming advertisements to secure patronage—Burial Grounds in Morristown—The "Bill of Mortality," by "Parson Johnes" and sexton William Cherry—"Time brushes off our lives with sweeping wings"—Many Revolutionary soldiers were interred in the Presbyterian burial grounds—Brass buttons have been found—Revolutionary soldiers were interred in the Baptist burial grounds—Buttons, pennies and wallet are found—The oldest stone in the Presbyterian burial grounds—The visit of an antiquarian to the oldest cemetery in Morristown—The oldest date she found, 1722—A friend said the oldest date was 1713 415-447

Errata ....
Addenda ....
Index of Persons ....

INTRODUCTION

Few will take up this book who do not know that Morristown is in Morris County in New Jersey, some thirty miles due west of New York. Few are aware, however, that the location of Morristown is absolutely unique, not in one respect only, but in three different ways. It occupies a geological site of remarkable interest. It was the westernmost colonial puritan church-town, the outpost of New England. In the revolutionary era, from the capture of New York to the capture of Cornwallis, it was the key of Washington's position, the one connecting link between the eastern and the southern states, like the stem of an hour-glass.

I.

The Morristown court house is on ground which has been solid ground since the world began. The Morristown green, near by, was for a long period under the waters of the ocean, as has been, at one time or another, nearly all the land within this country, and indeed most of the present land surface of the globe. From the hill on which the court house stands there could be seen, when the ocean last receded, no one of the numerous other hills now visible to the east and south. All that the ocean left behind it was a wide expanse of sandstone and shale. Melted rock, squeezing up later through cracks in the sandstone, was to form the hills that now shut in the Passaic valley, and others farther away.

When the ocean covered the site of the green, the coast line was continued to the northeast by Watnong, Boonton and Ramapo Mountains, but it did not extend in the opposite direction much beyond Bernardsville, Mine Mountain there forming a sort of promontory. Morristown is just on the ancient coast line. Were this all, the fact would be of interest, notwithstanding that there were many other points, along the line on the map which marks the boundary of the most ancient geological formation remaining in the world, besides that occupied by Morristown. But, besides this ancient line of the coast, and just here at right angles to it, there is another geological line of great importance known as the glacial moraine. This is a heavy deposit of "drift," consisting of sand, gravel, rounded stones, and boulders, which was left all along the southern margin of the great body of ice which covered the northern part of the globe during the glacial period. This line of drift running around the world crossed the ancient coast line precisely where Morristown now stands. It extended to the southeast as far as Staten Island, and thence eastward through Long Island. To the westward it is found across the continent. The greater part of Morristown is built on the glacial moraine, which is here of considerable depth, the site of the green being many feet above the shale and sandstone deposited by the ocean. In one field within the borough limits, on the southern side of the moraine, may be found three geological formations: ancient gneiss, shale, and glacial drift.

Enough has been said to show that Morristown occupies a unique geological position. What follows concerning geology is of local interest only. The Passaic Valley, extending from Morristown to Summit, and from near Paterson to a point below Bernardsville, originated in consequence of the formation of the range of hills enclosing it to the east and south. The waters of the valley found an outlet through a gap near Summit, then the bed of a river. The glacier filled the river bed with a body of drift which closed the gap as an outlet for the water of the valley and has kept it closed ever since. The valley south of the glacier having thus no outlet, the waters rose to about 360 feet above the present sea-level, when they were able to escape to the southwest and find their way to the Raritan. All parts of the valley below this level, and south of the moraine, thus became a lake, called by the geologists Lake Passaic. The shores of the lake are still marked, in place, by deposits of water-worn pebbles. After many years the glacier began to recede to the northward, and the lake became correspondingly larger until the time came when the water found a lower outlet to the northeast, by way of Little Falls, after which the present course of the Passaic River became established.

II.

Upon the crossing point of the two great geological lines just sketched there grew up a puritan settlement. The reader will find that, according to puritan custom, the early history of the town was substantially that of the church.

It is unnecessary to describe the puritan element, the most notable of those which went to the formation of American civilization. The puritan, the churchman, the Holland calvinist, the Scotch presbyterian, the lutheran, the catholic, the huguenot, all contributed their part, but the dominant element, in the north at least, was introduced by the puritan, whose settlements were known collectively as New England. Town after town was established on the puritan model, first on the coast, and by degrees in the interior, each town with its one church. If doctrinal differences arose in any church, one faction or the other would usually remove to another place and organize a new town. There were certain settlements outside of the legal limits of New England which were as truly puritan as any in Massachusetts or Connecticut, such as the Hamptons and Southold in eastern Long Island and Newark in New Jersey, with its offshoot Morristown.

Sometimes puritan settlements would be made amid uncongenial surroundings, and so lose speedily their peculiar characteristics. Among these were Westchester and Eastchester, Hempstead and Newtown, all under Dutch government and influences, and later under Church of England government and influences. In New Jersey, Woodbridge was settled from Massachusetts, but was soon invaded by Scotch and quakers, not to speak of Church of England influences from Amboy, the seat of government close by. Some who were born puritans were willing to remove to new homes without organizing a town and church after their own manner, and of such were the puritans who joined with others in building up Elizabethtown, Middletown, Shrewsbury, Monmouth and Cape May, Even Mendham, a semi-puritan village near Morristown, had its quaker meeting.

Newark, however, was wholly puritan, having its beginning in a revolt of some of the best men in New Haven colony when that colony was joined with Connecticut. They were distressed and scandalized by one result of the union, which was that godless men became entitled to vote, a right previously restricted by the laws of New Haven to church members alone. They accordingly exiled themselves and established a new town, to be ruled by its church. The early records of Newark show a thoroughly puritan intermingling of the affairs of church and state, such a thing as the election of a pound keeper being followed in the record by a vote for the call of a new minister. The laws were such when Morristown was settled, half a century later than Newark, that a town organization like that of Newark was no longer feasible. A wide territory called a township, sparsely settled and including several villages, had become the regular form of organization, as settlers no longer needed to cluster together for their common protection against Indians. Yet, at Morristown, church and village grew up together, and the people of both were puritans by birth and training, born in Newark, or eastern Long Island, or elsewhere, but all, with possible exceptions of no importance, sons of New England families. By this time all the puritan and semi-puritan churches of New Jersey, Newark included, had connected themselves with the presbyterian synod, under a compromise devised by the New England element, and the Morristown church was accordingly organized under the presbyterian name.

There were, no doubt, during the colonial period, villages to be found farther west than Morristown where New England ideas were uppermost, and among them notably a settlement in the Wyoming valley which might have become a Connecticut town, had it not been destroyed by the Indians. No other place of importance, however, was settled by the puritans west of the Hudson except Newark and Morristown, the latter being the advance post of New England, the church-town farthest west. This History will show how its church practically constituted the town during its first half century.

III.

For the better part of a century the little town secluded amid the Jersey hills maintained its character as the outpost of puritanism. It will be seen in these pages how such civic energy as there was came from the church, which, usually by formal vote of its trustees, supplied lands when needed for any public purpose, whether for a green or a court house, an army building or a drill ground. The revolution brought Morristown out of its seclusion, and the church-town at the crossing of the geological lines became the pivot of the war of independence.

The location of the district of which Morristown was the centre was such as to make its possession of supreme importance to the Americans. This district comprised, in addition to Morris County itself, the eastern hills of Somerset County, and might be described as the highlands between Essex County and the Raritan. The Somerset hills, to the eastward, are not far from Morristown, which is not five miles from the line between the counties. At that time there was really no town in Somerset, though New Brunswick, Princeton and Morristown were just beyond its boundaries on different sides. If the British could have taken and held the Morris district, the rebel colonies would have been cut in two, for such communication as might have been carried on through the forests to the northward would have been difficult and precarious. It was this opportunity, this danger, for one side or the other, that made Morristown so prominent during the revolution. It was this that kept the Morris district so constantly on its guard, that gave the militia of the Jersey hills so much more work to do than any other militia, and that created the need of the famous beacon system, including the "Fort Nonsense" beacon at Morristown itself. The British never succeeded in setting foot in Morris County, though their armies were repeatedly led up to the foot of the hills and repulsed; and only in one rapid cavalry raid, when General Lee was captured by them, did they enter the Somerset part of the district. Year after year they held off even from an attempt to advance, perhaps from undue caution, but certainly with the knowledge that on the signal all available men from Sussex, Hunterdon and Somerset on the one side and from Bergen and Essex on the other would rush to the defense of the middle hills, and that Washington and his army were always there or close at hand.

After taking New York in 1776, the British pursued Washington through the Jersey plains towards the Delaware, and were so confident or so careless that they delayed to secure the hill district. After winning his brilliant little victories at Trenton and Princeton with the remnant of his force, Washington turned unexpectedly to the hills and passed some months at Morristown, watching the enemy and reorganizing his army. From this point he could descend instantly to the plains if the British invaded Jersey, or march quickly, by interior lines, to defend the Hudson passes in case of need. From this time the cutting of the colonies in two was a main object of the British. In 1777 they hoped, with Burgoyne's help, to accomplish this object by taking and holding the line of the Hudson; but instead of advancing from New York to meet Burgoyne, with Washington in the way, they moved by water to the southward, drew Washington away, and took Philadelphia, not suspecting the fate to which they were leaving Burgoyne. Washington at Valley Forge protected the communication between the northern and southern colonies. When the British moved from Philadelphia towards New York, Washington moved also, always keeping between them and the hills, and striking a blow at Monmouth. The next three years he hovered in the hills, keeping them tied to New York. The first and second winters he quartered in the Morris district, the third on the west side of the river, but wherever he was the passes were steadily guarded, and the alarm guns and beacons were always ready. Then came the finish at Yorktown.

The Jersey plains were sometimes held by the British, and at other times were easily within their reach from Staten Island, which they always held in force. Communication between the Hudson and the Delaware, in order to be safe, had to go through Morristown. The road southwest from Morristown thus became a great thoroughfare; it was "the great road," as Chastellux called it in 1780.

The memory of the revolution is cherished at Morristown more faithfully, it would seem, than in any other town in the country, and this is indeed most fitting. A history of it has long been needed; and the present book, by an able writer deeply imbued with his subject, will surely meet a most cordial welcome.

Emory McClintock

ERRATA.

For "That the pioneers of Whippanong were chiefly English, or of English descent," on page 8, read: That the pioneers of Whippanong were chiefly of English descent.

For "Chapter VII," on page 139, read: Chapter VIII.

For "Thaddeus Koscinsko," on page 244, read: Thaddeus Koscinsko.

For "Down the straight road of the Revolutionary period toward the Basking Ridge road, about half the distance," on page 295, read: "Down the straight road of the Revolutionary period toward the Basking Ridge road, a short distance from the terminus of Jockey Hollow road."

ADDENDA.

Among the residents of early Morristown who served in the Revolution was James Rogers. He lived, as the author of this volume has been informed, in a house that stood on what is now South Street, about opposite the residence of the late Judge Vancleve Dalrymple. When about fourteen years of age he was a fifer in the Morris County militia. This statement will seem the less incredible when it is said that young Rogers was a tall, muscular and powerful boy. He was an ardent admirer of Washington. At one time during the Revolution James Rogers was employed as a bearer of despatches. While in the lower part of the State engaged in this service he put up at a tavern. He was in some way thrown into the company of several Hessian soldiers, and the conversation having turned upon Washington, one of them angrily exclaimed: "Damn Washington, and all his subjects!" Forgetful, apparently, of the "ticklish" business in which he was engaged, young Rogers fearlessly replied: "I am one of them"; and there is no record of the Hessians having molested the stalwart American patriot.

At the battle of Monmouth Rogers fought all day; and he subsequently remarked that several soldiers died from thirst on that memorable day.

After the close of the Revolution, out of which, as the writer is informed, Rogers came, at the age of about 23 years, as captain, he returned to Morristown. It was his special delight in response to the wishes of his fellow-townsmen, to carry the American flag in Fourth of July parades, and this he did until he was 90 years of age. He died about the year 1850 in the town in which he was born, and of which he had been a life-long resident.

The foregoing facts are obtained from a native and resident of Morris County who received them from Captain James Rogers himself.

ADDENDA

On page 483 of "Officers and Men of New Jersey in the Revolutionary War," by Adjutant General Styker may be found the following:"James Rogers, Fifer, Morris."

Hanover, N. J.
September, 1905.

There was a family living in the house near where I now live whom the "Morristown Ghost" wished particularly to interest his scheme. In the side of the house mentioned there was a window about 8 feet above the ground. On one stormy night the "Ghost" made his appearance at this window, made certain communications, and then vanished. In the morning following an examination of the ground about the house showed marks in the soft earth where some one had walked up to the house from the roadway on a pair of stilts, and back the same way. The marks in the road showed where a horse had been tied to the fence along the road. Further investigation proved that this horse had been used by the "Morristown Ghost" as a means of conveyance from the county seat to the scene of his midnight manifestations.

This is about the substance of what my grandparents knew about the episode above related. * * * The idea the "Ghost" wished to convey by walking on stilts was that he was a spirit floating through the air.

The following extracts from two of the numerous letters received by the author of this volume since the commencement, in the Saturday issues of the Newark Evening News, of the series of articles on "History of Morristown, New Jersey; The Story of Its First Century," on February 25, 1905, are here presented because of the interesting data therein communicated. The names of the writers of these letters are withheld, since their publication would be a breach of confidence on the part of their recipient. It should, however, be said that the writers of the letters from which the extracts are given, are well qualified to speak upon the matters involved:—

ADDENDA

"While I am writing, I recall being struck by your acceptance of a mythical story of a dance at Arnold's tavern in the spring of 1777. The tradition is no doubt true in spirit, but must relate to the spring of 1780, when there really were 'assemblies' in the Continental Store House, afterward known to Morristown people as O'Hara's tavern. (I have known earnest support of Morris's and Arnold's taverns as locations of the 1780 assemblies). In early 1777 Washington's army was nearer nothing than it ever was before or after—perhaps 2,000 or 3,000, scattered towards Battle Hill, and scourged with small-pox. There is no evidence, and no probability, that any one thought of dancing during those dreadful three months. * * * That the Jersey women knit stockings innumerable in the winter of 1779-80 is doubtless correct. The evidence you quote is good, and the need was great, among the Jersey troops at least. There is no evidence whatever that the entire army was ever short of any one article of clothing at the same time. * * * * * * * *

In the old Ms. letters, etc., that I have read in the past there were constantly two items cropping out: Our regiment, or our State troops, need so and so and the State clothier of Conn. or Penn., or some other State, will distribute shoes, or something else, at such a day and hour. (As these are not real quotations, I omit the quotation marks.) The Jersey stockings would naturally go to the Jersey clothier for distribution. There was a great diversity between the troops of different States in the matter of sufficient clothing. I recall no instance in which mention was made of the troops of one State being helped from the clothing supplies of another State. There was much State pride, which sometimes meant, of course, concealment of deficiencies of one's own State, along with private complaints in letters home. On the whole, barring the intense cold, my judgment is that the suffering in 1779-80 has been enormously exaggerated (on the whole), individual experiences and recollections being taken for universal facts. There is no question that the health of the army was particularly good."

* * * * "He (Rev. Theodore L. Cuyler, D. D.) wrote me that I must tell you that the picture of our patriotic ancestor, Joseph Lewis, was given to his mother by his grandmother whose maiden name was Anna B. Lewis, my aunt. Of course she knew how her father looked. Dr. Cuyler's mother was brought up in Morristown by the widow of Joseph Lewis. 'There is not a more genuine picture in existence than that was of my great-grandfather Joseph Lewis, who was Quartermaster-General of the Revolutionary army when it wintered over in Morristown. General Washington was often at his table.' I copied the above from Dr. Cuyler's letter so that you may know that it (the miniature portrait in oil from which the picture of General Lewis in this volume is reproduced) is correct."

INDEX OF PERSONS

INDEX OF PERSONS

D

INDEX OF PERSONS

INDEX OF PERSONS

N

O

P

INDEX OF PERSONS

R

S

INDEX OF PERSONS

INDEX OF PERSONS

Books of Andrew M. Sherman

Morristown in the Spanish-American War,

Large 8 mo. 200 pp. 75 illustrations. Cloth $1.50. Half Morocco $2.00. Postpage Prepaid.

"An accurate and reliable account of the part borne by historic Morristown, New Jersey, in the Spanish-American War."

"A timely and important contribution to local history."

Life of Captain Jeremiah O'Brien, Machias, Me.

COMMANDER OF THE FIRST NAVAL SQUADRON OF THE REVOLUTION. Introduction by Hon. John D. Long, Ex-Secretary of the Navy.

8 mo. 250 pp. 30 Illustrations. Cloth $2.00 net. Postage 16 cents.

"The heroic subject has been treated in a marvelously intertesting manner, resulting in a book of rare intrinsic merit and is a notable addition to the literature of the period."—*Providence Telegram.*

"Fully as interesting as a novel."—*Chicago Tribune.*

It is a thrilling story of an American sailor as typical and as original as Paul Jones or Decatur."—*St. Paul Dispatch.*

Mr. Sherman displays rare skill in the treatment of his subject. He has gone to original sources for his facts and possesses the true historical instinct. Without any doubt, the present work will run through several editions.—THOMAS HAMILTON MURRAY, Boston, Mass.

"It is the most important contribution to the local history of Maine that has appeared for some time and should be in every public library in the State, while collectors and historical students will at once add the volume to their shelves."—*Bangor (Me.) Commercial.*

Phil Carver; a Romance of the War of 1812.

8 mo. 300 pp. Picture of author. Cloth $1.25. Postage Prepaid.

"If action be not omnipresent its lack is compensated in entertaining descriptions of community life in New England during the early part of the past century. * * * The diction of the book is faultless."—*Chicago Tribune.*

"The scene of the story is in old Machias, Me., a town of great historic interest. Among the characters introduced is Captain (and subsequently, Colonel) Jeremiah O'Brien."—*New York Herald.*

"It is well written and interesting. * * * The story of the school conducted by Master Arthur, a graduate of Dublin University, is a capital sketch."—*Boston Transcript.*

"The plot of the story is laid in New England in the early part of the last century, and from tradition and personal observation the writer is enabled to set forth the life of the people of that period in a graphic manner."—*Newark (N. J.) Evening News.*

Memorials of the Hon. Joshua S. Salmon.

LATE REPRESENTATIVE IN CONGRESS FROM NEW JERSEY.

Large 8 mo. 200 pp. Two-thirds length portrait. Cloth $2.50. Postage Prepaid.

This book contains an authentic biography of the deceased Congressman, with specimens of his speeches, and the eulogies pronounced upon him in Congress, and has the endorsement of the family of the late Congressman.

Historic Morristown, New Jersey: The Story of its First Century.

Large 8 mo. Wide margin. 500 pages. Profusely illustrated. Cloth $3.50. Buckram $3.50. Half Morocco $4.50. Full Morocco $5.00. Gilt edges. Postage 25 cents additional.

Any of the above sent on receipt of price and postage by

The Howard Publishing Company

Morristown, New Jersey, U. S. A.

SPECIAL OFFER

The "Life of Captain Jeremiah O'Brien" and "Phil Carvey" (companion volumes) will be sent, postage prepaid, on receipt of $3.00.

CHAPTER I.

"Our forest life was rough and rude,
And dangers closed us round,
But here amid the green old wood,
Freedom was sought and found."

ORRISTOWN, New Jersey, was originally settled by a few persons from what is now Whippany, a manufacturing village in the present township of Hanover, situated about four miles to the eastward of the beautiful county seat of Morris County.

Before proceeding, however, to relate the circumstances under which Morristown was first settled by the whites, it seems desirable, particularly for the purpose of establishing, approximately at least, certain dates in connection therewith; and of ascertaining also, as nearly as is now practicable, the character of the early settlers, that the reader be made acquainted with the circumstances attending the settlement of Whippany by the whites, since the two occurrences, as will be seen, are intimately related.

A careful and unbiased examination by the writer of this history of all available sources of information bearing directly and indirectly upon the subject, has resulted in the conclusion that before the close of the seventeenth century—as early probably as about the year 1685—the whites had found their way into the region now known as Morris County, New Jersey. In corroboration of the above mentioned conclusion the following extract from the "Historical Collections of the State of New Jersey," by Messrs. John W. Barber and Henry Howe, published in the year 1844 is presented: "The township (Whippany) was first settled about 1685, soon after the settlement of Newark, and is supposed to have been the earliest settlement within the limits of what is now Morris and Sussex Counties." As nearest the bubbling spring on the hillside may be found the purest and most refreshing water, so, the writer ventures to say, in closest proximity to the event, the date of whose occurrence it is desirable to establish, may be found (in the conceded absence of clear evidence to the contrary) the most reliable and satisfactory information bearing upon the matter under consideration. The extract above quoted, the reader will notice, is from a history written sixty-one years nearer the date of the settlement of Whippany than the present fifth year of the twentieth century and is, therefore, presumptively, at least, more likely to represent the facts in the case than more recent expressions of opinion.

Whatever may have been the object of their coming, or whatever may have been the length of their stay in this region, the pioneers of 1685 can, however, be regarded as little else than adventurers. Indeed, one of the most reliable writers of local history says of these early pioneers: "My conjecture is that the original settlers (of Whippanong, now Whippany) may have been squatters, making iron from Succasunna iron ore, with the boundless forests in the region which they converted into coal." Rev. Dr. Joseph F. Tuttle, LL. D., from whom the extract just quoted is taken, and who, it may be incidentally remarked, has been justly termed "the father" of Morris County history, was a direct descendant of one of the early settlers of Whippanong. Of his direct paternal ancestor it has recently been said by a Morris County pastor (Rev. Edwin R. Murgatroyd, of the Presbyterian Church of New Vernon), in connection with commemorative dedicatory services in his own church: "It was here (at Whippany) that the grandfather of Rev. Dr. Joseph Tuttle, LL.D., president of Wabash College, hammered out a living at the forge." It is practically certain that one who was only two generations removed from the settlement of Whippanong, was in close touch with the early history and tradition of the village of which his paternal ancestor was an important factor in connection with its settlement and subsequent development. Add to this circumstance the fact that from the year 1847, till the year 1862—a period of fifteen years—Dr. Tuttle was identified, either as colleague or as pastor, with the Presbyterian Church at Rockaway, in the county of Morris, and that during that period he made an exhaustive study of county history, the results of which still abide to enrich the present and coming generations, and it must be conceded that Dr. Tuttle is deserving of no small measure of confidence when he speaks concerning the history of Morris County.

For about the same length of time, and during about the same period of Dr. Joseph F. Tuttle's Rockaway pastorate, his brother, Rev. Samuel L. Tuttle, was pastor of the Madison, New Jersey, Presbyterian Church; and it is a fact of no little significance that in an historical sermon delivered by the latter about the year 1850, he unqualifiedly stated that white settlers were in Morris County as early as the year 1685.

The impulse is irresistible to quote, in the present connection, the following, from a comparatively recent writer of local history, (Rev. Robert Aikman, D. D., pastor of the Presbyterian Church, of Madison, New Jersey) in confirmation of the reliability of the brothers Tuttle, as chroniclers of Morris County history: "To both these gentlemen (now deceased) every one who gains much knowledge of the early history of this portion of New Jersey, will have to confess indebtedness. Both were settled pastors in Morris County, and with genuine antiquarian enthusiasm improved their opportunities to gain information, while yet there remained among the living, aged men and women who remembered old historic scenes, or could repeat the recollections of their fathers or mothers."

It is highly probable, almost certain, indeed, that the early white explorers (or "squatters," as Dr. Joseph F. Tuttle aptly termed them) of what is now Morris County, carried back with them to the settlements whence they had come, information concerning the region explored by them, which led to its permanent settlement a few years later.

That the first permanent settlement by the whites of the region adjacent to what is now Morristown, was made not later than the early part of the eighteenth century, there can be, and is, in the minds of those conversant with the facts, no question; and that this permanent settlement was made in what is now the busy manufacturing village of Whippany is equally indisputable. In confirmation of the first statement it may be said, that on the opening pages of a book, now extant, used by the Rev. Jacob Green, the third pastor of the Presbyterian Church of Hanover, for the recording of baptisms, marriages and other parish data, there occur the following words, in the handwriting of "Parson Green."

"About the year 1710 a few families removed from Newark and Elizabeth Town and settled on the west side of the Pessaick River, in that which is now Morris County. Not long after the settlers erected an house for the public worship of God on the bank of Whippenung River (about three miles west of Pessaick River), about 100 rods below the forge, which is and has long been known by the name of the old iron works. There was a church gathered and in the year 17— Nathaniel Hubbell was ordained and settled there by the Presbytery of New York. About this time (1718 or 1719) the place obtained the name of Hanover and became a township, but the place was most commonly known by the Indian name Whippenung."

The entry above given, a facsimile of the original of which in the handwriting of "Parson Green" appears in connection with this history, it is important to bear in mind, was made in the year 1767, after the Rev. Jacob Green had been the pastor of the Hanover Presbyterian Church for the period of about twenty-one years; he having been settled over said church, according to his own statement, in the year 1746.

In the absence of more definite evidence with regard to the date of the permanent settlement of what is now Whippany—and the writer of this history has searched diligently, but in vain, to discover such evidence—the entry in the book above mentioned must be accepted as the only reliable and satisfactory starting point in the study of the early history of Morris County; so far, at least, as its permanent settlement by the English is concerned.

It may, however, be casually remarked, that about the year 1700, the Dutch from Bergen and New York, and from the early settlements at Kingston and Albany, on the Hudson River, made a permanent settlement in the northeastern portion of what is now Morris County, at or near what is now Pompton Plains.

It is said that the purchase, and subsequent permanent settlement of what is now Hanover Township, came about as follows: The first purchase of land from the Indians by the early settlers of Newark (or New Worke, as it was at first spelled) extended to the Passaic River on the east, and on the west, to the base of Wachung Mountain. In the year 1678 the western limits of the Newark purchase were extended to the top of Wachung Mountain, the consideration given the two Indians who deeded the extension to the whites, being: "Two guns, three coats and thirteen kans (cans) of rum." One of the more adventurous of the English settlers living on the east side of the Passaic River, climbed to the summit of Wachung Mountain, the height of which varies from 300 to 650 feet, and he was so delighted with the view of the Passaic Valley which greeted his eyes, that, returning to Newark, he reported in glowing language the result of his solitary survey. His description of the beauty of the valley upon which his eyes had feasted, and of the evident fertility of the soil, so impressed his fellow townsmen in public meeting assembled, that it was readily voted to purchase the goodly land from the Indians, which was subsequently accomplished; and its permanent settlement soon followed.

Whippanong—spelled also Whippenung, Whipponong and occasionally Whippening—is said to signify in the Indian language "the arrow." Along the banks of the winding river bearing the name from which the region first received its designation, there grew, and still grow, the graceful willows from whose smooth and slender sticks the aborigines made their arrows for hunting purposes, before the incoming of the "pale faces," with their guns and powder and shot, and destructive "fire water."

The settlers of Whippanong came from New England and Old England, by way of Long Island (then considered a part of New England), and from Elizabeth Town and Newark, the two latter places having been settled in the years 1665 and 1666, respectively.

That the pioneers of Whippanong were chiefly English, or of English descent, is clearly evident from the names borne by them, among which may be found those of Ball, Baldwin, Bowlesby, Cobb, Howell, Kitchell, Lindsley, Stiles, Thomas and Tuttle; all, as the reader will readily perceive, of Anglo-Saxon derivation. If further proof of the nationality, as above suggested, of these early pioneers were required, it might be added that a reliable chronicler of local history explicitly states that "Samuel and Joseph Tuttle were from the north of England, near the river Tweed, and that Joseph and Abraham Kitchell, brothers, and Francis Lindsley were all from England;" and these Englishmen just named, be it remembered, were among the early white settlers of Whippanong. It is a fact of no small significance in this connection that in Elizabeth and Newark the same names as those of the early pioneers of Whippanong, just mentioned, may still be found.

Another authority on local history says:

"The Tuttles, Kitchells and Lindsleys came from England, first to the New Haven and Connecticut colony, and migrated thence to New Jersey. * * * Robert Kitchell left England in the first ship that ever anchored in New Haven (then Quinnipiac) Bay. He and his son Samuel were two of the forty-one associates from Milford, Conn., who signed the 'fundamental (unchangeable) agreement' in 1667, which document the twenty-three associates from Branford, Conn., had signed the year previous. They each received their home lots in the town of Newark."

From an apparently reliable authority it is learned that the exact date of Robert Kitchell's departure from England, was April 26, in the year 1639. He is said to have accompanied a party of Puritan refugees, who were led by the Rev. Henry Whitfield. In the year 1666, Robert Kitchell, and his son, Samuel, and a few friends, removed to Newark, New Jersey. It was Samuel Kitchell's son, Abraham, who was among the early settlers of what is now Whippany. Rev. H. D. Kitchell, of Milwaukee, Wisconsin, published a few years since, a book, entitled: "Robert Kitchell, and his Descendants." From this book, whose statements bear the marks of authenticity, the present writer gleans several facts of special interest, among which are the following: The author states, in confirmation, as will be noticed, of the opinion of the Revs. Joseph and Samuel Tuttle (already quoted), that before the year 1710, a few pioneers from Newark, including Abraham Kitchell, settled on the banks of the Whippanong River west of the great Watchung, now Orange Mountain. The original settlement was made, in what is now the village of Whippany. The log house built by Abraham Kitchell was erected not far from the present (1905) residence of Charles M. Kitchell, in Whippany. From Abraham Kitchell to the present generation, one line of descent, is David Kitchell, Uzall Kitchell, Zenas Kitchell, Charles M. Kitchell, C. Ross Kitchell. Abraham Kitchell was a Lieutenant of militia in the year 1722, and a Justice of the Peace in the year 1725. He was a deacon of the Whippany church.

In Old England the early settlers of Whippanong—such of them, at least, as had come directly from the old country—may have become familiar with the iron industry; some of them, indeed may have been identified, either as employer or employe, with this branch of industry; and if such were the case, they were therefore, very naturally attracted to this portion of the New Jersey province by the reports which had presumably reached them from previous white explorers, during their temporary sojourn at Elizabeth Town and Newark, of the presence of vast quantities of iron ore embedded in the hills of this region. From the same sources they may also have learned of the abundance of forest trees, from which charcoal for smelting purposes could be advantageously made. The excellent water privileges afforded by the Whippanong River, and its confluents, were doubtless among the inducements, if, indeed, they were not the chief inducement to these early pioneers to settle in the particular locality chosen by them.

To those who came into this region after the iron

ndustry had been established, and the forests had been partially cleared for the manufacture of charcoal, the ertile soil, the genial climate, and the abundance of ish in the streams, and game in the surrounding coun-ry, were attractions of scarcely secondary importance. All kinds of game, as we are told, were abundant at hat early period—geese, wild ducks and pigeons being particularly abundant along the streams where now a in or a feather can scarcely be found.

"Passing the extensive Troy meadows, then no loubt a dense swamp covered with a growth of orig-nal forest timber, they (these early pioneers who had entered the region by way of Caldwell and Living-tone) were attracted by the high land of Hanover and Whippany"—such is the statement of a local historian Hon. Edmund D. Halsey, deceased); from which an-other inducement to the settlers of the region adjacent o what is now Morristown may be easily inferred—he high lands of Hanover and Whippany.

It was not long after the arrival of the sturdy Eng-ish pioneers in Whippanong, that some of the more enterprising of them erected there an iron forge, and n due course of time began the smelting of iron ore, and its manufacture into bars of iron for the market. Some of the company, however, as it is safe to infer, devoted themselves to the cultivation of the soil, which, owing to its rare fertility responded generously to their efforts. It is almost certain that, as in other portions of the American colonies, from the Indians then inhabiting this region the English settlers of

Whippanong learned the art of cultivating "maize," or "Indian corn," as it is known to the present day, and this "maize" was doubtless for some time their chief article of diet. In this connection it may be said that the "maize" which our fathers found so almost indispensable as an article of diet, was discovered by some Indian tribe in Central America, where it grew as a wild grass, and by the Indians it was brought to this portion of the continent and developed into form suitable for food. It is a circumstance worthy of mention, that at first the Indians of Whippanong furnished the early English settlers with game, skins and furs.

The first iron forge erected in Whippanong, which, it may be casually remarked, was at first a part of Burlington, and subsequently of Hunterdon County, and which included an extent of territory larger than the present township of Hanover; and, indeed, the first forge erected within the bounds of what is now Morris County, was, it is supposed, built by John Ford and Judge John Budd, and stood on the bank of the Whippanong River, just to the right of the upper end of the present bridge near the Presbyterian church, as one comes from Whippany toward Morristown.

In confirmation of the above statement concerning the location of the first iron forge in Whippanong, the words of a former resident of Whippany, who died about the year 1845, are here quoted: "I was born in 1778. I have seen old timbers said to have been a part of the old forge at Whippany. It stood at the west end of the cotton mill dam, between the river and the road. A saw mill and a grist mill were built upon the same ground after the forge went down." In this primitive forge, for many years known as the "Old Iron Works," which, tradition says, was a small and rudely constructed building, the pure iron was separated from the ore by the process known as "smelting."

That the iron industry in Whippanong was remunerative is evident from the fact that other forges were soon erected at several points along the course of the Whippanong River and its confluents, by the pioneers of this region; so that the entire region was for several years after its permanent settlement known as "Old Forges." The last of the iron forges to be operated in the vicinity of Whippany was at Troy, about two miles to the northward of the primitive settlement. Only a few years before the commencement of the Civil War the last bar of iron was manufactured at the Troy forge; and within a few years past the remains of the immense timbers of which it was constructed were to be seen lying prone upon its site. Some of the implements, also, used in the manufacture of the iron bars, rusty with age and neglect, were to be seen, reminding the observer of one of the most interesting periods of Morris County history.

The iron ore used in the early forges mentioned was for several years, after the settlement of Whippanong, procured without cost to the pioneer manufacturers, and was at first found on the surface of the earth, or, as a writer of local history tersely says, "Was to be had by simply picking it up." From another writer of county history, it is learned that: "At that time the ore protruded itself out of the ground, and even as late as the Revolutionary war a wagon could be driven up to ore beds and loaded without any preliminary hoisting. The appearance of the veins is very singular. It looks as if some powerful force from beneath had split the solid rock, leaving a chasm of from 6 to 25 feet, and that the ore in a fused state had been forced into it as into a mould."

From what is now the Dickerson mine, at Succasunna, about twenty miles to the westward of Whippanong, the ore was brought in leather bags thrown over the back of a horse; and after its manufacture into iron bars it was bent to fit the back of a horse, and in the same way transported to Newark and Elizabethtown, and thence by small sailing vessels and rowboats to New York. The journey from Whippanong to New York occupied about two and a half days. On the return trip various commodities used by the settlers were brought on horseback. The writer is reliably informed that several of the leather bags, used for the transportation of iron ore in the early part of the eighteenth century, are now (1905) in the possession of one of the iron manufacturing concerns in Dover, New Jersey.

Concerning the significance of the word Succasunna, just mentioned, Dr. Theodore F. Wolfe, of Roxbury Township, who has given much thought to the matter, says:

"The name was spelled Suckasunny (1808), Zukkazinny (1740), Zukkazunning (1710), Suckasunning (1715). It is derived from the Minsi-L. Suken, black, Ahsin, stone and ing, a locative suffix, and means 'the place of black stone.' It was primarily applied to the locality of the outcropping magnetic ore at Ferro Monte. Another tribe of the Lenape would have called the hill Sug-ah-sun-ing, and a third would have called it Suck-assuning."

It is a fact of no small interest that the iron ore utilized by the white settlers of what is now Morris County, had long been known to the native Indians, and had been worked by them in their rude way into implements of industry and war, many of which in recent years have been found in different portions of northern New Jersey.

The Indians who, prior to its settlement by the Dutch and English, occupied the region now constituting Morris County, were of the Delaware tribe, or, as they termed themselves, the Lenni Lenape, a term signifying "original people;" a title adopted by this tribe because of their claim that they were descendants of the most ancient of all Indian ancestors, a race of men which had existed unchanged from the beginning of time. In support of this claim, it may be said, that many associate Indian tribes accorded to the Lenni Lenape the title of "grandfathers," meaning thereby a people whose ancestors antedated theirs. The claim of the Lenni Lenape to being the "original people" seems to have been a just one, by reason of the fact that their language appears to have been more widely diffused than that of any of the other numerous Indian tribes of the Western Continent.

The Leni Lenape dwelt for the most part in villages, the wigwam sites being frequently changed, and new hunting and fishing grounds were thus sought as their necessities required. Among this tribe, of whom it is said there were at no period to exceed 2,000 in the entire State, there were no community houses, as among the Oneida Indians of central New York, but each family occupied a separate wigwam. The Indians of New Jersey are said by several writers to have been ruled by twenty kings or chiefs, some of the tribes having less than fifty subjects. A blanket or animal skin thrown over the broad shoulders, deerskin rudely fastened about the muscular legs, the feet covered with moccasins of the same material dressed in such manner as to be soft and pliable, and ornamented with quills and wampum beads—such was the dress of the Lenni Lenape Indians.

From the first, the Indians of what is now Morris County were hospitable and friendly in their intercourse with the early settlers, and these traits did not forsake them even after long association with their pale-faced neighbors. Among the Indians of the region under consideration there existed a code of honor—engraven on their hearts, as they claimed, by the Great Spirit—which would have put to shame some of their white neighbors, those in particular who attempted to corrupt and demoralize the aborigines by the introduction of "fire water," which attempt met with manly resistance on the part of the kings or chiefs of the various tribes. Notwithstanding this resistance to the introduction of the customs of civilization (?), the use of "fire water" among the Indians prevailed at length to such an extent that among the aborigines it was said: "Two of us die to every Christian that comes here." Because of the honorable dealings of the whites of this region with the Indians, in the matter of purchases of land and other business transactions, they dwelt together in uninterrupted peace; indeed, as already mentioned, during the first years of the settlement of this portion of the New Jersey Province, the friendly aborigines supplied the whites with game, skins and furs, thus materially lightening the rigors of a new settlement in a strange country and among an alien race.

The origin of the Indians of New Jersey, as understood by them, is deeply interesting from several points of view, but particularly as being remarkably suggestive of what is now known as the evolutionary theory of creation, which has come to be accepted by many scientists, and by not a few theologians, as well. Indeed, as will be seen, the Indian conception of their origin seems to have anticipated by many years the modern evolutionary theory of creation; for it was their belief that, previous to their incarnation in human bodies, they were in the form of beasts, and lived in caves under the surface of the earth. One of them accidentally discovered a hole leading out to the sunshine, and then they all followed him out and found it so pleasant that they began life anew. They gradually developed into the form of human beings, learned to hunt and fish, and in due course of time began, in a rude way, to cultivate the soil. The names "Sitting Bull," "Big Bear" and many others of a similar character since applied to Indians seem, by their suggestion of a beastly nature, to confirm the theory of creation entertained by the aborigines of New Jersey.

It is a matter of no ordinary interest that on the thirteenth day of August, in the year 1708, two years before the permanent settlement of Whippanong by the English, a tract of land consisting of several thousand acres, of which what is now Morristown was about the centre, was deeded by the Indians to the whites for what would, in these days at least, be considered an insignificant compensation. Said compensation was:

"Thirty pounds in cash, ten strandwater blankets, fifteen kettles, twenty axes, twenty hoes, ten duffills blankets, half a barrel of wine, three files, one gun-boer, one auger, four pistalls, four cutlasses, ten gunnes, one hundred barres of lead, half a barrell of powder, ten white blankets, twenty shirts, and one hundred knives."

This deed, executed on vellum and well preserved, is now in the possession of the New Jersey Historical Society at Newark, and is a particularly valuable document. Through the courtesy of the above named society the writer of this history was permitted to carefully examine this deed and to make tracings from the same. The signatures of the Indians, with their respective and varied marks, and the actual signatures of the whites on the original deed, are by no means the least interesting feature of this valuable document. Fac similes of these, and also of the beginning of the two first lines of the deed (enough to show the quaint, and for the times, really elegant, handwriting of the executor of the document), will be found in this volume, and will prove to be of deep interest to readers.

Not to dwell longer upon a subject, which, however interesting in itself, is not strictly appropriate to a history of Morristown, it may be proper to add that the Lenni Lenape were eventually settled on the Indian reservation in Burlington County, where they came to be known as the "Edge Pillocks."

The invitation to the remnants of the Lenni Lenape from the Mohicans of New York State, in the year 1801, to join them, is deeply significant as a striking illustration of aboriginal simplicity and hospitality:

> "Pack up your mats and come and eat out of our dish, which is large enough for all, and our necks are stretched in looking toward the fireside of our grandfathers till they are as long as cranes."

One brave and his faithful squaw of the Lenni Lenape tribe, remained in New Jersey after the remnants of the tribe had left the State, and twenty years afterward both died. The daughter of this lingering Indian couple, known as "Indian Ann," lived until the year 1894, and was therefore the last of the tribe in

New Jersey, which, in the early part of the eighteenth century welcomed with characteristic hospitality and friendliness the pioneers of what is now Morris County.

It is Hawthorne who writes of "the exquisite delight of picking up for one's self an arrow-head that was dropped centuries ago and has never been handled since, and which we thus receive directly from the hands of the red hunter. Such an incident builds up again the Indian village and its encircling forest, and recalls the painted chief, the squaws and the children sporting among the wigwams, while the little wind-rocked papoose swings from the branch of a tree."

Many arrow-heads, axe-heads and other Indian relics have been found in Morris County since the red men disappeared, and these are scarcely preserved by their present owners. Traces of an old Indian village are still (1905) discernible between Malapardis and Littleton, a few miles to the westward of Morristown. On the occasion of the delivery by the pastor of the Presbyterian Church of Whippany, in the year 1894, of an historical sermon, there were placed on exhibit in front of the pulpit desk an assortment of Indian relics found in the near vicinity of the village, which, in a most impressive manner, recalled the presence of the aborigines of this region, which now teems with the evidences of an advanced civilization.

"A moment and the pageant's gone;
The red men are no more;
The pale-faced strangers stand alone
Upon the river's shore."

CHAPTER II.

"The deeds of our fathers, in times that are gone;
Their virtues, their prowess, the fields they have won;
Their struggles for freedom, the toils they endured,
The rights and the blessings for us they procured."

MORE suitable introduction to the chapter of this history relating to the settlement, by the whites of what is now Morristown, New Jersey, could not be written, than the following extract from the "Annals of Morris County," by the Rev. Joseph F. Tuttle, D. D., LL.D., "the father" of Morris County history:

"Every community," he says, "has a history which, if properly related, must be interesting and even important at least to those who belong to it. Here the fathers of such a community fought the battle of life, wrestled with the problems of moral responsibility, loved the living, pitied the sorrowful, helped the weak, wept over the dying; here they laid the foundation of the social fabric as best they could, often in a very blind but honest method, lived life as we now live it, and they died leaving their graves to us as silent monitors not to permit them to sink into forgetfulness. Although not as great as many who have lived, they are our forefathers, and the work they did for us merits a grateful record at our hands."

The fact that Dr. Tuttle's ancestors were among the early settlers of what is now Morris County, and actively assisted in its material development, and in the shaping of its splendid history, gives special force to these words.

Following the course of the winding Whippanong River, or perhaps guided by the solitary crooked Indian path (Indian paths were invariably crooked) leading to the westward, some of the enterprising English settlers at Whippanong found their way to what is now Morristown, where they made a settlement. It is almost certain that this settlement, by the progressive pioneers of Whippanong, was made soon after their arrival at the last named place from the eastside of the Great Wachung Mountain—perhaps during the same year; or it may have been during the year next following the permanent settlement of Whippanong. It is a matter of sincere regret to students of local history, that extant historical records as well as tradition, are as silent as the Roman catacombs on the Appian Way, as to the exact date of the beginnings of what is now considered, by not a few world-wide travelers, the most beautiful city in the world—a city, also, about which there cluster historic associations almost unparalleled in interest in the annals of our great country. Nor is there any reliable history, or even trustworthy tradition, from which such data may be safely inferred; hence the student of local history is reluctantly compelled to accept some such vague statement as that of a former pastor of the historic First Presbyterian Church of Morristown (Rev. Rufus S. Green, D. D.), who says: "We cannot be far out of the way in placing the date of the first settlement of Morristown back nearly or quite to 1710:" or to accept the somewhat less vague conclusion of another student of local history, that "Morristown was first settled by the whites about the year 1710." If, however, "history makes us some amends for the shortness of life," then Morristown's "ample page which is rich with the spoils of time," most certainly makes us generous amends for the silvery haze which surrounds the commencement of her rare civic career.

The facilities for the prosecution of the iron industry offered by the Whippanong River, in the newly settled region, and perhaps the somewhat closer proximity of the iron ore at Succasunna, and the improvement in other respects of their material welfare, were apparently among the inducements to the founders of what is now Morristown to remove from the settlement at Whippanong, and make for themselves a new home in the inviting region chosen.

It will be far from uninteresting to the readers of this history to learn, that the particular locality to be first settled by the immigrants from Whippanong, was that in the near vicinity of the corner of the present Water and Spring streets, at the foot of Town Hill. This locality seems to have been chosen partly because of its proximity to the Whippanong River, flowing but a few rods to the eastward, which was to be utilized for the carrying on of the iron industry; and partly because of the ample protection from the winter winds afforded by the bold hills to the northward and westward of the spot selected. Inasmuch as what is now Morris street, as also the present Spring street, were at the early period now under consideration, the Indian path leading from Whippanong eastward toward Roxiticus, which is now Mendham, it is probable that the particular locality chosen by the Whippanong immigrants was selected also with a view to keeping as near as practicable to the only apology for a road then known in the vicinity.

The first iron forge to be erected by the early settlers of what is now Morristown, probably stood near, and perhaps upon, the identical site of a portion at least of what is now known as "Flagler's mill," and by some as "Durling's mill," which is situated a little to the north of the present Water street, and at the lower end of what was once known as "Pochontas Lake." This body of water was for many years, and until the complete destruction of the dam by a great freshet about ten years since, the peculiar pride of the young for swimming, boating and skating, not to mention the pleasure it afforded those of piscatorial tastes, who occasionally landed from its quiet waters a handsome black bass of no ordinary weight.

Near the primitive iron forge may have stood the gristmill and sawmill, both of which, as a means of supplying the imperative needs of the infant settlement, were doubtless built a little prior to the erection of the iron forge. Several other iron forges were subsequently erected at different points on the Whippanong River, the remains of one of which, if local tradition is to be relied upon, are still (1905) to be seen on the northern bank of the stream nearly opposite the site of the present new roundhouse of the Lackawanna Railroad Company. It is said that about the year 1777 there were in Morris County nearly 100 iron forges in operation, and that Washington, during his first sojourn in Morristown, expressed his disapproval of the employment of the large number of able-bodied men which the operation of these forges required, while the depleted ranks of the American army were left unreplenished. All the iron forges on the Whippanong River within the bounds of Morristown were, however, so far as their operation is concerned, extinct as early as about the year 1823.

The houses, or huts, as they might more properly be called, first erected by the immigrants from Whippanong, it is almost superfluous to remark, were rude structures, being constructed for the most part of logs, but they afforded satisfactory shelter from the elements, and protection at night from the wild beasts which then roamed at will through the newly-settled region.

We have seen that the early settlers of what is now Morristown, first erected their rude log houses near the intersection of the present Water and Spring streets. It was not long, however, before a few log houses were erected in clearings along what is now Morris street. A few years later—it may have been during the year 1718 or 1720—the energetic settlers found their way up the hill (Town Hill, known for many years as "the gully," because of its condition as the result of frequent washings out by the rains) to the locality now occupied by the Green, and the churches and business blocks surrounding it. In those early days this section of Morristown was part of a dense forest composed of giant oaks, chestnuts and other native species; but in clearings made by the sturdy woodman's axe, the enterprising settlers erected their houses on the plateau which is nearly 400 feet above the ocean level. It is highly probable that among the considerations which moved the settlers to this change of habitation to the above-mentioned plateau, was the improved state of the atmosphere, as compared with the dampness and miasma of the low lands adjacent to the Whippanong River, where the original settlement had been made.

The red men of the Whippanong tribe, be it remembered, still lingered amid the scenes and associations of their revered fathers. They doubtless viewed with amazement the rapid strides of their pale-faced neighbors, away from simplicity and barrenness, toward the higher civilization to which their racial instincts impelled them. From the pretty Whippanong stream these peaceable aborigines procured, with bow and arrow, and with rude spear, the fish with which its waters then abounded; and over the wooded hills and through the beautiful vales, now dotted with the signs of twentieth century civilization, they hunted wild game which then constituted the basis of their daily diet. Under the same somber moon that now, in his season, sheds his pale light upon the earth, swarthy lovers plighted their troth each to the other; since love is love, whatever be the shade of complexion, or whatever be the place or period. After having lived in harmony with the whites for half a century, the Indians of Morris County emigrated, a decimated band, to the West, about the year 1740, having been compensated by the State for the territory relinquished.

It has seemed meet, while the early history of what is now Morristown was passing in review before us, to drop a tear to the memory of our red-faced brothers who once inhabited the region, but who have melted away before the rising sun of civilization.

Wild beasts, including the bear, the panther, the wolf and the wildcat, roamed in the neighborhood unmolested, save as they now and then encroached upon the humble habitations of the white settlers. The presence of these marauding enemies of civilization necessitated the careful herding in pens of the sheep and other stock by night, while by day, they were protected by the vigilance of their owners, whose unerring aim laid not a few of the stealthy prowlers low. At length the few surviving beasts slunk away from the human habitations which, year by year, were increasing in number, and the period of local history when "wolves in great numbers answered each other from the neighboring hills," soon became only an interesting memory.

The quaint deed by which the land now embraced in Morristown's centre (the entire tract containing 2,000 acres), was, in the year 1715, conveyed to one John Keys, or Kay, is of too much interest to be omitted; hence a verbatim copy is here presented:

"By virtue of a warrant from ye Council of Proprietors, bearing date ye tenth day of March last past, I have surveyed this Tract or Lott of land unto John Kay within ye Western Division of ye Province of New Jersey, in ye Last indian purchases made of ye Indians by ye said Proprietors; Situate upon & near a Branch of Passamisk River, Called whipene, beginning at a small hickory corner, standing near a Black oak marked K, ten cha. distance from a corner of Wm. Pens Lands; thence Northwest one hundred sixty & five cha; crossing ye said Whipene to a corner white oak marked also K; thence South west one hundred twenty and seven cha. & twenty-five link to a poast for a corner under ye side of a hill called mine mountain; from thence South east one hundred sixty & five cha. to a poast; then North East one hundred twenty-seven cha. & twenty five links, & by ye bound of Govn. Pens land to ye place of beginning. Containing Two thousand acres of land besides one hundred acres allowance for Highways, surveyed April ye 28th, 1715 pr me R. Bull Survy.

"Ye 22 of August 1715 Inspected and approved of by ye Council of Props. and ordered to be Entered upon Record.

"Tests, JOHN WILLS, Clerk."

In the same year (1715), 1,250 acres of land embracing what is now Morristown, and Morris Township, were surveyed, and deeded by the same Council of Proprietors to Joseph Helby and Thomas Stevenson. Helby's land lay to the east and north, and Stevenson's to the south and west of the present Morristown Green. Neither Kay, Helby nor Stevenson, however, settled in West Hanover, as Morristown was then called, and the large tracts of land owned by these early speculators were soon sold in farms and building lots, to those who had established themselves in the village and vicinity which, all unknown to them at the time, was destined to become famous in the annals of America.

From the fact of the transfer by the Council of Proprietors to Helby, Kay and Stevenson, in the year 1715, of the land embracing that on which the immigrants from Whippanong first settled at the foot of "Town Hill," it is a safe inference that these immigrants had either purchased their homesites and mill-sites and garden-plots from the friendly Indians (which seems improbable), or that they were "squatters," as were the first white explorers of Whippanong during their temporary sojourn in the region near the close of the seventeenth century. It is an equally safe inference that the industry of the founders of Morristown—the industry which "sweeteneth our enjoyment, and seasoneth our attainments with a delightful relish" —was soon rewarded with the means with which the more frugal of them were able to purchase such lands as were deemed necessary. Thus the 4,500 acres and more of land owned by three men in the year 1715 were, a few years subsequently, in the possession of numerous residents who were "here to stay," and in whose honored descendants they are still with us as interesting links with the eventful past.

It should be said at this point that the handful of immigrants from Whippanong who had settled West Hanover, was supplemented by frequent arrivals of English direct from Newark, Elizabethtown and New England, which is apparent from the fact of the newly added names which soon afterward appeared on the rolls of the village church.

Concerning the first frame house built in West Hanover, the following note, taken from a manuscript of the late Rev. Dr. Joseph F. Tuttle, is of more than ordinary interest: "Rev. Baker Johnson some years ago conversed with a Mr. Shipman (father of Lawyer Shipman, of Belvidere), whose father aided in building the first house in Morristown, somewhere on the stream. It was in 1727, as Mr. Johnson thinks, Mr. Shipman stated."

The character of the early white settlers of Whippanong, and hence of West Hanover, may be inferred from the fact that almost simultaneously with their entrance into the region contiguous to what is now Morristown, they inaugurated religious services. At first they gathered for divine worship in their humble homes, and it may be in the rude barns of the period, the services then being conducted for the most part by some of their own number selected for their superior gifts and graces. It is highly probable that the village schoolmaster, whose coming into the new settlement was not long delayed after the first log hut was raised, and who was easily, before the arrival of the minister, the most highly respected of the settlers, was among the number selected to lead the worship of men and women who, even at that early period, cultivated "the presence of God." To the Whippanong schoolmaster we shall have occasion to refer by name at a subsequent stage of this history. It may be that, as was the case in other early settlements in the province of New Jersey, the Whippanong people assembled, when the state of the weather permitted, in the open air for divine worship, with only the blue canopy of the skies for a roof. Occasionally, as seemingly reliable tradition informs us, a minister from the older settlement at Newark was present to conduct the services for the Whippanong worshipers. It is not improbable that Rev. John Prudden, pastor of the Newark church from the year 1692 to the year 1699, and who may have been a resident of Newark after his dismissal from this pastorate officiated now and then for the congregation gathered in Whippanong before a pastor was called by them. Such, indeed, is the opinion of those who have digged deeply into Morris County history. Of Rev. Mr. Prudden's Newark pastorate, which continued but seven years, it is recorded that it was "not a smooth one," and if he occasionally officiated for the Whippanong worshipers his visits to that quiet hamlet were doubtless an agreeable relief from the memory of his troublesome pastorate in Newark.

The religious services inaugurated by the pioneers of Whippanong, led to the organization, probably in the latter part of the year 1717 or in the early part of the year following, or even earlier, it may have been, of a church at Whippanong, the first of any kind to be organized in what is now Morris County. It was, in a sense, the mother of the numerous churches of the different sects whose edifices, many of them costly and imposing, now lift their spires heavenward from the hills and valleys of this region. It is said, however, that soon after the settlement of Whippanong an unsuccessful attempt was made to establish an Episcopal chuch. As early, indeed, so it is said, as the year 1710, an Episcopal missionary from Newark held occasional services in or near Whippanong; "but they were soon discontinued."

In the early autumn or winter of the year 1718, a house of worship was erected in Whippanong, on land given by the village schoolmaster, John Richards, which land is now the burial ground for the village of Whippany. It is situated on the right hand of the road leading through the village from Morristown, as one goes toward Hanover. The original deed conveying the land on which the mother church edifice was erected is still (1905) in existence, and in excellent condition. The substance of this quaint document is as follows:

"I, John Richards, of Whipponong, in the county of Hunterdon, schoolmaster, for and in consideration of the love and affection that I have for my Christian friends and neighbors in Whipponong, and for a desire to promote and advance the public interest, and especially for the public worship of God, give three and one-half acres of land, situate and being in the township of Whipponong, on that part called Parcipponong, on the northwestern side of Whipponong River; only for public use, improvement and benefit, for a meeting-house, schoolhouse, burying yard and training field, and such like, and no other."

This deed was dated September 2, 1718, and the witnesses thereto were Jedidiah Buckingham and John Cooper.

Dying in the month of December, in the year 1718, at the age of sixty-three years, the remains of Mr. Richards were the first to be deposited in the tract of land so generously given by him for a "burying yard," while living. His headstone, composed of red sandstone, is still to be seen in the older portion of the Whippany burial-ground, and the sight of this ancient landmark kept free from moss by some friendly hand, so that the inscription is always discernible, arouses one's slumbering reverence for the past.

The history of the Richards deed deserves at least a passing notice. The document, as might be supposed, originally belonged to the mother church at Whippanong; but while other records and papers belonging to the parish were removed to Hanover, when, in the year 1755, the new house of worship was erected there, this deed, for some reason now unknown to the writer, was retained at Whippanong. Among the papers of Calvin Howell Esq., of Whippany, found after his decease, was the Richards deed. It was discovered in a sort of secret drawer in an old desk. For many years it was in the possession of William H. Howell Esq., a son of Calvin Howell, the former of whom was sheriff of Morris County about twenty years ago. Upon the decease of William H. Howell, the deed came into the possession of his family. The writer had the privilege a few years ago of carefully examining this rare document. It has since been presented to the Washington Headquarters, in Morristown, New Jersey, where it may now be seen by the visitor.

CHAPTER III

"Dissensions, like the small streams are first begun,
Scarce seen they rise, but gather as they run;
So lines that from their parallel decline,
More they proceed the more they still disjoin."

HE house of worship erected in Whippanong in the year 1718, traces of the foundation of which were discernible as late as the nineteenth century (as the writer has been informed by an aged resident, now deceased), was a small square structure, covered on all four sides and on the roof with shingles, and was without cupola or spire. By at least one local historian this primitive church is said to have had galleries which were reached by an outside flight of stairs. The building stood to the left of, and somewhat back from, the present front entrance to the Whippany burial ground. To this church, at first of the Congregational order, apparently, and later of the Presbyterian, the people of what are now Morristown, Madison, Chatham, Parsippany and other surrounding hamlets, went each Sunday, through the almost unbroken wilderness, for nearly a score of years for divine worship.

Of the Whippanong church the first pastor was the Rev. Nathaniel Hubbell, a native of New England, and a graduate of Yale College. He may have been settled as pastor of the church in the month of December, 1718, almost immediately following the decease of "John Richards, schoolmaster." After a pastorate, as near as can now be ascertained, of about twleve years, Mr. Hubbell was succeeded about the year 1730, by the Rev. John Nutman, also a graduate, in 1727, of Yale College. He was the son of James Nutman Esq., of Edinburgh, Scotland, by his second wife, Sarah, daughter of the Rev. John Prudden, of Newark, and hence was a grandson of the last named gentleman.

He may, therefore, have been introduced to the people of Whippanong by his grandfather, who had probably, as we have seen, officiated occasionally in the church. Mr. Nutman is said to have been a man of excellent scholarship for his day. Soon after the installation of Mr. Nutman as pastor of the church at Whippanong—it may have been during the year 1731 or the year 1732—there began a discussion among the congregation over the matter of the erection of a new house of worship. The structure in which they worshiped was, if tradition may be regarded as trustworthy, considered by a portion at least of the worshipers as "old and dilapidated." This is a claim, however, which seems to have had little or no basis in reason, when it is remembered that the structure had at the time been used only about fourteen years, and was occupied as a house of worship for about twenty-three years subsequently. It is a claim that appears to have been, as all the circumstances of the case are recalled and impartially considered, a mere pretext on the part of certain elements in the congregation for the removal of the church organization to a part of the extensive parish which would more completely gratify their desires in the matter. There is little doubt that the church edifice in Whippanong was getting too small to accommodate the growing congregation; but the natural remedy for that was the enlargement of the primitive building. The failure of the project to abandon the old house of worship at Whippanong resulted in a determination on the part of that portion of the congregation residing at West Hanover, to withdraw from the mother church and organize a separate church at that point. The reasons urged by the people of West Hanover in favor of a separate church organization were, the inconvenience of attending divine services at Whippanong, owing to the long distance and imperfect facilities for travel, and the material increase of population at West Hanover, which rendered the support of a pastor practicable. To the proposal to organize a separate church at West Hanover the majority of the Whippanong congregation was stoutly opposed.

The West Hanover people were determined, however, upon a separation, and as a means of adjusting the growing difficulty it was at length resolved by the several parties in the congregation at Whippanong, to submit the decision of the matter to the casting of lots, each party agreeing to abide by the result.

After much prayer the lots, with great solemnity, were cast. The result of the lot-casting was, that the mother church was to remain undivided; and if a new house of worship was erected, it should be upon the old site, in the burial lot given by "John Richards, schoolmaster." Contrary to agreement, however, the West Hanover people refused to accept this result, and the greater portion at least of the dissatisfied ones ceased attending the services at Whippanong.

Two versions of this episode have been given. One is, that the portion of the congregation living at West Hanover did not agree to abide by the result of the lot, and that they objected at the beginning to the employment of that means for the adjustment of the difficulty confronting the parish. The other is that there was a general agreement to abide by the result of the vote. The reader is left to decide for himself, from facts to be presented later, which is the correct version.

It is probable that religious services were soon afterward inaugurated at West Hanover, in private houses. Some of the West Hanover people who had worshiped at Whippanong may have begun almost immediately to attend the services at Basking Ridge, which seem to have been inaugurated about the year 1720, two or three years later than the organization of the church at Whippanong.

The alienation of the West Hanover people from the mother church, as might have been anticipated, seriously crippled the latter organization, rendering it difficult for those who remained to suitably provide for the support of their clergyman, Mr. Nutman. At the annual meeting of the synod of Philadelphia, within whose ecclesiastical jurisdiction the Whippanong church then belonged, held in the year 1733, Mr. Nutman sought relief from pecuniary embarrassment, which seemed to threaten the speedy dissolution of his pastoral relation with the mother church, over which he had but recently been installed. He pleaded for the exercise of the influence of the synod for a reunion of his divided parish. At this session of the synod, that body expressed in strong terms its disapproval of resorting to the casting of the lot for the settlement of church difficulties, which were susceptible of adjustment by appeal to the constituted judicatories of the ecclesiastical body with which they were identified.

The synod evidently did not approve of the organization of another church at West Hanover, for the people of that part of the parish were advised to join themselves, temporarily at least, with the congregations at Basking Ridge and Whippanong. This arrangement was to continue, however, only until the churches at East Hanover (Whippanong) and Basking Ridge should reach a condition of self-support, and until the growth of population at West Hanover should justify the establishment of a self-sustaining church, in that section of the parish. If it should, after proper effort, be ascertained that a reunion of the people of West Hanover with the mother church was impracticable, then the people of the former place were to be left at liberty to organize a new church. The fact that Mr. Nutman, at the same meeting of the synod as that above mentioned, and after the expressions of opinion by that body already referred to, requested dismission from his presbytery and the termination of his pastoral relation with the church at Whippanong, seems to indicate that his understanding of the temper of the West Hanover people led him to the conclusion that a reunion of the two sections of the parish was not to be expected. The presbytery of East Jersey, of which Mr. Nutman was a member, was recommended by the synod to exert its good offices on behalf of a reconciliation between the two portions of the dismembered parish, with the proviso that if such reconciliation could not be effeced then the presbytery was to be at liberty to dismiss the clergyman, upon his application.

At the meeting of the Synod of Philadelphia, in the year 1734, the Whippanong and West Hanover church difficulty was again before that body. The use of the lot in the settlement of church difficulties was formally condemned by the synod. The opinion was also expressed by this ecclasiastical body that "we are afraid that much sin has been committed by many, if not all, the people in the profane disregard of said lot, and therefore excite them to reflect upon their past practises in reference thereto in order to their repentance."

This deliverance of the synod only widened the breach between the two sections of the Hanover parish, and to thoughtful observers a reconciliation seemed among the impossibilities. The synod met again in the year 1735, and at this session the West Hanover people made application for the ordination to the Christian ministry of John Cleverly, a graduate of Harvard College, who had recently come among them. This application, it will be noticed, was in evident disregard of the recommendation of the synod at its meeting of the year before. The matter of the ordination of Mr. Cleverly was referred to the Presbytery of Philadelphia. Meanwhile Mr. Cleverly remained in West Hanover and probably conducted the religious services held there.

In the month of May, 1736, the Presbytery of Philadelphia met, and at this session the people of West Hanover, by their representatives, urged upon that body the ordination of Mr. Cleverly. They were instructed to appoint a day, giving due notice to the presbytery, that they might attend to the matter in proper form. For reasons which do not appear upon the record no day was appointed for the ordination of Mr. Cleverly.

The meeting of the Presbytery of Philadelphia in the year 1737 was held at West Hanover, and when the matter of the ordination of Mr. Cleverly came before that body there was found to be opposition to its consummation. This opposition appears to have originated among the people of Whippanong, or East Hanover, as it was also called. They were apparently determined to embarrass the establishment of another church at West Hanover, and this they could effectually do, temporarily at least, by preventing the ordination and settlement of Mr. Cleverly as pastor of the congregation at West Hanover. It was not, as it appears, that the people of East Hanover were opposed to Mr. Cleverly personally. They were simply opposed to the settlement of any individual as pastor of what they considered a faction which had wrought havoc in the mother church. In view of the determined opposition to his ordination, the presbytery deemed it inexpedient to proceed further in the matter; the congregation was excused for its failure to appoint a day for his ordination, and Mr. Cleverly was advised to seek another field of labor. He chose, however, to remain in West Hanover, and he probably continued to conduct the services there, for the most part at least, until the year 1742, when a pastor was called and duly installed. It is said that during his residence in West Hanover, Mr. Cleverly preached, occasionally at least, in the Presbyterian church at Turkey, now New Providence. Indeed, the writer has seen the statement that before coming to West Hanover, he supplied the Presbyterian pulpit at Turkey. Mr. Cleverly remained unmarried all his life. He died in 1776, aged eighty-one years, and was buried on the last day of December in the yard in the rear of the First Church, where his headstone may be seen.

The synod had with commendable prudence and

tact dealt with the difficulty which had so long existed between the people of East and West Hanover. The difficulty, however, still remained. Being desirous of bringing about a reconciliation between the estranged sections of the parish, a large committee was appointed at the meeting of the synod, held in the year 1738, and to it the entire matter was submitted for final consideration. On July 26 of that year this committee met at Hanover, almost certainly in the "old and dilapidated" house of worship in the burial ground at Whippanong. The Rev. Gilbert Tennent, of New Brunswick, one of the brothers famous in ecclesiastical annals for their religious trance experiences, was selected to preach the sermon, which he consented to do. He took for his text words found in the eleventh chapter of Ezekiel, nineteenth verse: "I will give them one heart." From these words, in the selection of which the preacher was unquestionably guided by other than human wisdom, Mr. Tennent, whose reputation as a profoundly religious man had doubtless preceded him to Whippanong, delivered a sermon. The moral effect of it upon the hearts of his hearers may be inferred from the subsequent conduct of the parties involved in the long-standing difficulty existing between them, and from the prompt and happy settlement of the trouble to the entire satisfaction of all concerned. We notice first the consequent pliable disposition of the people of East Hanover, who expressed a desire for a reunion, if it could be had on reasonable terms. The West Hanover people were, however, indisposed toward a reunion, because, as they declared to the committee, their numbers had increased since the separation from the mother church, about the year 1732, and they as a result were better able to support a pastor. Recognizing the force of these allegations of the West Hanover people, and having drawn, by questionings, from the East Hanover people, the admission that they, too, were in better condition to support Mr. Nutman than formerly, the committee, on behalf of the synod, concluded that no further efforts for a reunion be made, but that there be two separate churches. To this all parties agreed, and harmony once more prevailed. Doubtless an appeal, at the outset, to the better nature of the parties concerned would have resulted in a more speedy settlement of the difficulty between them, and saved the cause of religion from the reproach which fell upon it.

In the autumn of the year 1738, or early in the year 1739, a Presbyterian church was formerly organized in West Hanover, or Morristown, as about that time it came to be known. During the year 1739 the county was laid out and given the name of Morris, in honor of Governor Lewis Morris. It then included what are now the counties of Warren and Sussex; and what for more than a quarter of a century had been called West Hanover came to be known as Morris Town. The first official reference to West Hanover as Morris Town, however, is to be found in the book of records in the county clerk's office, under date of March 25, 1740, when the county was divided into townships by the court.

It is a fact greatly to be regretted that from the organization of the First Presbyterian Church of Morristown, to the summer of the year 1742, when a pastor was called, there were no records kept, or if kept, are unavailable. As already remarked, John Cleverly, who was still in Morristown, continued to supply the pulpit of the newly organized church occasionally, and probably continuously, until the coming of one whose name is still revered—Rev. Dr. Timothy Johnes, who, in the two or three succeeding chapters, becomes one of the central figures of Morristown's rare history.

The Presbyterian church of West Hanover, or Morristown, as it had already come to be popularly called, was, as previously stated, organized in the autumn of the year 1738, or near the opening of the year 1739. The present writer is of the opinion, however, that the organization of this church was effected almost immediately after the meeting of the large committee of the Synod of Philadelphia, held in the primitive house of worship at East Hanover (Whippanong) July 26, 1738, at which time and place the long-standing difficulty between the two sections of the extensive Hanover parish was finally and satisfactorily adjusted; and that by the close at least of the month of September of the year last mentioned the First Presbyterian Church of Morristown, New Jersey, had commenced its famous career as a regularly organized ecclesiastical body.

As near as can now be ascertained the church was organized with a membership of about 100, and was from the beginning self-supporting. It was within the bounds of the Presbytery of New York, which had been constituted during the same year as above mentioned, by the union of the presbyteries of Long Island and East Jersey.

In the mind of the writer there is scarcely a doubt that Rev. John Cleverly, bachelor, who continued to reside in West Hanover after his failure of installation, conducted the services of the newly-organized church most of the time from its inception until the settlement of a pastor, about four years later. It will be no reflection upon the character and professional attainments of Mr. Cleverly, for the writer to express the opinion, that but for eccentricities, the exact nature of which are not now ascertainable, he may have been the first, of a by no means short list of installed pastors, who have served the First Presbyterian Church of Morristown during the past 162 years of its remarkable history.

The first house of worship in what is now Morristown, was erected probably during the year 1740, or about two years after the organization of the church. It is said to have stood on the site, or nearly so, of the present substantial stone manse of the First Presbyterian Church, upon a piece of land given to the church by two of its well-to-do members—Benjamin Hathaway and Jonathan Lindsley for a parsonage and burial-ground. It is understood to have faced what is now Morris street.

It was a nearly square structure, and small, and is by some said to have been a frame building, shingled on its four sides, as well as on the roof. By others we are told that it was a "log meeting-house." The writer is inclined to accept the former opinion, for the reasons following: It is a well authenticated fact that as early as the year 1727 the first frame house was erected in West Hanover. It is highly probable that by the year 1740 frame houses were becoming numerous in what had then come to be known as Morristown. And one can scarcely be charged with jumping to conclusions if he infers, that a house of worship erected at that period was a frame structure, whose sides and roof were shingled. It is quite probable that this house of worship was a sort of duplication in form, if not also in dimensions and general appearance, of the first house of worship previously erected in the older settlement of Newark; since, among the projectors of this primitive house of worship then identified with the Morristown Presbyterian Church, there were probably not a few persons who, prior to their removal to the last named place, had attended the Newark Church, and hence were familiar with the character, capacity and cost of the latter structure. That, in the construction of the original house of worship in Morristown, the suggestions of these former members of the Newark Church were taken into consideration, is a most natural inference. It is to be regretted that there is extant no reliable representation of this house of worship; but it would not be far from the truth to say, that it was in form and dimensions a duplicate of the primitive house of worship in Newark, of which an apparently accurate picture is to be seen among historical collections.

Among the many commendatory patriotic services rendered by the Daughters of the American Revolution, through its various chapters, was the placing, on November 10, 1904, of a stone tablet which is said to mark the site of a corner of the original house of worship in what is now Morristown. One of the most interesting features of the occasion of the formal placing of this marker was the circumstance that a great-great-granddaughter of Rev. Timothy Johnes, Miss Little, performed the ceremony of unveiling the tablet. This stone tablet, which is about two feet in width and three feet in length, and elevated about four inches above the surface of the ground, bears the following inscription: "This stone marks the site of the original church built in 1740, used as a hospital for the Revolutionary soldiers in 1777. Erected by the Morristown Chapter, D. A. R., 1904." The picture of this memorial tablet, which appears in this volume, is from a photograph taken by Frederick F. Curtis, of Morristown, about the middle of November, of the year 1904. The stone work conspicuous in the background of the picture is a portion of the First Church edifice.

In the year 1764 a steeple, 125 feet in height, as we are informed, was added to the original house of worship, which by some is said to have been built in the middle of the structure; the more probable theory, however, is that it was attached to one end of the modest building. By no means the least interesting fact concerning the erection of this steeple is this: that to Colonel Jacob Ford Sr. was assigned, by the trustees of the parish, "the care, management and oversight" of the work. Hitherto the people had assembled for divine worship on Sunday, for the space of nearly a quarter of a century, without the use of a bell, but after the completion of the new steeple, a bell was placed in its tower. On this bell, which has been used from the year it was first placed in position until the present time, a period of 141 years, is the impress of the British crown, and also the names of the makers, "Lister & Pack, of London fecit." Tradition informs us that this bell was presented to the Presbyterian Church of Morristown by the King of Great Britain. This bell, it is said, was brought from Elizabeth Town to Morris Town, by Benjamin Freeman; he who was subsequently the proprietor of the tavern formerly kept by Jacob Arnold, and who, late in the seventeenth century, ran a stage coach to Elizabeth Town. Although since the time of its first hanging in the tower of Morristown's historic church, this bell has been twice recast in consequence of its cracking, it has since been used to summon the congregation for worship in the handsome stone edifice standing upon ground made sacred by the associations of a truly eventful past. Owing to its great age and the rich historical associations which cluster about it, this bell has become an object of veneration on the part of those acquainted with its remarkable record. It is in some respects a most singular fact, that now, (1905) for the third time, this bell is cracked, and will again require recasting.

The growth of the Morristown church, during the

decade following the erection of the new steeple and the hanging of the imported bell, necessitated the enlargement of the primitive house of worship, which was accomplished in the year 1774. It is said that the original structure was separated in the centre (sawn asunder, it may be said), the two sections thus made, moved away from each other and the open space left between them filled in by the construction of a new part. The entire building when completed was about thirty by fifty feet. At each end of this house of worship was an entrance for the accommodation of attendants coming from different directions to attend divine services. The main entrance was on what is now Morris street.

The seats in this enlarged house of worship were enclosed, leaving a square space within, which resembled in appearance more a pen than church pews. These pen-like pews were made for the accommodation of an entire family. A single flight of stairs led up to the dizzy heights of the "cup-like" pulpit.

In the summer of the year 1742, commencing with the thirteenth of August, the pulpit of the Presbyterian church of Morristown—at that time the congregation, as will be seen, worshipped in the original structure erected about two years previously—was for six consecutive Sundays supplied by Rev. Timothy Johnes, a graduate of Yale College, and a licentiate of the Congregational body in New England. From an interesting paper read by Mrs. Isaac R. Pierson, at the sesquicentennial celebration of the First Baptist church of

Morristown, in the year 1902, the following extract is presented:

> "The Indian name for the country around was Rockciticus, as late as the arrival of Parson Johnes, in 1742. Pastor Johnes was one of the prominent historical characters of the times. Previous to his coming to Morristown he had several other calls, and he was perplexed as to which to accept, so he referred the matter to Providence—deciding to accept the next one made. He had not risen from his knees, when two old men came to his house and asked him to become pastor of a small congregation at Rockciticus (now Morristown). He consented and after traveling a long distance, through the forest, he inquired of his guides: 'Where is Rockciticus?' The reply was. 'Here, there and everywhere.'"

It is, perhaps, superfluous to say, that "Parson Johnes" came to Morristown on horseback. So satisfactory were the preaching and personality of this young theologue that at the termination of his engagement as a temporary supply, a call was extended to him to become the pastor of the newly organized church. This call, after due consideration, he accepted. and in the spring of the year 1743 he removed his family, consisting of a wife and two children, to Morristown. On the ninth of February, of the year of his removal to his new parish, Mr. Johnes was installed by the Presbytery of New York as pastor of the church, which for more than half a century he served most faithfully and efficiently. Prior to the coming of Mr. Johnes to Morristown, no record of church proceedings had been kept, or if any had been kept, they have not since been available. But almost immediately after the commencement of his services as a supply with the church of which he was to become the pastor, he began a record of its proceedings, which was continued until his decease. The title which appears at the beginning of this record, written by Mr. Johnes himself, is worthy of presentation, and is as follows:

> "The Record of the Church, in the town of Morris, from the first Erection and founding of it there;—and, under Christ, as Collected, and Setled, and Watered (in much weakness) by Timo. Johnes, Pastor; who first came, Aug. 13th, 1742, stayed 6 Sab., and then fetched my Family, and was ordained, Feb. 9, 1743."

CHAPTER IV

"I love the memory of the past, its pressed but fragrant
flowers,
The moss that gathers on its walls, the ivy round its towers."

T the time of the installation of the Rev. Mr. Johnes, the Presbyterian church of Morristown had a membership of somewhat over 100, of which, in view of its rare genealogical importance, a complete list is here appended:

"John Lindley, Elizabeth Lindley, his wife; John Lindley, Jr., Sarah Lindley, his wife; Jacob Fford, Hannah Fford, his wife; Joseph Prudden, Joanna Prudden, his wife; Caleb Fairchild, Anna Fairchild, his wife; Joseph Coe, Judith Coe, his wife; Joseph Coe, Jr., Esther Coe, his wife; Solomon Munson, Tamar Munson, his wife; Benjamin Pierson, Patience Pierson, his wife; Stephen Freman, Hannah Freman, his wife; Matthew Lum, Susanna Lum, his wife; Peter Cundit, Phebe Cundit, his wife; Philip Cundit, Mary Cundit, his wife; Joseph Howard, Mary Howard, his wife; Sarah, wife of Samuel Ford; Benjamin Bailey, Letitia Bailey, his wife;

Samuel Nutman, Abigail Nutman, his wife; James Cole, Phebe Cole, his wife; Benjamin Coe, Rachel Coe, his wife; Thomas Kent, Ebenezer Mahurin and his wife, Uriah Cutler, Timothy Mills, Job Allen, of Rockaway; John Clarke, Abigail Clarke, his wife: Benjamin Beach, of Rockaway; Abner Beach, of Rockaway; Jonah Arstin and his wife; Zeruiah, wife of Isaiah Wines, 'now of Captain Samuel Day;' Sarah wife of Isaac Price; Martha, wife of Cornelius Arstin; Susanna, wife of Caleb Tichenor; Sarah, wife of James Frost; Mary, wife of Isaac Clark; Elizabeth, wife of David More; Ann, wife of Alexander Robards; Ann Allen, widow; Sarah wife of Abraham Hathaway; Bethiah, wife of Thomas Wood; Experience, wife of Benjamin Conger; Charity, wife of Benjamin Shipman; Phebe, wife of Shadrach Hathaway; ——, wife of John Jonson; Catherine, wife of Peter Stagg; ——, wife of Eliacam Suerd; Mary Burt; Comfort, wife of Joseph Stiles; Joanna, wife of Peter Prudden; Samuel Sweasy, Susanna Sweasy, his wife; Hannah, wife of Joseph Fowler; Hannah, wife of Jeremiah Johnson; Martha, wife of John Fford; Abigail, wife of Jonathan Conklin, 'now of Samuel Bayles:' Charles Howell, daughter (?) of Charles Howell; Deborah, wife of Charles Howell; Dr. Elijah Jillet; Jane, wife of Dr. Jillet; Elder Morris, of Basking Ridge; Mary, his wife; Sarah, wife of Abraham Campfield; Phebe, wife of Joshua Ball; Elizabeth Kermickle, widow; Nathan Ward's wife; Jemima, wife of Deacon Matthew Lum; Samuel Baldwin, of Mendham; Rebecca, wife of Zechariah Fairchild; Elizabeth, wife of Captain Clark; Sarah, wife of Samuel Mills: Elizabeth, wife of David Gauden; Mattaniah Lyon, ——, his wife; Alexander Johnson's wife; Silas Halsey, Abigail, his wife; Bathiah, wife of Benjamin Halsey; John MacFeran, Elizabeth, his wife; Nathan Price, Peter Prudden."

As explanatory of the composition of the list of names above presented, it should be said that in connection with the list, as recorded in the book of the First Presbyterian church of Morristown, there appears, in the neat handwriting of Mr. Johnes, the following heading:

> "The number and names of the persons that were in full communion when the church was first collected and founded, together with the number of those that came since from other churches."

The following entry upon the membership roll of the young church in Morristown—the first to be made after the entry of the long list above given—is of such special interest that it is here presented:

> "August 15, 1765, Naomi, wife of John Laporte, turned from the Anabaptists and received on ye foot of her being a member of that ch. in good standing."

West Hanover, afterward Morristown, was probably settled under the following regulations made by the Duke of York for all settlements in the province of New Jersey:

> "Every township is obliged to pay their own minister, according to such agreement as they shall make with him, and no man to refuse his own proportion; the minister being elected by the major part of the householders and inhabitants in the town."

In strange contrast with the salaries received by ministers of the Gospel in the twentieth century (insufficient as, in the writer's judgment, they are), the salary, in money, promised Mr. Johnes at his settlement, or installation as we would now call it, was twenty pounds, which at that period was equivalent to about $50 per year; we must, however, rely upon tradition in the acceptance of this statement. It could not have been long after the settlement of Mr. Johnes as pastor of the Presbyterian church of Morristown, that he was able to furnish his table chiefly from the products of the parsonage plot, which covered the piece of land bounded by the present Morris, South and Pine streets, and extending down to the Whippany River.

Just when Mr. Johnes began to occupy the parsonage cannot now be definitely stated; but it could not have been long after his settlement as pastor of the Presbyterian church. This parsonage stood on the site now occupied by the Memorial Hospital, on the left of Morris street, as one goes "from town" to the station of the Lackawanna Railroad. It was the writer's privilege to frequently see this interesting old building while it stood upon its original site. The old parsonage building has been moved to a place almost directly across Morris street, and now stands somewhat back from the sidewalk. It is occupied by a private family.

The farmers of the parish plowed the ground, planted the seed and gathered the crops, for "the parson;" and furnished and cut the wood used in his house. The periodical parish "bees" furnished the parsonage with liberal supplies of necessaries for the table; and on the return of the beloved pastor from his social visits over the parish he was not permitted to be empty-handed. It has been said that "every imaginable article, from a riddle to a squire's publishment of a marriage, has been found on the account books of ministers (of 'ye olden times') as having been received in partial payment of stipend." Could the account books of Mr. Johnes their secrets unfold, they would doubtless relate a similar story; a story which would make extremely interesting reading for the present generation.

Reference has already been made to the casting of lots at Whippanong, as a means of deciding the long mooted question whether the primitive church organization should remain there, or be removed to another part of the extended parish; to the refusal of that portion of the Whippanong church, residing at West Hanover, to abide by the decision of the lot that the church organization should remain where it was originally established, notwithstanding their solemn agreement so to do; and to the fact, also, of the premature establishment of religious services at West Hanover, regardless of the counsel of synod and presbytery, and the wishes of the brethren residing at Whippanong.

The sequel to the ecclesiastical irregularities above mentioned could not have been particularly agreeable to the active participants therein; for almost immediately following the settlement of Rev. Timothy Johnes, as pastor of the young church at Morristown, they were called to an account for their conduct in the matter. The citation of the following extract from the records of the First Presbyterian Church of Morristown, will suffice, without note or comment, for our enlightenment upon this interesting subject:

"An accompt for Public Confession. A public confession at the settlement of the ch. for a transgression Relating to a Lot Cast with Reference to the Settling of a house for Public Worship between Hanover & this town. Ye persons that confessed are Joseph Coe, John Lindley Jr., Joseph Prudden, Matthew Lum, Uriah Cutler, Stephen Freeman, Peter Cundit, Jacob Fford, Joseph Howard, Benj. Bailey, Philip Cundit, Benjamin Coe, Ebenezar Mahurin, Samuel Nutman, Timothy Peck, Cornelius Arstin, Solomon Munson, Caleb Fairchild, Joseph Coe, Zachariah Fairchild, Joseph Tichenor."

That the Morristown church, and its conscientious young pastor, did not regard these fellow-members as totally and irremediably depraved, is clearly apparent from the fact that five of them were subsequently elected to the eldership, in which capacity they rendered most excellent service to the church, which may be facetiously spoken of as having been "born out of due time." The names of these elders, who seem to have composed the first session of the First Presbyterian Church of Morristown, were: Joseph Prudden, Matthew Lum, John Lindsley, Joseph Coe and Jacob Ford, the latter, the son of John Ford, Esq., of what is now known as Monroe, situated about two miles to the eastward of Morristown. One at least of these church officials, Jacob Ford, played a conspicuously important part in the civic affairs of a town which is now famous, the country over, because of its rare Revolutionary history. Of Jacob Ford it has been said by a local historian of high repute (the late Edmund D. Halsey, Esq.): "He was no doubt the leading man in Morristown"; but close behind him, it should be said, come not a few other Morristonians, whose names and deeds materially aid in illuminating the pages of its local history.

Almost from the time of its first settlement by the whites, about the year 1710, what is now Morristown, was called West Hanover and New Hanover, interchangeably; and it was a part, at first of Burlington, and later of Hunterdon County. The following extracts from the minutes of the Hunterdon County Court, under date of June 5, of the year 1722, held at Trenton, then the county seat, will serve as a link between the original settlement of what is now Morristown, and its subsequent history as a separate township officially bearing that name:

"Whereas, there is no assessor returned to this court to serve for the inhabitants of the township of Hanover, it is, therefore, ordered by the court that Elisha Bird serve as assessor for the said township of Hanover for the ensuing year, to assess the tax to be levied upon the said inhabitants towards the support of his Majesty's government; and it is hereby ordered accordingly."

Additional links between the periods mentioned, will be found in the several facts following: At the sessions of the same court, held in the years 1723, 1724 and 1725, other officers were appointed for the township of Hanover, which, it should be borne in mind by our readers, included what is now Morristown. Commencing, however, with the year 1726, the Hanover Township officers were elected by the people in town meeting assembled, in genuine New England fashion. The record of the first town meeting convened for the election of officers in Hanover Township, is of too much interest to be passed over, hence it is given, verbatim:

"It being the General Town Meeting appointed by Law for Electing their town Officers, and the Inhabitants of our Said County being met on that acct., proceeded to chose as follows: John Morehouse assessor for ye Governor Tax, Joseph Lindsley Collector, Morris Morrison and Joseph Coe Freeholders, Abraham Vandine and Jonathan Stiles commissioners for laying out roads, Benjamin Beach and Matthas Van Dine, Thomas Huntington, Nathaniel Cogswell and John Courter overseers of ye Highway, John Morehouse Town Clerk."

In the year 1729 the following persons were elected to the office of constable: Ephraim Rue, Stephen Tuthill and Paulus Berry. Among the associate judges who sat at the October term, in the year 1737, of the Hunterdon County Court, was Abraham Kitchell, a resident of what is now Whippany.

In the year 1739 a new county was laid out within the bounds of what had been Hunterdon County, to which was given the name of Morris County, in honor of Governor Lewis Morris, the first Chief Magistrate of New Jersey after its separation from New York. The act of the Legislature, passed on the fifteenth day of March, in the year 1739, by which Morris County was established, declares that:

"All and singular the lands and upper parts of the said Hunterdon County lying to the northward and eastward, situate and lying to the eastward of a well-known place in the county of Hunterdon, being a fall of water in part of the north branch of Raritan River, called in the Indian language or known by the name of Allamatonck, to the northwestward of the northeast end or part of the lands called the New Jersey Society lands, along the line thereof, crossing the south branch of the aforesaid Raritan River, and extending westerly to a certain tree, marked with the letters L. M., standing on the north side of a brook emptying itself into the said south branch, by an old Indian path to the northward of a line to be run northwest from the said tree to a branch of Delaware river called Muskonetkong, and so down the said branch to Delaware river, all which said lands being to the eastward. northward and northwestward of the above said boundaries, be erected into a county; and it is hereby erected into a county, named and from henceforth to be called Morris county, and the said bounds shall part and from henceforth separate and divide the same from the said Hunterdon county."

The Morris County of the year 1739, as above defined, included what are now Morris, Sussex and Warren Counties, containing 1,360 square miles, with a population of nearly 2,000. Morristown, owing in part to its central location, and in part, no doubt, to its importance as a town, by reason of the high character of its citizens, became, almost inevitably as it appears, the county seat of the newly constituted county.

The sessions of the Morris County Court, or Court of Common Pleas, as it is now generally known, whose institution followed promptly the establishment of the new county, were at first held in the tavern of which

Jacob Ford, Esq., one of the justices at the time, was the proprietor. This tavern may have been situated in the neighborhood of the original settlement at the foot of Town Hill; it may have been somewhere in the vicinity of what is now the Green; or, what seems more probable to the writer, it may have been in the neighborhood of the "Washington Headquarters," at some point on what is now Morris street, which even as early as the period under consideration had doubtless become something of a thoroughfare for travelers east and west. This theory as to the situation of Jacob Ford's tavern, finds support in the fact, that Jacob Ford Sr., built the house now known as the "Washington Headquarters," the foundation of which was laid in the year 1772, and which was completed in the year 1774, and the same year occupied by Judge Ford and his family. It is a matter of record (and this fact seems to be even more positively corroborative of the theory above suggested) that as early as the year 1731, Jacob Ford became the owner of a large tract of land, a portion of which lay to the eastward of what is now the Lackawanna Railroad. The writer had the privilege of examining a copy of the deed by which this tract of land was conveyed to Mr. Ford, on the "Thirty-first day of May In the fourth year of the Reign of King George the Second Defender of the faith Annoquo Domini One Thousand Seven Hundred and Thirty one." The witnesses to this deed were: Jonathan Osborn, Zachariah Fairchild and John Morehouse.

The first session of the Morris County Court of

which, so far as is now known, any record has survived, was held on March 25, in the year 1740. In the minutes of this initial session of the court it is referred to as the "General Sessions of the Peace," and the first matters to receive its attention were the laying out of the townships of Pequonock, Hanover and Morristown. From the minutes of the Morris County Court above mentioned, now bearing the marks of age and of continuous usage, the following extract is presented, showing the action of the "General Sessions of the Peace" of the infant county, by which Morristown, as a township was originally established:

> "And that a certain road from the bridge by John Day's, up to the place where the same road passes between Benjamin and Abraham Persons, and thence up the same road to the corner of Samuel Ford's fence, thence leaving Samuel Ford to the right hand, thence running up the road that leads from the old Iron Works toward Succasuning, crossing Whippening bridge, and from thence to Succasuning, and from thence to the great pond on the head of Musconecong, do part the township of Hanover from the township of Morris, which part of the county of Morris lying as aforesaid to the southward and westward of said roads, lines and places is ordered by the Courts to be and remain a township, district or precinct, and to be called and distinguished by the name of Morristown."

Thus it will be seen that what had almost from the day of its settlement by the whites, about the year 1710, been called West Hanover and New Hanover, and, beginning with about the year 1738, had come to be popularly called Morristown, was, on March 25, of the year 1740, officially and legally named Morristown, by the "General Sessions of the Peace," of Morris County, New Jersey.

The composition of the Morris County Court at its initial session, held as we have seen on March 25, of the year 1740, does not appear in the book of minutes; but as given in the minutes of the second session of the court, held on March 26, in the same year, it was composed as follows: "The justices were: John Budd, Jacob Ford, Abraham Kitchell, John Lindsley Jr., Timothy Tuttle, Samuel Swesey." At the session of the county court last mentioned, the following township officers were appointed for the term of one year: "Zachariah Fairchild, Town Clark and Town Book-keeper; Matthew Lum, Assessor; Jacob Ford, Collector; Abraham Hathaway and Joseph Coe Jr., Freeholders; Benjamin Hathaway and Jonathan Osborn, Overseers of the Poor; Joseph Bridden and Daniel Lindsley, Surveyors of the Highways; Stephen Freeman and John Lindsley, Esq., Overseers of the Highways; Isaac Whitehead, Alexander Ackerman and William Duglas, Constables." At the same session of the court a license was granted Jacob Ford for the keeping of a tavern and inn in Morristown.

Before presenting the form of the license as granted by the County Court of Morris, to Jacob Ford, it may be said that at the May term of the Hunterdon County Court, held at Trenton, in the year 1738, petitions were presented by Jacob Ford and Abraham Hathaway, asking for the renewal of their licenses to keep a tavern and inn at New Hanover for the year ensuing; and both were granted. The license granted Jacob Ford at the second session of the Morris County Court, in the year 1740, was really, therefore, a renewal of the license granted him at Trenton about two years previously. Following is an exact transcript of the license:

"Jacob Ford, Esq., Presenting A petition to the Court Pursuant to A Late Act of the General Assembly of this Province for the Granting him A License to Keep a publick house and Inn in Morris town where he Now Lives the Court on reading the Same Ordered the Same to be filed & he having Entred into A Recognizance pursuant to Said Act the Court grants Said Jacob Ford Said License for one year now next Ensuing. Jacob Ford, Joseph Howard and David Wheeler Entered into recognizance Pursuant to the Directions of said Act."

In the year 1752, the number of "freeholders" or real estate owners in Morris County, was about 450; which estimate is based upon a census "taken by virtue of a rule of the Supreme Court by John Ford Sheriff of the County of Morris, this thirty-first day of August, A. D. 1752." Of this number of freeholders, nearly two-fifths were residents of Morris Town. A practically accurate list of the freeholders of Morris Town is here appended:

"George Armstrong, Charles Allin, Ebenezor Allen, Jonah Allin, William Armuld, Samuel Armund, Robert Arnuld, Benjamin Baley, David Brant, Herick Benjamin, Henry Burg,

John Beadel, Jacob Beadle, John Brookfield, John Burwell, Solomon Bates, Soloman Boyles, Samuel Baley, Thomas Bridge, William Broadwell, Benjamin Coe, Benjamin Conger, Benjamin Carter, Daniel Cooper, David Comton, Ezeakiel Cheevers, Ellis Coock, Frances Caterlin, Francis Caterlin, Jr., Jacob Carle, Joseph Coe, Jonathan Conklin, Isaac Clark, John Cramer, James Colwell, Jacob Cline, Joseph Coe, Jr., John Clark, James Cole, Peter Cundict, Philip Cundict, Peter Cline, Robart Chambers, Seth Croell, Stephen Conkling, Thomas Coe, Thomas Cleverly, Thomas Canem, Uriah Cutler, William Crane, William Cumton, John Day, Samuel Day, Thomas Darling, Hir Esborn, Richard Easton, Richard Easton, Jr., Benjamin Fowler, Benjamin Freeman, Ebenezor Fairchild, Gorshom Fairchild, John Feper, Jacob Ford, James Frost, Joseph Fairchild, Joseph Fouler, Richard French, Samuel Frost, William Frost, Zacheriah Fairchild, David Goddin, Henry Gardner, Jonas Gobel, Jacob Garagrace, Robart Gobel, Simeon Gobel, Thomas Gurin, William Gardner, Jr., Zopher Gildersleave, Abraham Hatheway, Abraham Hatheway, Benjamin Hatheway, Benjamin Halsey, Seth Hall, Benjamin Hatheway, Jr., Daniel Hayward, Ezra Halsey, Gilbort Headey, Jonathan Hatheway, John Holoway, Joseph Hayward, Isecker Hunterton, Shadrach Hayward, Samuel Hutson, Simeon Hatheway, Jeremiah Johnson, Peter Kimbol, Thomas Kint, Cread Ludlum, Daniel Lindsley, David Lum, David Leonard, Juniah Lindsley, John Lindsley, Josiah Lee, Joseph Lacey, Mathew Lum, Peter Layton, David Moore, David Muer, James Miller, John Marsh, John Muchmore, Soloman Munson, Samuel Munson, Timothy Mills, William Miller, Abraham Person, Benjamin Parker, Daniel Prost, Henry Primrose, Isaac Price, Joseph Prudden, Joseph Person, John Parkest, Nathaniel Parker, Zebulon Potter, Daniel Rattan, Daniel Roberts, Giddeon Riggs. Jonathan Reaves, John Robart, James Rogers, Nathaniel Rogers, Peter Rattan, Richard Runyon, Samuel Ross, Samuel Robarts. Daniel Sears, Joseph Stiles, Jonathan Stiles, Samuel Sutton, Samuel Sayer, Benoney

Thomas, Caleb Tichnor, David Trobridge, Jesper Totten, Jesper Totten, (Jr. 2), Mathias Tyson, Samuel Totten, Samuel Tuttle, Sylvenus Totten, Thomas Tomson, William Tharp, Bliker Witenac, Daniel Walling, Henry Wick, John Wade, Joseph Wood, Isaac Whitehead, Jonathan Wood, Joseph Wingit, Luis Wiens, Rubin Wingit, Samuel Whitehead."

We have seen that the sessions of the Morris County Court were at first held in the tavern of which Jacob Ford Esq. was the proprietor. How long this arrangement continued it is difficult now to determine with certainty, although it is safe to presume that the court continued to sit at the Ford tavern, and, possibly, at the residences of other Judges of the Morris County Court, in Morristown, until the erection of a courthouse. It was during the year 1755 that the first courthouse, a rude log structure, was erected near the centre of what is now the Morristown Green; we say, "What is now the Morristown Green," for it then had no existence, not even, so far as is now known, in the imagination of the fathers. What is now the Morristown Green was probably as late as the year last mentioned, simply a vacant, and nearly square, lot, comprised in the large tract of land, then owned by the Presbyterian church, and known as the "meeting house land," the "parsonage land," and "the green."

This primitive courthouse served the purpose, also, of a jail, and here, for a period of fifteen years "impartial justice," it is to be hoped, "held her equal scales;" until the year 1770, when a new building was erected on land purchased of the First Presbyterian church, as may be learned from the following entries in the trustees' book of said organization:

"May 17, 1770, the trustees being Duely Called and met at the county hous (the log structure erected in the year 1755, near the middle of what is now the Green), and agreed to Convey a Part of the meating hous Land to the freeholders of the County of Morris for the Benefit of the Court hous." "June 7, 1770, the trustees met & Gave a Deed for one acre of Land on which the Court hous (the log structure near the middle of what is now the Green) standeth to three majestrets and the Freeholders of the County of morris."

The new courthouse and jail erected in the year 1770, was a one-story frame structure, about thirty-five feet in depth and forty-five feet in length, shingled on all four sides, and on the roof. It extended out to about the centre of what is now the street passing in front of the United States Hotel, and faced to the northwest, or toward the present site of the above named building. By way of confirmation of this statement as to the location of the old Morris County courthouse, it may be said, that when, a few years since, the macadam road was in process of construction in front of the United States Hotel, some of the foundation stones of the old courthouse were discovered about one-third of the distance out from the curbstone of the present Green walk.

Underneath the front veranda of the above named hotel may be seen several oaken timbers which once formed part of the old jail on the Green. These timbers are filled with wrought iron, handmade nails, driven into them to prevent the escape of prisoners by cutting their way out.

The narrow lane running in front of the new, or second, courthouse, was dignified by the name of Court street. Of the courthouse of the period now passing under review, it has been said by an antiquarian: "Nor was the old Court House any way inferior to these (other buildings around the Green) as a relic of antiquity, a sort of curiosity shop, standing in its enclosure on what then and for many succeeding years was called 'the Green,' perhaps because no grass grew on its face."

Near the courthouse and jail stood the pillory, which, however, owing to the increase of enlightenment, was not used after the year 1796, although as late as the year 1803, its decaying stump remained as a silent reminder of a heathenish mode of punishment inflicted upon men created in the image of God.

Five pounds, we are informed, was the price paid by the county of Morris for the one acre of land, "strict measure," on which the new courthouse and jail was erected—a building, the story of which would alone make to all lovers of local history, particularly, a volume of thrilling interest. The reader may be willing to tarry a few moments at this juncture of our story to listen to the relation of a single incident—that of one Uriah Brown, and his mysterious disappearances from the "debtor's room," which was one of the special features of the old courthouse. Uriah, as may be inferred, was a victim of the infamous law requiring imprisonment for debt, which, with advancing civilization, has disappeared from the pages of our statute books. In the apartment where Brown was confined, was a large, old-fashioned fireplace, about half way up the massive chimney of which strong iron bars had been placed, to prevent the escape of prisoners by way of that sooty exit. For several nights in succession, loosening one of the iron bars, Brown would stealthily ascend the spacious stone chimney, and by way of the low roof (the building at that period was, the writer presumes, only one story in height) gain terra firma, where he doubtless accomplished all the sweet pleasure of his will. Early in the morning following, however, the deputy sheriff, who had rooms in the building, would be rudely roused from his uncompleted slumbers, by a knock at his door. Hastening, on the first morning, at least, to ascertain the nature of the urgent business requiring his untimely awakening, he would be blandly greeted by the migratory jailbird, who, fearing arrest as a jail-breaker, was naturally solicitous to resume his comfortable day quarters in the "debtor's room." Failing to draw from Uriah Brown the explanation of his escape, the deputy sheriff was left to infer that some accomplice had stolen his keys, and permitted the prisoner to go free. The repetition of Brown's disappearance and reappearance resulted in the conclusion on the part of the officials that he was devil-possessed, and only the expressed resolution of the said superstitious officials to bind him with chains, forced from Uriah's lips the confession that the removal of one of the iron bars in the great chimney flue made the open door for his mysterious escapes. As will be seen at a later stage of our story, the Uriah Brown incident just related, interesting in itself as it may be to our readers, is insignificant in comparison with the series of important events and occurrences associated with the courthouse and jail, and its auxiliary, the detested pillory, in subsequent years. A second story, it may be here remarked, was added to the courthouse and jail of which the reader has just heard, during the year 1776. A cupola and bell were also among the improvements made in connection with the raising of the one-story structure. The addition of the second story to the courthouse and jail, as will in due time appear, was a necessity required by the exigencies of the critical period through which Morris County was then passing.

Thanks to the patriotic spirit of the Morristown Chapter of the Daughters of the American Revolution, the site of one corner—the southwest—of the Morris County courthouse and jail of the Revolutionary period, is now marked, approximately at least, by an upright, unhewn stone, to whose face is fastened a bronze tablet bearing the following suggestive inscription: "1770-1827. Here stood the Court House and Jail at the time of the American Revolution. Marked 1904 by the Morristown Chapter D. A. R." The dedicatory exercises were of an interesting character and may, at a later stage of our story, receive the attention due the importance of the occasion.

It will be noticed in the picture of the Morris County courthouse and jail, as a two-story structure, with its quaint cupola and vane, and as it appeared between the years 1776 and 1827, that the detested pillory is represented as standing a few feet in front of the northwest corner of the building. There is ample evidence, however, upon which to base the unqualified statement that the pillory stood about seventy-five feet due south of the courthouse and jail, which, from a point of the sidewalk in front of and across the street from the present (1905) postoffice, would locate the pillory about forty feet back from the sidewalk in the direction of the parsonage of the Methodist Episcopal Church.

In the picture of the courthouse and jail will be noticed, also, a well-curb, with an old-fashioned sweep, represented, and rightly, as the writer believes, as having been situated a few feet in the rear of the building in question. By whom, or when this well was dug, it is doubtless impossible now to definitely determine; as to the when, however, the index finger of probability seems to point in the direction of the theory that almost simultaneously with the erection, in the year 1755, of the primitive log courthouse on what is now the Morristown Green, the springs thereof were loosed, and its refreshing waters began to flow, and to entitle it to the application to itself of the following words of Miss Eliza Cook, the poetess:

Traverse the desert, and then you can tell
What treasures exist in the cold, deep well,
Sink in despair on the red, parch'd earth,
And then ye may reckon what water is worth.

At the risk of the seeming prematureness of the offering of the following suggestions—if they have a basis in fact we confess our inability to substantiate them—they will, notwithstanding, for lack of a more opportune time, be here presented: For nearly two score years prior to the opening of the Revolution, the waters from the "old well" on the Green may have quenched the first of the then loyal Jersey subjects of King George. During the smallpox epidemic in Morristown, in the year 1777, when many of Washington's soldiers were confined in the Presbyterian and Baptist houses of worship, then used as hospitals, the cool waters from the "old well" in the rear of the courthouse and jail, may have assuaged the burning thirst of not a few of the victims of the dire disease which had fallen relentlessly upon the hamlet nestled among the hills of northern New Jersey. It is a well-established fact that during the Revolution several Tories were hanged in Morristown, probably from the limb of some convenient tree in the vicinity of the courthouse and jail; and that their untimely exit from this fair world was rendered more comfortable by the administration of a "cup of cold water" from the depths of the "old well" on the Green, is but a reasonable tribute to the quality of mercy existent in the breasts of their executioners.

Nor is it, by any means, outside the bounds of reason to presume, that during his frequent walks across the Green, during the years 1777, 1779 and 1780, the immortal Washington may have lingered long enough to refresh himself with a draft from "the cold, deep well."

With the rapid flight of years the primitive well-sweep gave way to the more convenient well-curb, with overhead wheel, and rope and bucket to bring the sparkling waters from the quiet depths below. This means of water drawing was in due course of time succeeded by the more modern pump, by which the needs of its numerous patrons were supplied—patrons, who, as the years rolled on, had come to cherish a commendable sentimental regard for the "old well" on the Green, whose beginnings had been in the dim distant past "whereof the memory of man runneth not to the contrary." To the ears of the writer there has come the report that nearly a quarter century ago a few interested (?) citizens of Morristown, dominated apparently more by the spirit of commercialism than by the spirit of sentimentalism, insisted that the water in "the cold, deep well" on the Green was unwholesome, and hence its use as a beverage for man should be discontinued, and the well be obliterated by filling in, as a means of escape from a much "talked of" epidemic. The writer wonders—this much in parenthesis—whether the epidemical fear of two and a half decades ago was the forerunneer of the epidemical panic in our fair city of more recent years, the subjects of which insisted (and successfully) upon the obliteration, by the filling in or draining, of several pretty bodies of water, which for many years had furnished amusement for our youth, and gratification for the esthetic. If, as a recent author says: "Within yourself lies the cause of whatever enters into your life. To come into the full realization of your own awakened interior powers, is to be able to condition your life in exact accord with what you would have it"—it may be the cause of the apprehended epidemic above alluded to, may lie within rather than without.

To return to "the pump on the Green"—it is reported that peremptory steps were taken to remove it, and fill in the well; which was prevented, however, by the prompt and energetic action of sentimental residents of Morristown, who had the water chemically analyzed, and found to be pure and wholesome. The "pump on the Green" was subsequently made an issue in local politics, with the result that the old iron pump is still standing, and the well it not filled in. Shall it not be permitted to remain as a suggestive landmark for "generations yet unborn," that

> When to the sessions of the sweet silent thought
> I summon up remembrance of things past,

they may, in national crises which it is not impossible may come, be animated by the same measure of patriotism which carried the fathers through the times that "tried men's souls?"

CHAPTER V.

"Sincerity,
Thou first of virtues, let no mortal leave
Thy onward path, although the earth should gape,
And from the gulf of hell destruction rise,—
To take dissimulation's winding way."

MONG the early settlers of what is now Morristown there were a few persons, at least, of the Baptist belief, who until their organization into a church, may have occasionally attended the Presbyterian services inaugurated, as we have seen, as early as the year 1734 at the place above named. In his history of the Baptist Church in America, Benedict says:

"As early as 1717 one David Goble, with his family of the Baptist persuasion, removed to this place (West Hanover) from Charleston, S. C., and some ministers of the same order began to preach at their house; a small company, after many years of patient effort, were collected as a branch of old Piscataway, which in 1752 was formed into a distinct church."

The writer is of the opinion that the first date (1717) mentioned in the above-cited extract may be inaccurate; that the arrival of Mr. Goble in West Hanover, and the inauguration of Baptist services there, may have occurred somewhat later than the year 1717. Of the accuracy of Mr. Benedict's statement, however, with the exception of the date in question, there is apparently no reason to doubt. At the period under consideration West Hanover, as our readers will doubtless be interested to learn, extended from what is now the quiet hamlet of Monroe, with its pretty chapel, on the east, to the Passaic River at Van Doren's mill, on the west; and from what is now Morris Plains, on the north, to the edge of the Great Swamp, on the south. In view of the meager population of the period, it will readily be seen that the settlement, which a few years subsequently became Morristown, was but sparsely inhabited. The Baptists of West Hanover resided, for the most part, on what is now known as the Mountain Road, or Mt. Kemble Avenue, as it is also called, leading toward Basking Ridge and New Vernon. The centre of the Baptist population, however, seemed to have been in the neighborhood of what is now popularly known as the "Brick Schoolhouse" (situated about three miles south of the Morristown Green), in which religious services are now frequently held. These Baptist pioneers in West Hanover were as tenacious of their doctrinal beliefs as were their brethren of the Presbyterian faith of theirs; hence our readers need not be greatly surprised to learn that for several years—probably a score—they not infrequently worshiped on Sunday with those of their own persuasion at Piscataway, in the vicinity of New Brunswick, of which church some of them, at least, were at the time members.

The Baptist church at Piscataway was organized in the year 1689, and it is, therefore, in point of age, the mother of the numerous churches of the same persuasion now existing in New Jersey. A journey of about fifty miles, on horseback, and perhaps on foot, through a wilderness broken only by their own blazed path, to enjoy the privilege of worshiping God according to the dictates of their own individual consciences, furnishes a most impressive illustration of the profound sincerity of those pioneers of the Baptist faith in Morris County; sincerity of which Lady Cudleigh says:

> Oh, that I could to her invite
> All the whole race of human kind;
> Take her, mortals, she's worth more
> Then all your glory, all your fame;
> Than all your glittering, boasted store,
> Than all the things that you can name.
> She'll with her bring a joy divine;
> All that's good and all that's fine.

On the eighth day of June, in the year 1752, eleven persons of the Baptist faith residing in Morristown, obtained letters of dismissal from the mother church at Piscataway, for the avowed purpose of organizing a church of their own faith at the first named place; and on the eleventh day of August, of the same year, "The Baptist Church at Morristown" was regularly organized by Elders Isaac Eaton, Benjamin Miller and Isaac Steele, all members of the mother church. By the addition of six new members by baptism, on the day of its organization, the membership of the infant church was increased to seventeen, representing eleven families. The names of the eleven persons dismissed from the mother church at Piscataway—who constituted the nucleus of the young church—were Daniel Sutton, Jonas Goble, John Sutton, Melatiah Goble, Jemima Wiggins, Daniel Walling, Ichabod Tomkins, Sarah Wiggins, Mary Goble, Naomi Allen and Robert Goble. All these Gobles may have been and probably were the children of the David Goble, who, as historian Benedict states, removed from Charleston, S. C., to West Hanover, in the year 1717.

At the first business meeting of the newly organized Baptist Church, held on the nineteenth day of August, in the year 1752, a deacon and church clerk were chosen, and arrangements were also made for the supply of the pulpit, and the administration of the ordinances. It could not have been long after the organization of the church that a meeting-house was erected on land said to have belonged to the David Goble already mentioned, as having removed from Charleston, S. C. This meeting-house, a small frame structure, shingled on sides and roof, stood about 100 yards below the present brick schoolhouse, on the same side of the road, leading toward Basking Ridge, and near what is now known as the "Mills Bailey" house. Indeed, it is the opinion of some students of local history, that it stood on the site of the house mentioned. If this were true, the conjecture that a portion of the old Baptist meeting-house was used in the construction of the "Mills-Bailey" house, is not without a reasonable basis. With reference to the Morristown Green, the location of this primitive Baptist meeting-house is about three miles distant in a southerly direction.

For a period of about two years the pulpit of "the Baptist Church at Morristown" was supplied by several persons, including Revs. Isaac Eaton, James Manning, Benjamin Miller and John Gano. Mr. Gano, who was still pursuing his studies at Princeton College (located at Newark), also conducted religious services in private houses in the hamlets adjacent to Morristown. The Rev. Isaac Eaton mentioned was the founder of Hopewell Academy, the first Baptist theological school in America, which was subsequently removed to Rhode Island, where it was developed into what is now Brown University. The Rev. James Manning here mentioned, became the first president of Brown University. The first pastor of the Baptist Church at Morristown was Rev. John Gano, and his introduction to the church may be learned from the following extract from the extant Morristown Baptist Church records: "1754, May. Mr. John Gano came to us and continued to preach for us till October following, when he went on a journey to Carolina." Mr. Gano was then but twenty-seven years of age. His subsequent return to the pulpit of the Morristown Baptist Church is evidenced by the following extract from the church records: "1755, June. Mr. J. Gano returned from Carolina and again went on to preach for us." From the extract following, the conclusion of Mr. Gano to become the permanent pastor of the Morristown Baptist Church may be learned: "October (1755) Mr. Gano, at the earnest request of the church, concluded to settle with us for the sum of forty pounds a year." After his marriage to Sarah, daughter of John Stites, Esq., Mayor of Elizabeth Town, which followed close on his settlement in Morristown, Mr. Gano purchased a farm in the vicinity of the primitive house of worship.

During his brief pastorate, Mr. Gano frequently conducted religious services in the districts adjacent to his parish, including Basking Ridge, Mendham, Morristown (at the central village), and Hanover. The first convert under Mr. Gano's labors in Morris County, was Hezekiah Smith, who is said to have resided in Hanover then a separate township. Young Smith was baptized by Mr. Gano on the twenty-sixth day of February, in the year 1756. He subsequently entered the Baptist ministry, and attained to eminence in his profession in New England. Of the Haverhill (Mass.) Baptist Church, of which he was the founder, he was the beloved pastor for the period of forty years.

Mr. Gano's characteristic reference to the conversion of young Smith is worth quoting. He says:

> "At one of these places there was a happy instance of a promising youth (by name Hezekiah Smith), who professed to be converted, and joined the church, who appeared to have an inclination for education. * * * He went through a collegiate education at Prince Town College, and came out a zealous preacher, and, to appearances, a useful one. The church at Morristown gradually grew and the congregation increased."

In the sentence last quoted the success of Mr. Gano's pastorate is comprehensively summed up. Passing over intervening events in connection with his Morristown pastorate, the following extract from the church books is cited:

> "1757, June 24. Elder John Gano returned from Carolina But instead of being willing to remain with us, he now requested liberty from the church to remove to Carolina and settle there. And a meeting of the church being called to consider upon it, they concluded that if he thought it his duty to go there and leave them, he might go, but they would give no other consent, leaving it to his own conscience." "September 25. Elder Gano, thinking it his duty to go, moved from us to Carolina after disposing of his property in Morristown."

Both Mr. Gano and Mr. Smith were chaplains under Washington in the Continental army during the Revolution. From the diary of the Rev. Mr. Smith, the following extracts, having more or less reference to

Morristown and Morris County, during the early years of their history, will be found of deep interest:

"1764. Feb. 27. Preached in Morristown and after hearing Mr. James Manning preach, I administered the Sacrament. Monday, March 5. Preached at Jeremiah Sutton's at Long Hill. In the evening gave an exhortation after Mr. Manning had preached.

"1764. Nov. 6. I went by water (from New York) to the Point and from thence in a chair to Jeremiah Smith's. Wednesday, 21. I preached in the Morristown meeting house. Thursday, 22. Preached in Mr. Green's meeting house. (Hanover). Friday, 23. Went to Morristown and in the evening I preached at Mr. Oliver's. Saturday, 24. Preached in the Baptist meeting house and in the evening at Deacon Gobel's.

"1765. Wednesday, Sept. 11th. Went to my father's. Friday, 13th. In the evening I preached at Happy Cook's Saturday, 14. Went to Capt. Brookfield's in Morristown and preached there that night. Sabbath, 15. Preached two sermons in the Baptist meeting house at Morristown. In the evening I preached at Mr. Brooks's. Wednesday, 25. Went to commencement at Princeton and took my Master's degree.

"1766. Monday, Oct. 6. I preached at my father's a sermon from Ps. 23:1. After sermon I baptized my mother in the Passaic River. In the evening I preached at Happy Cook's."

No less interesting are the following extracts from a timely article, entitled, "Rev. Hezekiah Smith, D. D. A Morris County Boy of the Early Day. One of Washington's Chaplains," by Rev. Norman Fox, D. D., which appeared in The Jerseyman, in the year 1904:

"He is widely known as one of the Chaplains of the Revolutionary Army. He was always interested in civil as well as religious matters. In his journal for 1766 we find the following entry:—'Thursday, July 24th. Preached two sermons, one in my meeting house and the other at New Rowley. It was a good Thanksgiving Day, which day was by authority set apart as a day of thanksgiving on account of the repeal of the Stamp Act.' But this slight clearing of the sky was followed by ever thickening tempests and in 1775 we find him with young men of his town among the troops around Boston. Among his papers is a somewhat extended outline of a sermon on 'The Soldier's Spiritual Armor,' which according to a note at the end was 'composed to preach the 18th of June, 1775, at Cambridge, amongst Col. Nixon's regiment, in consequence of an invitation by letter from the Colonel himself.' Had not this been carefully written out the world might have lost it, for on Saturday the 17th, came the battle of Bunker Hill and it is doubtful if the next day the excitement had so far subsided as to allow the men to give due attention to this well-prepared discourse.

"Under date of July 12th, 1775, the church records say:—'Voted,—That our pastor shall comply with the request of Col. Nixon and supply as Chaplain the quarter part of the time for the future in his regiment.' In this regiment were many from Haverhill. Col. John Nixon was present as a soldier at the siege of Louisburg in 1745; was a captain in the attack on Ticonderoga and in the battle of Lake George; was at the head of a company of minute men at Lexington, and at Bunker Hill received a wound from which he never recovered. He was made Brigadier General, Aug. 9th, 1776, and placed by Washington in command of Governor's Island. He was again severely wounded at Stillwater, receiving permanent injuries. He and the Chaplain were warm personal friends.

"Chaplain Smith's letters to his wife give many vivid details of Washington's siege of Boston. When the army was transferred to New York, he went as Chaplain of Nixon's and Reed's regiments, arriving there April 15th. When the latter was sent to Canada, Webb's took its place. The next December, after an absence from home of a year and eight months, he took a furlough.

"Among the papers left by him is a commission signed by John Hancock, President of Congress, constituting and appointing Hezekiah Smith, Gentleman, 'to be Chaplain of a battalion whereof John Nixon, Esq., is Colonel in the Army of the United States,' etc. Later he appears as Brigade Chaplain.

"In a list of twenty-one Brigade Chaplains in the army, Aug. 17th, 1778, there are two Episcopalians, three Presbyterians, five Congregationalists, five whose church relations are not given, and six Baptists, nearly a third of the whole, viz., Gano, formerly of Morristown; Smith, formerly of Morris county; Jones, Rogers, Thompson and Vanhorn. There were other Baptist chaplains in the army and when it is remembered that the Baptists of that day were but a handful of people it will be seen that their record is an exceedingly honorable one.

"Having rejoined the army at Peekskill, Chaplain Smith set out with Gen. Nixon on July 5th, 1777, for Albany and the Burgoyne campaign. His journal gives some vivid descriptions of the battles of Stillwater and Saratoga. For the next three years, with some long furloughs, he was on service with the army on the lower Hudson.

"It is evident that he commanded the respect of men of all ranks. From his papers we learn that on Sept. 14th, 1777, in preaching to his brigade, he had among his hearers Gen. Gates, Gen. Glover, Gen. Poor and other prominent officers. We read also,—'Sabbath, Aug. 2d.—I preached a sermon to our brigade from Malachi 2:5. His Excellency General Washington attended. I dined with him the same day.' 'Monday, Nov. 1st.—I went to West Point. Dined with Washington.' Washington corresponded with Chaplain

Smith after the war. His grand-daughter speaks of remembering among the family papers a package of twenty or thirty letters from Washington, which were given away to friends in days when such documents were not so highly regarded as at present. When Washington visited Haverhill in 1789, he called on Chaplain Smith at his house."

The second pastor of the Baptist Church of Morristown was Rev. Ichabod Tomkins, who was a member of the local church, and was ordained to the ministry and assumed the pastoral charge of the church on the sixth day of November, in the year 1754. His pastorate closed with his decease, in consequence of smallpox, on the eighth day of January, in the year 1761. Among the present membership of the Baptist Church, of Morristown, are descendants of Mr. Tomkins. On the seventeenth day of June, in the year 1767, John Walton was ordained to the ministry, and at the same time installed as pastor of the Baptist Church of Morristown.

A score of years had scarcely elapsed since the organization of the infant Baptist church at Morristown, when its membership was increased to nearly a hundred —eighty-five to be exact. On the fifteenth day of February, in the year 1769, therefore, during Mr. Walton's pastorate, a meeting of the church was held, at which time it was concluded to draw up and circulate as soon as possible, subscripition papers for raising money for a new meeting-house to be erected "on Morristown Green." Among the subscribers to the fund for a new Baptist meeting-house, was John Brookfield.

Upon his decease, at Spring Valley, there was found among his papers a memorandum book, kept by him while living. This came into the possession of his son, Job Brookfield, who died in the year 1877. When last seen the writing in this memorandum book was as legible as if it had been executed within a decade, the ink being of a dark color, and distinct. From this memorandum book the followingg extract is presented:

"February 15, 1769.

"At a meeting of Business of the Baptist church at Morris Town, it was concluded that subscriptions be drawn up as soon as possible for the building of a new meeting house on Morris Town Green and to be sent out and if we can git £200 signed exclusive of what the church members will give, to go on with the building.

	£.	s.	p.
Zopher Gildenshaw	0	13	11
Jeams Brookfield	0	10	10
Jeams Miller	0	1	9
Benjamin Goble	0	9	8
Robard Goble	2	0	5
Elijah Person	0	9	2
Capt. Stark	3	3	9
Ephriem Goble	8	0	1
John Linsly	0	6	2
Fradreck King	2	16	2
Joseph Wood	2	10	6
Garshom Goble	3	6	10
John Brookfield	5	2	9
Samuel Serin and Zopher Freeman, in part	1	18	9
Moses Monson	1	5	10
Anais Holsey	6	10	4
Gilbard Allien	1	4	3

William Goble	I	9	9
Hanah Lincton		5	6
Jonathan Wood		13	5
Solomon Monson		4	2
Solomon Southard	3	18	6
Aaron Stark, Jr.	6	13	11
Peter Jollomons	6	3	3
John Stark	I	I	0
Jacob Alien and John Alien	3	17	0
Daniel Congar	0	5	I
Abraham Person	0	2	0
John Lepard	0	9	9
Thomas Wood	0	2	0
Waitstill Monson	0	19	6
Gorge Goble	0	I	I
Joseph Fairchild	0	5	11
Anney Wilkinson	I	2	2
Benjamin Goble by Jeminey Day	I	7	7
Moses Person	I	16	6
John Conkling	I	3	0
John Shadwick	0	I	I
Abraham Ludlow	0	10	9
Jeams Hill	I	15	8
Robard Goble	0	13	5
William Cullen	3	0	0
	76	19	0

Aaron Curnit also gave £8. 0. 0. Proc. and £12 Lite."

It will be noticed that several of the above named subscribers to the fund for a new Baptist meeting-house on the "Morris Town Green," were of the Presbyterian faith; from which it is evident that ecclesiastical comity is no novelty in the twentieth century.

The Rev. Mr. Walton, during whose pastorate the

movement toward the raising of money for a new meeting-house began, died in the year 1770, and on his headstone, in the Presbyterian burial grounds, is the following inscription: "In memory of Rev. John Walton, who was minister of the Baptist Church in Morristown, and who died October the first, 1770, aged thirty-five years.

The burying ground of the primitive Baptist Church of Morristown (whose commencement may have antedated several years the organization of the church) was situated on the opposite side of the road from the meeting-house, and a few rods farther north in the direction of the Morristown Green. This burying ground seems to have commenced at some point between the present residence of John S. Green, and that of Lewis P. Baird; and, as necessity required, was extended northward along the road leading "toward town." In recent years the remains of interments have been found as far north as the rear of Lewis P. Baird's residence. Headstones have also been found in the same locality. It was the writer's rare privilege (he speaks as a lover of local history and tradition) to see, not long since, on the premises of John S. Green, two headstones, which once marked the burial place of some family interred in this ground. We say "some family," for Mr. Green informed the writer that in close proximity to the two headstones mentioned, were two or three smaller stones, the whole number being in a row, and the natural inference is that the two larger stones marked the resting places of the parents, and the smaller ones those of their children. These headstones were removed by Mr.

Green, personally, about twenty-two years ago. Some of these stones had settled into the ground so as to be nearly out of sight, while one or two were a few inches above the surface of the ground. One of the two stones seen by the writer was about four feet in length by one foot in width and three inches in thickness; the dimensions of the others were somewhat smaller. All the stones mentioned were of common field stone, and, so far as could be seen, bore no inscription, and probably never did. A wooden stake—thanks to the thoughfulness of our informant—now marks the spot where these rude headstones once stood. Inasmuch as the house now occupied by John S. Green, was, as early as about the year 1750, the residence of Robert Goble, one of the original members of the Baptist Church of Morristown, it is probable the headstones found in the rear of Mr. Green's house, marked the graves of members of Mr. Goble's family. It may be that the graves were those of Mr. and Mrs. Goble, and two of their children, in other words it may have been the family burial ground. In seeming confirmation of this conjecture it may be said,—so the writer has been informed by one who was born, and for not a few years lived in the neighborhood in question (our fellow townsman, John D. Guerin),—that on the same side of the road leading toward Basking Ridge, but some little distance below the Robert Goble place, there is a family burial ground. Still farther down the same road, and on the same side, but lying at a considerable distance back from the road, is another family burial ground, sheltered by a handsome copse of trees.

It is by some thought that during the encampment of Washington's army in the vicinity of the old Baptist burying ground, in the winter of 1779-80, not a few of his deceased soldiers were interred therein. This conjecture is by no means without a reasonable basis. The proximity of the encampment to the burying ground, and the consequent convenience of interment therein, would of itself furnish excellent ground for such conjecture. But to this there may be added the fact of the numerous interments made in this old burying ground, as evidenced by the large number of mounds visible, some of them at least, not many years since; as well as by the unusual extent of the interments to the northward; all of which circumstances render it improbable that local casualities could have entirely furnished the inhabitants for this populous city of the dead.

During the construction of their new meeting-house on the "Morris Green," the Baptist people, who by this time had mostly removed "into town," held divine services in the new courthouse erected, as we have seen, on the Green, in the year 1770. The Baptist meeting-house, when completed, was about forty feet in length by thirty feet in depth, and stood on a slight elevation, a little farther back from what is now Speedwell Avenue, than the more pretentious structure of a later date. We say "what is now Speedwell Avenue" because at the period under consideration, there was no road where Speedwell Avenue now is.

The picture of the Baptist meeting-house, appearing in

connection with our story, is an accurate representation, having been made from a description of the structure furnished, indirectly, it is true, by those who saw it while standing. For this accurate representation of the Baptist house of worship of 1771, our readers are indebted to George W. Howell, surveyor and civil engineer, now deceased, and one of his talented daughters, Miss Rachel Howell.

On the second Sunday in May, of the year 1771, the new meeting-house was formally dedicated by exercises appropriate to the occasion, which was one of rare interest to those present. It is a circumstance, for a knowledge of which present and future generations of Morristonians, particularly, should congratulate themselves, that the dedicatory sermon was delivered by the Rev. John Gano, the first pastor of the church; John Gano, of whom Henry Clay is reported to have said: "Of all the preachers I have ever listened to, he made me feel the most that religion was a divine reality."

The first pastor of the Baptist Church on "Morris Green" was the Rev. Reune Runyon, who in the month of December, 1771, began his labors, as a licentiate. He was ordained to the Baptist ministry in the month of June, in the year 1772. Mr. Runyon was the pastor of the Morristown Baptist Church during the Revolution; and he is said to have been an ardent patriot, brave and true. Of this church more will be said at the proper time.

CHAPTER VI.

"And often a retrospect delights the mind."

"There are not unfrequently substantial reasons underneath for customs that appear to us absurd."

HE period of Morristown's local history lying between its settlement, and the opening of the Revolution, presents a picture, the examination of which, in contrast with present conditions, will doubtless prove of great interest, especially to the young, and to others who may be unacquainted with the customs and habits of those early days.

True to their Old England and New England training, the early inhabitants of Morristown regarded Sunday, or the Sabbath as they then almost invariably called it, as the chief day of the week; and attendance upon the services of the sanctuary was to them a sacred duty, which was not, except under extraordinary circumstances, to be neglected. Neither extreme distance from the house of worship, nor the inconvenience of primitive modes of conveyance; not even the long and tedious services of the period, were sufficient to deter these God-fearing pioneers from regular attendance upon the public means of grace.

Wagons and carriages as modes of conveyance were rarely seen in Morristown until after the Revolutionary period. During the Colonial period, however, a family might now and then be seen on the Sabbath, riding in a cart to the house of worship. Usually they were seated on a sheaf of straw, placed crosswise in the springless vehicle, drawn, perchance, by a well-broken yoke of oxen. Most of those who lived at too great a distance from the house of worship to walk, rode on horseback, especially the women and small children. The sight of a father occupying the saddle, and driving the horse, with a mother seated on a pillion (the pad or cushion attached to the hinder part of a saddle, as a second seat), and the children hanging on as best they could, and in this manner pensively wending their way to the house of God, was by no means infrequent in the early days of Morristown's local history.

In marked contrast to the custom of the present century, the women of the early days were seated during divine service on one side of the broad aisle, running north and south in the Morristown Presbyterian meeting-house, and the men on the opposite side. The aged of both sexes occupied the seats directly in front of the pulpit, in part, no doubt, to facilitate hearing. In one of the two side galleries, each reached by a separate flight ɔf stairs, sat the unmarried women and girls; while in :he other sat the unmarried men and boys.

As a means, not invariably effectual, however, of :ontrolling the buoyancy of youth, certain men—"tith-ng men" they were called in early New England, and n Old England, "beadles"—were employed; their com-ɔensation perhaps consisting of the assiduously culti-ʻated consciousness of being "drest in a little brief au-:hority," or what is more charitable to suppose, of the ceen gratification of enforcing what was then deemed .he proper observance of the Sabbath—the day of which he poet says, and truly, too: "The week were dark, but 'or Thy light; Thy torch doth show the way." The ithing men of New England found it necessary to equip .hemselves with an emblem of authority—an ecclesias-.ical wand, we will call it—with which, by a slight tap ɔn the shoulder or head, they not infrequently awakened he drowsy worshiper to a realization of his sanctuary ɔrivileges; and if they now and then used it with force ;ubdued upon the cranium of some seemingly incor-'igible youth of the masculine sex, it was, of course, 'or "the glory of God." Whether the "overseers of ;rave character" employed in Parson Johnes's "meetin'-ıouse" in early Morristown, were similarly equipped, ɔr whether, if they were, they ever found it necessary o similarly apply the aforesaid emblem of authority, he chroniclers of local history, for reasons best known o themselves, have omitted to mention—because, per-:hance, of their belief that:

> Historians, only things of weight,
> Results of persons, or affairs of State,
> Briefly, with truth and clearness should relate.

Two services on the Sabbath, one commencing at 10:30 o'clock in the forenoon, and the other at 1:30 o'clock in the afternoon; with an hour's intermission, spent in social converse absolutely devoid of course, of what is now known as gossip; and in munching an improvised lunch, including a liberal supply of aromatic fennel (Latin, foeniculum), that the adolescent youth of the gentler sex might "smell of sweetest fennel"—such, in brief outline, was the program of the primitive day of worship in early Morristown, so far as church attendance was concerned.

The writer distinctly remembers when the custom of a morning and afternoon preaching service prevailed in New England, with the Sabbath-school sandwiched in between; his recollection, however, of the excessive demands upon his vitality necessitated by two preaching services, and the conduct of a Bible class of young men of an inquiring turn of mind, between—with only sufficient spare time to run to the nearby parsonage for a bite and a sip, to restore jaded nature—is not without a lingering protest against a custom which constrains not a few of its victims of other days now to exclaim:

> Ah! what avail the largest gifts of heaven,
> When drooping health and spirits go amiss;
> How tasteless then whatever can be given!
> Health is the vital principle of bliss.

And then the extreme length of the sermons, and indeed, of the entire service of the early days of Morristown's history—why, the mere contemplation of it throws over one the weariness induced by an extensive journey. Even Parson Johnes, much as he was beloved by his large flock, and earnestly as he proclaimed the eternal verities, as he understood them, must have found it well-nigh impossible to woo his drowsy hearers from:

> Man's rich restorative; his balmy bath,
>   That supplies, lubricates, and keeps in play
> The various movements of this nice machine,
> Which asks such frequent periods of repair,
>   When tir'd with vain rotations of the day.

But the sermons of the early days, their extreme length notwithstanding, constituted the chief and engrossing topic of conversation in the homes of Parson Johnes's scattered parishioners during the week, where every conceivable phase of them, from "firstly" to "lastly" was earnestly discussed. The writer wonders, as he reviews the early years of Morristown's history, whether there would not now be a similar reverence for the Lord's Day, and a similar interest in the weekly ministrations of the pulpit, if the pulpit of the twentieth century courageously led the people in their thought of things eternal.

To be permitted to see, in his own handwriting, the notes of a sermon delivered by "Parson Johnes" (as we write his name, a feeling of inexpressible awe broods over us) during his long and eminently useful pastorate of the Presbyterian Church of Morristown, will, we believe, be esteemed a rare privilege by readers who are following the story of the first century's history of this truly famous town.

The notes of such a sermon (abbreviated, as will be noticed, for the purpose, undoubtedly, of economizing space) are presented in this volume. It was a sermon delivered in the year 1755, after Mr. Johnes had been settled over his flock about twelve years. It will be noticed that only a single page, the first of the sermon notes, is presented. The complete notes of this sermon, however, occupy eight pages. The handwriting of the sermon notes presented is, in the original, considerably smaller than the handwriting of Dr. Johnes in general: hence, it has been thought well to somewhat enlarge the original, to facilitate reading. For the truly rare privilege of looking upon the photographic reproduction of this page of Dr. Johnes's sermon notes, the readers of this story are indebted to the courtesy of a direct descendant—a great-grand-daughter, now residing in Morristown, who for many years has sacredly preserved this precious souvenir of a period of our local history, which will increase in interest as the years roll on.

There is one custom of the early years of Morristown's history, the mention of which should not be omitted. This is the peculiar style of singing in connection with the services of the sanctuary, known as "lining." A man was employed to stand, usually on the floor in front of the pulpit, and read a line of the hymn—Watt's hymns were for many years almost exclusively used—after which it would be sung by the congregation; another line would be read, and then sung, and so on to the close of the long musical composition. The fact that not all the devout worshipers of those primitive days could read, either type or notes, accounts in large measure for the quaint custom of "lining" to which allusion has been made. If traditional reports of the public singing of the early years are to be credited, its effect upon those of musical ear in the congregation, could scarcely have been such as Pope describes in speaking of the delights of music:

> I seem through consecrated walks to rove,
> I hear soft music die along the grove.

To Dr. Johnes is given the credit of having introduced a choir and choir-singing into his service; not, however, without objection on the part of some of his flock, one member of which was so indignant as to absent himself for a long time from the communion.

The days of which we are speaking were the days of fireplaces in the homes of the people; stoves were unknown until many years afterward. With rare exceptions, however, the meeting-houses of the early years did not enjoy the luxury even of a fireplace. By means of perforated tin foot-stoves, filled with live coals, the women and children were made comfortable, shall it be said, or were they simply prevented from freezing? Upon a good blood circulation, induced by outdoor occupation during the week, the men were able to remain during the tedious services without serious injury to health. It may be, too, that certain phases of the preaching of those early years assisted in keeping up the circulation. One chronicler of local history informs us that when stoves were first introduced in the "Baptist Church on Morris Green" the stovepipes were run out through a window. As for means of church illumination in the "good old days," if an evening service were held, the worshipers brought a tallow candle in a hand candlestick, which was held until the benediction was pronounced. The wall candlestick for the illumination of the meeting-house in the evening was a later innovation. "The women," we quote again from the entertaining paper read by Mrs. Isaac R. Pierson, at the sesqui-centennial celebration of the First Baptist Church, of Morristown, in the year 1902, "were clothed in the home-spun of their own industry. It was steady work with them, as all had to be supplied with clothing; and this constant spinning gave the name of 'spinster' to the unmarried daughters of the family. Every farmer raised his patch of flax which, when cured and properly dressed was spun with a greater or less degree of fineness, according to the purpose for which it was intended, and was then woven into cloth and bleached on the grass in the sun. This made a linen cloth which was used for table or bed linen, etc. Many of us possibly have these mementoes of the olden time. The tow, which was the coarser part of the flax, was used for ropes and harness, and a portion of it was spun and woven into a coarser cloth for men's wear. The cloth called 'linsey woolsey' was made of linen and wool, and used for women's wear. The woolen cloth for the men was dyed with a preparation of butternut bark, which gave it a peculiar shade of brown. It was then fulled and napped and dressed.

The men wore knee breeches, long stockings, and shoes with silver buckles. The woman's dress consisted of a 'linsey woolsey' petticoat and short gown, with a kerchief pinned over the shoulders.

"In the days of our ancestors, carding, spinning, weaving and knitting was the employment alike of the common people and the ladies of fashion. It was considered an honor to appear in home-made apparel. Pins were almost unknown, and thorns were used in their place.

"A shoemaker went from house to house, making the shoes for the family, at stated times. The flint and steel were the only means of getting fire. The fires were made of wood on the ground; or if in a log house, on the wide stone hearth. When bedtime came enough live coals were buried in the ashes, for rekindling in the morning, but in case the fire should die out, resort must be had to the flint, steel and tinder box. In the absence of these, the musket was used by placing powder in the pan of the lock, and flashing it against a bunch of tow, an article found in every home in those flax-spinning days. When these failed, one had to fetch fire in an iron pot from a neighbor's."

Those days of long sermons, "lining," cold meeting-houses, foot-stoves, tallow candles or dips, spinning-wheels, fire-places, linsey-woolsey, etc., are gone, and we look back upon them merely as curiosities of the undeveloped past.

For nearly a score of years following its organization, the Presbyterian church of Morristown seems to have been without legal standing. The church and congregation had meanwhile greatly increased in numbers and in influence. Recognizing the necessity of a legal standing, and guided in the matter by their sagacious pastor, a petition was drawn up and duly presented to his excellency Jonathan Belcher, Esq., Governor of the New Jersey province, requesting incorporation. The extreme length of the charter granted by Governor Belcher forbids that it be given in full, hence the opening and closing lines only are presented. They are as follows:

"George the Second, by the Grace of God, of Great Britain, France and Ireland, King, Defender of the Faith. To all to whom these presents shall come, Greeting:

"Whereas, the advancement of true Religion and virtue is absolutely necessary for the promotion of Peace, order and prosperity of the State,

"And Whereas, it is the duty of all Christian princes and Governors by the law of God, to do all they can for the encouragement thereof,

"And Whereas, Sundry of our loving Subjects of the Presbyterian Persuasion Inhabitants of an (d) about the Township of Morris, within our Colony of New Jersey, by their humble petition presented to our Trusty and well beloved

Jonathan Belcher, Esq., our Captain General and Commander in Chief of our Province of New Jersey and Vice-Admiral in the same, showing that the petitioners and others of the same persuasion Inhabitants, in and about the Township of Morris aforesaid, do make up a very large and considerable congregation, that the most advantageous support of religion among them necessarily requires that some persons should be incorporated as Trustees for the community that they may take grants of lands and chattels thereby, to enable the Petitioners to erect and repair public buildings for the Worship of God, and the use of the Ministry and School Houses and Alms Houses, and suitably to support the Ministry and the Poor of their church, and to do and perform other acts of Piety and Charity, and that the same Trustees may have power to let and grant the same under a Publick Seal for the uses aforesaid, And that the same Trustees may plead and be impleaded in any suit touching the premises and have perpetual succession. * * *

"In Testimony Whereof, we have caused these, our Letters to be made Patent, and the Great Seal of our said Province of New Jersey to be hereunto affixed.

"Witness, our Trusty and well beloved Jonathan Belcher, Esquire, Governor and Commander in Chief of our said Province of New Jersey, this Eighth day of September, in the Thirtieth year of our reign, and in the year of our Lord one thousand Seven hundred fifty and six.

CHARLES READ, Secr'y.

"I have perused the above charter and find nothing therein contained inconsistent with the honor and interest of the Crown. September 7th, 1756.

"C. SKINNER, Att'y Gen'l.

"Let the Great Seal of the Province be hereunto affixed.

"J. BELCHER.

"To the Secretary of New Jersey.

"Recorded at Trenton, Oct. 5, 1774, in Book C, 3, of Commissions, page 7, etc."

A complete copy of this charter may be found in "Record and Combined Register First Presbyterian Church, Morristown, N. J., 1742 to 1891."

The following extracts from the trustees' book of the Presbyterian church of Morristown, will be found particularly interesting to our readers. It will be noticed that the extract immediately following, is the first entry to be made in the trustees' book after the receipt of the charter of incorporation:

"A Record of the Transactions of the Trustees in and for the Presbyterian Chh & Congregation at morristown, in Vertue of a Charter granted to the said Chh & Congregation by his Excellency Jonathan Belcher, Esqr., Captain General and Governor in Chief in and over his majesties Province of Nova Cesarea or New Jersey and territories thereon Depending in America Chancellor and Vice admiral in the same, &c., which Charter was granted the eighteenth of September, in the twenty ninth year of his majesties Reign 1756, the Expence of which Charter being about seven Pound Proc. was Raised by Publick Contribution Excepting the writing of Sd Charter, which was Generously done by Ezekiel Cheever, member of Sd Society.

"The Incorporated Trustees, Viz.: messiurs Benjamin Hatheway, President; Benjamin Bayles, Thomas Kent, Benjamin Coe, Charls Howell, Sam'l Robarts & henry Primrose, on the Receiving the Charter at the ministers hous from the hands of Mr. Johnes, who had Been Desiered and was Principally Concerned in obtaining the Sd Charter, the Trustees by a Vote did then and there appoint Sam'l Robarts the Corporation Clark.

"The President according to Charter appointed a meeting of the trustees at his own hous January 18, 1758, all the members being Present it was agreed that as the President had heretofore given a Deed for the Parsonage to mess, mathew Lum, thomas Cleverly & Timothy mills that it might now fall under the Priviledges of the Charter, and it was agreed that Sd Parsonage Land by a Quit Claim be Conveyed to the trustees it was also agreed to take a Quit Claim Deed for the meeting hous Land which is now in the hands of Joseph Pruden & the Heirs of John Lindsley Deceased Both of the town of morris.

"apriel 2 1759 the trustes met at ye Presidents hous according to the appointment All Present Except Benj Bayles at which time the President Received his Quit Claim of Said matthew Lum timothy mills and Thomas Cleaverly and accordingly Gave a warrantee Deed to the trustees

"apriel the 9 1759 the Clark by appointment of the Trustees Received a Quit Claim Deed for the meeting hous Land of Joseph Prudden * * * * * * * * * * *
may the 1 1761 the Trustees met on the Green But Capt. Stiles absent and agread to Lay out into Lots and Sell Som Part of the Pairsonag Land Lying before the meeting hous Dore.

"June the 8 1761 the Trustees met eh icn Court hous and agreed upon a Price for three Lots the first which they then Conveyed to Joseph King was Sixteen Pound taen Shilling and Seald the Conveyance with the Shape of a man's head and the Second or midle Lot is Likewise Sixteen Pound taen Shilling the third or corner Lot twenty Five Pound which two Lots remain yet not sold * * * * * * * * * *

"apriel the 6 1762 the trustees met at Doct hatheways and Conveyed the third Lot to Isaac Bobet for twenty-five Pound and Sealed it with the Seign of a Sheaf and that Same Day Agread and Bought that same Seal for the use of the Charter."

The following brief extracts from the records of the Presbyterian Church of Morristown, so carefully kept by the beloved pastor, are presented chiefly as illustrations of the unceasing watchfulness exercised by the church over the conduct of its members, and of the means employed to restore the erring to the path of rectitude. Names are in some instances purposely suppressed by the writer.

"Monday 12 of April—56. 2 'o P.M. at Y House. B'r——— was inquired of as to the Reason of absenting from the Lords Supper and upon Examination judged his Reasons altogether groundless being but a Private suspicion of a certain Brother's sincerity—and Exhort him to a careful and Impartial Examination and Prayer that he may escape the snare of our grand Adversary and invite him again to take his place at the Communion.

"Jan. 18-58 * * * Also was resumed the case of Br. ———, & after much Reasoning and debating could not remove his Scruple Tho' we Judge him Still to be in error in makeing a Private Judgement the ground of Omitting a Publick duty yet as we would shew all Tenderness in points of Conscience we would only recommend him to a more critical Study of those Precious rules of Scripture that refer to Chh. fellowship, & to God by earnest Prayer for direction & Light, & that the Moderator do Dehort, & Exhort, him from his Neglect, to his Duty. * * * January 3d 1760, Mr. ——— and wife for partaking of stolen water-melon;" "July 26 1766, ——— for a premeditated fist quarrel;" "January 1 1772, ———, for taking hold of an antient man & member of ye ch., and shaking him in an unchristian & threatening manner."

It is almost needless to say that the above unnamed persons were disciplined by the church for their alleged misconduct, as was also the individual referred to in the following extract:

"June 30, 1786, ——— ——— and wife for ye premature marriage of wife's sister after first wife's death."

With the following extract, cited as will be noticed somewhat out of chronological order, we must deny our readers of further pleasure in the perusal of the quaint and in some instances pathetic records of church proceedings, in an age which at best enjoyed but "a dim religious light," in comparison with the effulgence of the twentieth century.

"June 10 1773. The Elders duely noticed Met at the Ministers House accordingly present Dea. Prudden Dea. Lum Jno. Ayrs Esqr., Cap. Timo. Mills, Cap. Jno. Lindsley Mr. Ezra Halsey, & the Modr Timo. Johnes. The Session was opened by prayer, after which there was a dispute laid before us, respecting the title of a certain tract of land in Hanover, in which several parties were concerned, Viz. Col. Ford, Dea. Matthias Burnet, Joseph Ketchel Esqr., in behalf of Joseph Baldwin, & Alexander Car-michael, who all agree'd that the Judgement of the Elders should be finally decisive, and that each of them would abide their determination. —— This question disputed is that Dea'n Burnet for him Selfe & y'os connected with him complain that Col. Ford has laid a Proprietor-right on Lands that were Surveyed in the year 1715, & therefore were not vacant when the Colonel laid his right upon them, after Hearing the parties, and Evidences distinctly, & reasoning upon the matter we deferred the further consideration of it to thursday next to meet at 2 'o clk. to deliberate further on the subject ——— concluded with Prayer ———

"Thursday June 17, 1773. the Elders met according to adjournment, present all the Members & Parties, except Joseph Ketchel Esqr., and after Prayers the above Matter was resumed, and after hearing what the Parties could say, and the evidence that could be produced, the Mod'r before the Session made their judgment, recommended it to the parties Viz Col. Ford, Dea. Matthias Burnet, & Mr. Alexander Cermichael, to retire by them Selves, with mutual benevolence and condescention, to make proposals for accomodation, they accordingly after a proper time of deliberation, came in, and to our great satisfaction, appeared in a friendly manner, and declared to the Session, that they had come to an entire agreement in the disputed matters, and superceeded the necessity of our Judgment. ——— Concluded w'h Prayer."

Again we quote from the trustees' book of the Presbyterian Church of Morristown, this time concerning the establishment of schools in the village:

"January 12 1767 the trustees Being called and met at the school hous henry Primrose Joseph Stiles and Benjamin Coe absent Proseaded and chose Benjamin Bayle President and Gave Lieve that a school hous might be Built on the Green Near whair the old hous Now Standeth."

The early settlers of West Hanover had apparently followed the example of New England, from whence many of them had either directly or indirectly come, and "near the schoolhouse built the church."

Indeed, this, the writer ventures to suggest, may have been literally true, for he is of the opinion that the "old house" mentioned as standing on "the Green," may have occupied a portion of the ground now owned by H. H. Davis, on Morris street, in the rear of the Presbyterian manse. Or, it may have stood on the opposite side of what is now Morris street from the manse, not far from the office of the Daily Record.

From the entry just quoted it will be seen, that prior to the year 1767, a school had been established in the village of West Hanover, and from the fact that in less than a decade after the settlement of Whippanong a school was established there, under the management of "John Richards schoolmaster," it will constitute no violence to reason to assume that as early at least, as the year 1725, the settlers of West Hanover, believing that

> "Learning by study must be won,
> 'Twas ne'er entail'd from sire to son,"

had erected a "school hous" and employed an instructor, such as the times afforded, to impart to youth knowledge, which if the Bard of Avon is to be accepted as authority, is "the wing with which we fly to heaven."

Of the interest of the people of early Morristown in the matter of education, there could be no more convincing proof than that furnished by the fact that in the year 1769, as may be learned by reference to the sessional records of the Presbyterian church, the sum of one hundred and fifty pounds and five shillings were contributed by the pastor and members of the above mentioned organization, toward the support of the College of New Jersey, now known as Princeton College. The contributors to the college mentioned were:

"Rev'd Tim. Johnes	£ 9	0	0
Jacob Ford, Esq'r	21	0	0

Dea. Matthias Burnet	9	0	0
Cap. Tim Mills..........................	6	0	0
Elder Daniel Lindsley	3	0	
Abr. Ogden, Esq'r.......................	3	0	0
Elder Jno. Lindsley	3	0	0
Joseph Wood	6	0	0
Henry Gardiner	0	16	0
Nathan Reeve	3	0	0
John Ayres, Esq'r.......................	9	0	0
Thomas Kenney	3	0	0
Will'm De Hart, Esq'r...................	3	0	0
Thomas Morrell	4	10	0
Jonas Phillips	4	10	0
Isaac Pierson	3	0	0
Jonathan Cheever	1	0	0
Peter Condict	2	11	0
Peter Prudden	2	11	0
Moses Prudden	2	11	0
Joseph Prudden	2	11	0
Benjamin Pierson	9	0	0
Samuel Tuthill, Esq'r...................	3	0	0
Slias Condict	3	0	0
Ezra Halsey, elder	12	0	0
Samuel Robarts	3	0	0
Augustine Bayles	3	0	0
Wid. Phebe Wood	3	0	0
Jonathan Stiles, Esq'r..................	1	15	0
Cap. Benjamin Halsey	0	10	0
	140	5	0 Proc.

BENJAM'N LINDSLEY."

The omission of the following entry, to be found in the sessional records of the Morristown Presbyterian Church, would render the preceding quotation incomplete; so it is appended:

"April 27, 1773. The Elders being met, Mr. Sergeant, the Treasurer of ye College receit for £140 Proc. was seen and acknowledged by the Elders and the overplush was allowed for incidental charges, testified in behalf of ye Rest by

JACOB FORD.

"Sept. 29, 1787. Then presented to the Trustees of Nassau Hall for the education of poor and pios youth as followeth, viz:

Caleb Russel, Esq.	22	dol.	& 45	ninetieths
Joseph Lewis, Esq.	11	"	& 5	"
Silas Condict, Esq..............	42	"	& 1	"
Icabod Cooper, ...	1	"	& 1	"
Dea. Gilbert Allen...............	1	"	& 80	"
Philip Lindsley	3	"	& 66	"
Jonathan Dickerson, Esq........	16	"	& 12	"
Col. Benoni Hathaway	3	"	& 30	"
John Mills	9	"	& 2	"
	—		—	
	£41		3. 9	

"For which they received the thanks of the Board of Trustees.

Test. TIMO. JOHNES."

From the following entry in the trustees' book of the Presbyterian Church of Morristown, there may be gleaned several facts of more than ordinary interest, with regard to schools in the township:

"Octob 7 1771 the trustees met at Doct tuthills Esq. Sam Robarts absent and agreed that the money that Mr. Watt Left to the town Should be Laid out towards Purchasing utensils for the communian Table also that the school hous now on Peter Mackees Land be Removed onto the Parsonage Land and there to Remain During the Pleasure of the trustees and then Lyable to be Removed."

Where "Peter Mackee's land," with reference to the Presbyterian house of worship, was situated, it would be interesting to know; that it was in the near vicinity of that house of worship is highly probable, and that it may have been in front of the "meeting house Dore" is possible. As to the residence of "Doct tuthill Esq.," we can speak with certainty; it was situated on the left hand side of what is now South street, and about midway between what is now the southwest corner of the Green and what is now James street; or, to be somewhat more definite, it stood about opposite where Boyken street intersects with South street. Inasmuch as he was a leading man in the community, the reader will be interested to learn a few facts concerning "Doct tuthill Esq." And first as to his bearing the double title of "Doct," and "Esq." After his graduation from Yale College, he evidently studied medicine, which accounts for the application of the former title. On the nineteenth day of March in the year 1759, when he was thirty-five years of age, he was appointed a judge for Morris County, by Governor Barnard, and on the twenty-first of April, in the year 1768, he was reappointed to the same office; and here we have the explanation of the title of "Esq.," applied to this prominent Morristonian of former days.

It would be exceedingly interesting to know who were the teachers in Morristown's early schools; but this is a pleasure our readers are required to forego, since there is now, apparently, no way of ascertaining. We do know, however, that in the year 1779, there appear on the roll of membership of the Presbyterian Church of Morristown, the names of "Mrs. Dow" and "Dorothea Cooper, school madams," who had evidently united with the church by certificate from some sister organization; and from this circumstance we may be permitted to infer that they were teachers in the schoolhouse on the parsonage land, wherever that may have been. Of the schoolhouse on the Green, no description has come down to us, nor is there now any knowledge of the methods employed in teaching. From the following description of a school situated a few miles from Morristown, at the period under consideration, given by an aged eye-witness, there may, however, be drawn an inference of the *modus operandi* of the school on the Morristown Green. This gentleman of four-score years and two (Mahlon Johnson) thus spoke, just prior to the opening of the Civil War:

"The school building was constructed of logs, and instead of glass for windows sheep skins were stretched over apertures made by sawing off an occasional log. These windows had one virtue—they were an effectual screen to prevent pupils from being interrupted in their exercises by what was going on outside. The time was regulated by an hour-glass, and they drank their water from a tumbler made of cow's horn or ground shell. Arithmetic was not taught in classes, but the pupils ciphered when they were not reading, spelling or writing. The latter branches were taught in classes. A chalk line or a crack in the floor was the mark they were required to toe. The common school was hardly considered a school in those days unless the whack of the ruler or the whistle of the whip was frequently heard."

The taverns and tavern-keepers of early Morristown were more numerous than the average resident of this now historic town apprehends, as may be inferred from the following announcement in the year 1764:

"Whereas Samuel Tuthill, of Morris Town, in Morris County (the identical Samuel Tuthill of whom we have just been speaking) purposes to leave of the Business of Tavernkeeping, he will sell the Farm where he now lives, containing about 90 Acres, being well proportioned with Wood Land, plough Land, and Meadow, and a fine Stream of Water running through the Whole; with a good Orchard on the same, consisting of 257 bearing Apple Trees, besides a Variety of other Fruit Trees; and also a large Dwelling House on the Place, convenient for a Tavern and other Public Business; standing about Twenty Two Rods from the Court House, in Morris Town, being in the most publick Part of the Country. Any Person inclinning to purchase, may apply to Samuel Tuthill, on the Premises, who will give a good Title."

Before bidding adieu to the period of Morristown's history so briefly reviewed, let us draw aside a little wider the veil separating the past from the present, and take a final view of affairs in Morristown as indicated by the following extract from the New York Mercury of December 20, in the year 1762:

"On the 25th. of November last broke out of Morris County goal, in New Jersey, a prisoner named John Smith, an Irishman, tall, slender, and thin visaged, much pock marked, about 35 years of age, with brown hair: Had on, a brown jacket, a check shirt, and linen trowsers. Whoever shall take up the said Smith, and bring him to me, or my goaler, in Morris Town, shall have five pounds reward, and all reasonable charges, paid by

"SAMUEL TUTHILL, Sheriff."

That the "good old days" in Morristown's history were not exempt from crime, is a fact that, in a striking manner, is brought home to those of the present generation, by such announcement as the following, from the New York Mercury of April 30, in the year 1764:

"Morris Town, April 19, 1764.

"FIFTY POUNDS REWARD.

"Whereas my House in Morris Town, was broke open on Monday Night the second Instant, the Lock broke off my Desk, and my Pocket Book taken out, with about £27 in Cash, and several Writings of the greatest Consequence to me: Particularly some Receipts, one of which was from John Tuttle to me, for £200 York Currency; and as a certain Person was heard to say (that Morning before this Theft was made) that the above Receipt would never be seen again, I have the greatest Reason to suspect this infamous Robbery has been committed on Account of the aforesaid Receipt, with a villanous design to defraud me of the Money depending on said Receipt, together with my Character: Therefore whoever will discover the audacious Perpetrator of this horrid Crime, shall receive on Conviction the above Reward, from

"DAVID GOULD."

"Contentment, rosy, dimpled maid,
Thou brighest daughter of the sky—"

must have been a stranger to the individual named in the announcement: "Runaway a few days ago from the subscriber of Morris Town, in East New Jersey, a servant man, named Ebenezer Haulbeet, a carpenter by trade, about 25 years old, about 5 feet 8 or 9 inches high, light complexion, flax colour'd straight hair; rode a white horse, which it is supposed he would soon part with, as he is very fond of swaping horses. He is supposed to be gone to Connecticut, somewhere near or about Sharon, where he has relations of the same name. Whoever takes up said servant, and secures him in any county goal, so that I may obtain him again, shall have five pounds reward, paid by me.

JOSEPH KING.

"June 18" (no year given, probably 1764).

CHAPTER VII.

"Who swerves from innocence, who makes divorce
Of that serene companion—a good name,
Recovers not his loss; but walks with shame,
With doubt, with fear, and haply with remorse."

HE oft-repeated saying that "truth is stranger than fiction" was never more aptly, nor, indeed, more amply illustrated than in the following condensed account of the counterfeiting operations of Samuel Ford, and his partners in the crime, which was carried on by them in Morristown, chiefly, during the decade immediately preceding the commencement of the Revolution.

Samuel Ford, the leader of this notorious gang of counterfeiters, was the son of Samuel Ford, whose father was John Ford, who, in the year 1721, settled in what is now known as Monroe, situated about two miles to the eastward of Morristown, upon a large tract of land given him by John Budd as an inducement to open up a settlement in that region. From one of Samuel Ford's blood relations, who was familiar with his personal appearance as a young man, we learn that "he was a handsome man," but as we shall in due time ascertain, he did not become a shining exemplification of the significant saying that "Handsome is that handsome does;" indeed, to quote again from the relation mentioned, "he was a great grief to his friends." Samuel Ford, Jr., married Grace, the daughter of Joseph Kitchel, Esq., of Hanover Township, and she was a sister, therefore, of the Hon. Aaron Kitchel, who was United States Senator from New Jersey from the year 1807 until the year 1811, and who, before and during the Revolution, had played an important part in county affairs. Colonel Jacob Ford, Sr., was an uncle of Samuel Ford, Jr., who, as may be inferred from the fact of his highly respectable family relations on both sides, was the one "black sheep" of the flock.

Prior to the year 1765—it may have been as early as the year 1762—we find Samuel Ford, Jr., engaged in the iron industry at what is now known as Hibernia, four miles north of Rockaway, in company with Lord Stirling and Benjamin Cooper; the latter the son of Daniel Cooper, one of the early judges of the Morris County Court. It is said that the Hibernia works were originally built and owned by Samuel Ford, Jr., and Lord Stirling, and that Benjamin Cooper joined them in the business subsequently. If the declaration of Samuel Ford, made in after years, is accepted as truthful (and the writer recognizes no reason for doubting it), Benjamin Cooper, during a period of financial embarrassment in their business at Hibernia, suggested to him the idea of making and using counterfeit money to enable them to meet their pecuniary obligations, and so continue the business. It is not improbable—indeed, the writer ventures the opinion that it is highly probable—that either Samuel Ford, alone, or in conjunction with Benjamin Cooper, soon afterward began the manufacture at "Hiberny" of counterfeit money, but with what measure of success as to the execution or circulation of it the writer has no opinion to express.

It is a matter of record that on the twenty-eighth day of October, in the year 1765, Samuel Ford sold several tracts of land at Hibernia to James Anderson and Benjamin Cooper. His wife Grace joined with him in the transfers. The deed given to Anderson was acknowledged "before me, Joseph Tuttle, Esq., one of the Judges of His Majesty's inferior Court of Common Pleas, held at Morristown, July 9, 1766." To this latter circumstance special reference will be made at a later stage of this history, in connection with the endeavor to account for the absence of the records of the Morris County Court from the year 1754, to the year 1796—a most significant fact when considered in the light of the highly sensational occurrences of the intervening period, one of which, we are about to relate. That Samuel Ford disposed of his interest in the iron business at Hibernia in the year 1765, seems evident from the consideration of two facts; first, that the conveyance of the tracts of land above mentioned to James

Anderson speaks of "outhouses, buildings, barns, furnaces, &c., mines and minerals, &c.," as included in the deed; and, second, that as early as the year 1768 the firm conducting the Hibernia iron works is spoken of as "Benjamin Cooper & Co.," and Lord Stirling was understood to be the "Company." For the property sold by Samuel Ford at Hibernia, he received from James Anderson the sum of £265 13s. 4d., and from Benjamin Cooper the same, having sold to each the same quantity of land.

Not long after the sale of the above-mentioned property at Hibernia—it may have been late in the same year (1765), or early in the year following, probably the former—Samuel Ford made a trip to Ireland, and from the circumstance of the close proximity of the two occurrences, it is safe to infer that this sale of property was made for the express purpose of raising funds with which to defray the expense of his transatlantic trip. At the period under consideration, Ireland was reputed to have the most skilful counterfeiters in the world. The object of Samuel Ford's visit to the Green Isle was, as subsequent events clearly disclosed, the perfection of himself in the business of making counterfeit money, and in this branch of business he became, as we shall shortly learn, an expert. While in Ireland he won the affections of an interesting Irish girl, whom, with undue haste, he married. She is said to have had a respectable sum of money, which we may reasonably assume was appropriated by the bridegroom in the conduct of his unique business. Ford remained n Ireland several months, returning with his young Irish bride to America, as near as can now be ascertained, in the early part of the month of June, in the year 1766.

Upon learning that Ford had a wife and children n this country, his bride of a few months was almost beside herself with grief and disappointment; and that she promptly separated herself from one who had so basely deceived her, it is almost superfluous to mention. There is good authority for adding that this brokenhearted Irish girl subsequently married one of her own countrymen, and for many years resided in Whippany, New Jersey.

It is a fact pregnant with significance that simultaneously with the landing of Ford in this country, on his return from Ireland, there appeared in one of the New York periodicals the announcement of the arrival at that port of a ship with "a large sum of counterfeit Jersey bills of credit." Equally significant is the fact that on the twenty-eighth day of June, in the year 1766, the Governor of New Jersey issued a warrant on the New Jersey Treasury to the Honorable John Stevens, for dispatching an express into the province to inform the inhabitants of a large sum of Jersey bills of credit having arrived in a vessel from England; the vessel evidently set sail from some port in the country last named. This counterfeit money was unquestionably the product of Samuel Ford, and his instructors, in the Emerald Isle.

In the year 1767, Samuel Ford was a resident of New

York, and here he was arrested "on a charge of uttering false New Jersey bills of credit." There is no record, however, of his having been brought to trial for his alleged crime.

With the consummate skill as a maker of counterfeit money acquired in Ireland, Ford now resolved to engage in the business—"a money-making affair" he pleasantly termed it—on an extensive scale; and we next find him living in a secluded spot on what is now the Columbia road, a little more than half a mile beyond the "Washington Headquarters." The house in which he lived with his wife and children, whom he had meanwhile joined, has disappeared, and on its site there now stands another dwelling. His counterfeiting quarters was a hut or shop situated on a small island about in the centre of what has for many years been known as the "Hammock." The "Hammock" was in Samuel Ford's day a piece of swamp land, which, during the greater portion of the year was covered by a foot or more of water; indeed, a gentleman who for many years has resided in the vicinity, says: "I have seen five feet of water on the 'Hammock.' I have hunted ducks there." This same gentleman when asked by the writer how long this piece of swamp land has been known as the "Hammock," replied, with apparent irritation, that its long-continued designation should for a moment be questioned. "Why, bless you," he exclaimed, "ever since I was a baby I have known it by that name," and he has reached three-score and ten, after honorable service in the Civil War, and thrilling adventures in the extreme West. Lest some of our readers, in expectation of fine sport and buoyed also by dreams of well-filled game bags, set out on some auspicious morning for the "Hammock," the writer will promptly inform them that it was long since filled in. Its location, however, and the location of the miniature island once rising in its centre, upon which Samuel Ford's shop was situated, are still discoverable.

While engaged in his counterfeiting business at the "Hammock," Ford was in the habit of leaving his home at daylight each morning with gun over his shoulder, as if starting out on a hunting expedition. His real objective, however, was the little shop on the Hammock Island, where he was wont to attend to his "money-making affair." In order to reach this shop it was necessary for him to crawl on his hands and knees, a portion of the way at least. Owing to his reputation in the neighborhood for idleness, his peculiar course of life aroused no suspicion. The one unaccountable thing in connection with his life which impressed his neighbors was the fact, that a man with no ostensible means of livelihood, save a few acres of swamp land, could dress well, live well and always have plenty of money. Doubtless Ford could have solved the knotty problem for his wondering neighbors had he been so disposed; that he was not disposed was undoubtedly owing to prudential considerations. There is evidence, which cannot, the writer believes, be gainsaid, that Ford's counterfeiting shop was visited, once at least, by Thomas Kinney, of Morristown, who was subsequently the sheriff of Morris County. Mr. Kinney's visit (or visits?) to the counterfeiting establishment of Samuel Ford, was not, of course, generally known at the time. It is not improbable, and this opinion is not expressed save as the result of thorough and impartial investigation, that other men of prominence in Morristown and Morris County (the mention of whose names even suggestively might produce at least a mild sensation) visited the little shop on the "Hammock" while hunting ducks or other more precious game, perchance.

In the year 1768—it was probably during his residence near the "Hammock"—Ford, on the night of July 21, with the aid of accomplices, robbed the treasury of East Jersey, then situated at Perth Amboy, the account of which follows: In the office adjoining the sleeping-room of Mr. Skinner, the treasurer, was an iron chest containing the provincial funds then in his custody. It was the purpose of Samuel Ford and his accomplices—comprising, according to seemingly reliable evidence, three soldiers employed as guards on the premises—to carry off this chest and afterward open it and secure its contents. If this failed, the robbers were to take the key to the iron chest from Mr. Skinner. The desperate character of this robbery, as deliberately planned by the perpetrators, may be inferred from the fact that it was resolved that, if necessary to the success of their undertaking, Mr. Skinner, the treasurer, or any other person obstructing the execution of their plans, should be murdered. It was also mutually agreed that if the prospective robbers were suspected, or discovered, and brought to trial, they should turn "King's evidence" and endeavor to implicate Mr. Skinner as an accomplice in the crime. The penalty for the contemplated crime was, at the time, death by hanging; and when one of the gang, apparently more humane than the rest, expressed his disapproval of trying to implicate the treasurer, Samuel Ford exclaimed: "No, d—n him, he will only be condemned; he has friends enough to save him from the gallows."

Finding that the iron chest containing the coveted money was too heavy and too large to carry off, the robbers concluded to open it on the premises, and then and there rifle its contents. This was accomplished by means of an old rusty and cast-off key, accidentally found in the drawer of an old desk which the robbers had broken open, in the expectation of finding money. The key in use for opening the iron chest was in the room occupied by Mr. Skinner, presumably somewhere about the clothing he had laid aside for the night. It is the opinion of not a few persons familiar with the details of this crime, that the accidental finding of the cast-off key to the iron chest containing the provincial funds, was the means of preserving the life of the sleeping treasurer, who, upon awakening, would not have given up the key to the iron chest without a struggle for its possession, which would almost certainly have resulted in his death at the hands of four desperate robbers, three of whom had basely betrayed the trust of guardianship reposed in them by the treasurer. But, by the aid of the old key the iron chest was opened, and its contents secured and carried off by the robbers. It is safe to assume that of the sum secured, £6,570, 9s, 4d, in bills and coin—Samuel Ford received the lion's share. The three soldiers were doubtless suitably rewarded for the valuable assistance rendered by them.

Benjamin Cooper, Samuel Ford's former partner in the iron industry at Hibernia, received, as he subsequently acknowledged, £300 of these ill-gotten gains. But why should Benjamin Cooper receive a portion of the fruits of this daring robbery if he had not been a partner, either active or silent, in the crime whose penalty was death by hanging? Or, did he receive it as "hush money?" That other persons in Morris County, one at least of the number a Morristonian, were connected directly or indirectly with the robbery of the treasury at Perth Amboy and shared in the ill-gotten gains, there is in the mind of the writer scarcely a doubt. One, as we have seen, confessed to having received a portion of this stolen money; but how many more did not make a confession? Let us find the answer to this query in the words:

> "Justice is passionless and therefore sure;
> Guilt for a while may flourish; virtue sink
> 'Neath the shade of calumny and ill; justice
> At last, like the bright sun, shall break majestic forth,
> The shield of innocence, the guard of truth."

The failure of the provincial authorities to discover the perpetrators of the Perth Amboy robbery, in close connection therewith, is a sufficient explanation of the fact that Ford and his accomplices in the crime were unapprehended, and the circumstances of this highly sensational occurrence were not made public until several years afterward under the shadow of the scaffold.

There is some evidence that soon after the Perth Amboy robbery, Ford made a second trip across the Atlantic, going this time to England. No account of the particulars of this second transatlantic trip, however, so far as the writer is aware, has descended to us.

Early in the year 1773, large quantities of counterfeit money, consisting of bills of credit and coin, were found to be in circulation in the New Jersey province. By reason of a combination of circumstances, which will now be particularized, suspicion was at length fastened upon Samuel Ford, Jr., as the person chiefly responsible for this alarming state of affairs. On the sixteenth day of July, in the year 1773, therefore, he was arrested and placed in the Morris County Jail on the Green. It will be remembered that the Morris County Courthouse, a portion of which was used as a jail, was at the time mentioned a one-story structure, with the large, old-fashioned open fire-place and immense chimney, spoken of in connection with the account of Uriah Brown's mysterious nocturnal escapes. Simultaneously, or nearly so, with the arrest of Ford, several other persons were also arrested on suspicion of having been identified with him in the manufacture and circulation of counterfeit money. Their names were Benjamin Cooper, of Hibernia; Dr. Bern Budd, of Morristown; Samuel Haynes and one Ayers, both of Sussex County, and David Reynolds, a native presumably, of the Emerald Isle—an Irishman certainly. These were likewise lodged in the jail on the Green. If the arm of the law had been long enough and strong enough, doubtless this quintet of suspects would have been considerably swelled, but—well, the words following have, at least, some measure of application to this case:

> Laws are like spider webs, small flies are ta'en,
> While greater flies break in and out again—and some flies that ought to be in, never get in.

One of the most unfortunate features of this counterfeiting affair is the fact, that most of the persons implicated and arrested were well connected, and some at least of them moved in the best society of the day.

On the night of his arrest, or on the day following, Ford escaped from the county jail. That he was aided in effecting his escape was the common opinion of the day; and that one John King, who seems to have been at the time under-sheriff, or jailer, at the Morris County Jail, was Ford's confederate in the occurrence, was also the prevalent opinion. Certain it is that in the month of February following, Deputy Sheriff King was cited before the Privy Council of New Jersey. Nor was the sheriff of Morris County at the time, Thomas Kinney, free of suspicion, as a confederate of Ford, in effecting his prompt escape from the old, one-story jail on the Green. In this connection one can scarcely avoid the conclusion that Samuel Ford did not have to climb up chimney to make his escape. Subsequent developments, as will be seen, more than confirmed the grounds of suspicion that Sheriff Kinney had a hand in Ford's escape, and it would be gratifying to the writer to be able to say, or to think, that the developments above suggested do not encourage the belief that Sheriff Kinney, as an individual, had also been an accomplice, silent, it is true, with Ford, in his long-continued counterfeiting operations. Ford might have been captured, after his escape from the Morris County Jail, but for the circumstances about to be related. He made his escape on July 16 or 17, 1773. For more than a month thereafter it was quite generally known that he was secreted in the near vicinity of Morristown. In this knowledge, it is practically certain, the High Sheriff of Morris County, shared. On August 5—nearly three weeks, it will be noted, after Ford's slick escape—Sheriff Kinney publicly offered a reward for the apprehension of the escaped counterfeiter. Not until the month of September, did the Pennsylvania Gazette begin to publish items concerning the pursuit of Ford, and the same periodical did not get the Governor's proclamation for publication, until December 1, 1773. But we will now

> Search not to find what lies too deeply hid,
> Nor to know things where knowledge is forbid.

Ford, after his escape from jail, fled to a lonely spot on the mountains in the vicinity of Hibernia, where he had once been engaged in the iron industry. Here he secreted himself in a deserted colliery cabin known as "Smultz's Cabin," and here we will for the present leave him, where, quoting the apt lines of Longfellow:

> The leaves of memory seem to make
> A mournful rustling in the dark.

At a special session of the Court of Oyer and Terminer of Morris County, held on the fourth of August, in the year 1773, a preliminary examination of witnesses was conducted. The evidence then and there adduced against the persons confined in the county jail, for alleged complicity with Ford in his counterfeiting operations, was such that their trial and conviction became a foregone conclusion. In view of this latter fact, presumably, Benjamin Cooper, one of the prisoners, on the fourteenth day of the month last named, made a partial confession. This he was moved to do in the hope of a mitigation of his evidently anticipated punishment. A second confession, by another prisoner, presumably Dr. Bern Budd, included a complete and explicit account of all the details of the "money-making" scheme. There is evidence which indicates that this latter confession was suppressed. It is a matter of record that "In 1773, Lord Stirling complained that Samuel Tuttle and Colonel Samuel Ogden had acted in an unfair and partial manner 'in taking the examinations and depositions of several witnesses of and concerning several criminal matters,' inquired into by them as Judges of the Morris County Court of Oyer and Terminer; he also charged that they had 'suppressed the testimony of some material witnesses (in connection with the Ford counterfeiting operations?) for bringing certain criminals to Justice.' These charges being made to the Council of the Province, Col. Ogden in behalf of himself and Judge Tuthill demanded an inquiry. But Lord Stirling withdrew the charges, and the matter was dropped." These confessions led to an examination of the shop on the "Hammock," where a press and plates for printing the bills, not only of New Jersey, but of Maryland, Pennsylvania and New York, were found. A quantity of type and other material used in the counterfeiting business, as also a leather wrapper in which the false bills were kept, were among the fruits of the raid on the "Hammock."

After Ford's flight from New Jersey, and settlement elsewhere, of which an account will, in due course, be given, his former home near the scene of his criminal operations was purchased by Sheriff Robertson. While subsequently repairing the house, counterfeiters' tools were found secreted in the walls.

On the nineteenth of August, in the year 1773, the trial of Cooper, Budd, Haynes and Reynolds was begun in the Morris County Court; Ayers was tried and convicted in Sussex County. The Morris County Court room was crowded during the trial, by an eager and sympathetic throng, nearly every one of whom was related, in some way, to the prisoners who were being tried for their lives. To the indictment found against them, each prisoner pleaded guilty, and they were sentenced to be hanged on the seventeenth of the month following. One of the judges of the court which had tried and sentenced these men, was the father of Benjamin Cooper. The writer has seen the statement that the sentences were passed upon the prisoners in the "meeting-house," by which is doubtless meant the Presbyterian meeting-house. It is said that when Mrs. Budd heard of the sentence of her husband, she started at once for Perth Amboy, where, on her knees before the Governor, she pleaded for her husband's pardon, with what effect, however, is not known. Quite different was the deportment of Dr. Budd's mother, a woman of extraordinary dignity and stateliness. When she witnessed the grief of her daughter-in-law, she remarked, by way of reproof: "He has broken the laws of the land, and it is just that he should suffer by them." Mrs. Budd, the doctor's mother, was, however, a kind-hearted, sympathetic woman. The day fixed for the execution of the sentenced criminals arrived. The scaffold had been carefully erected on the Green. Over the business of executing four men Sheriff Kinney is said to have been greatly excited—so excited, indeed, as to be almost beside himself. But before he was required to perform the dreaded execution, an order arrived at Morristown, from Governor Franklin to remand Budd and Cooper and Haynes to jail. Reynolds, however, the least guilty of the number, for lack of "friends at court," was executed on the day set—September 17. The fellow-Irishman upon whose tesimony Reynolds was arrested shed bitter tears of regret when he was informed of the sentence of his acquaintance. To the last moment Reynolds protested his innocence. Among the witnesses of the execution of Reynolds was David Gordon, a nephew of Sheriff Kinney. From Rev. Dr. Joseph F. Tuttle, the following is quoted:

> "My aged friend, Mr. Gordon (the Gordon above mentioned), says he remembers that Reynolds, one of the four condemned counterfeiters, protested to the last his innocence. He admitted that it was right that he should die, for he had done many things worthy of death. One of his great crimes as rehearsed on the scaffold, and only one made an impression on Mr. Gordon's mind. With much feeling, Reynolds recurred to his boyhood. His grandmother sent him to procure her some snuff. He performed the errand, but only expended a part of her money, as she ordered. With the rest he procured some cake or candy for himself. He said that dishonest act had distressed him greatly, and if guilty of no other crime, for this he ought to die. 'But as for the indictment on which I am convicted and sentenced I am entirely innocent.'"

Mr. Gordon informed Dr. Tuttle that the scaffold on which Reynolds was executed was erected "immediately in front of the courthouse," by which, as the present writer believes, he means, on the side of the court house nearest the Presbyterian Church. Inasmuch as, at the period under consideration, there was a road on the easterly side of the courthouse, it is easy to conceive that by "immediately in front of the courthouse," Mr. Gordon refers to what was really the rear of that structure. That the scaffold was erected literally in front of the courthouse would mean that it was erected in the public highway; for the courthouse, as a matter of fact, fronted on what was then known as Court Street, a narrow road to the westward of the courthouse. An examination of the map made in the year 1777, by order of Washington, will confirm the view above stated. Another incident related by Mr. Gordon is given in the words of Dr. Tuttle:

> "It seems that (just previous to the hour fixed for the executions) a son of the Sheriff, a lad of some ten or twelve years of age, and himself (Mr. Gordon), forgetful of the dreadful nature of the business in hand, were indulging themselves in some athletic sport. Mrs. Kinney called her son into the house, and rebuking him for his shameless levity at such a time, severely chastised him. The sheriff coming up just at that moment, nervous and agitated with the hanging business, seized the boy by the arm, and called out spitefully: 'Why don't you put it on him?' His wife very wisely concluded, that however well calculated he might be in that mental agitation to hang four men, he was not at all fitted to advise concerning the whipping of one boy, and she forthwith desisted. As for Mr. Gordon, he thought the Sheriff would be at him next, and he was greatly frightened about it."

In the month of December, 1773, after several respites, Governor Franklin granted a complete pardon to Budd, Cooper and Haynes.

Such was Dr. Budd's reputation for skill in his profession, that notwithstanding his conviction and sentence for crime he promptly resumed his practise in Morristown. One of the first patients he was called to attend was a woman who was supposed to be near the end of her life. Dr. Budd had scarcely crossed the threshold of the sick room, when the woman summoned sufficient strength to inquire, with unaffected simplicity: "How did you kind of feel, doctor, when you came so near being hanged?" Turning with a smile, and a blush to her husband, the doctor remarked: "Well, well, I guess your wife has a fair chance to recover."

About the middle of September, 1773, after Samuel Ford had been in hiding for nearly two months Sheriff Kinney repaired quietly to Rockaway (it was on Sunday), where he leisurely summoned a posse for the pursuit of the escaped counterfeiter. Kinney, apparently for the purpose of making a showing of earnestness, pressed into service as a guide Abraham Kitchel, a brother of Samuel Ford's wife, Grace.

Kitchel, while the posse was on its way to Hibernia, remarked to Sheriff Kinney: "I know where Ford is, and will take you to the spot, but you know you dare not, for your own sake, arrest him." This remark has but a single meaning, which our readers will not be slow in discovering. A boy—James Kitchel, son of Abraham—upon seeing the sheriff arrest his father as a guide to Ford's hiding place, was so frightened, that he started on a run for home; but on the way he stopped at the house of Joseph Herriman long enough to tell him of the occurrences of the morning. Herriman at once threw off his coat, and ran at the top of his speed by a short cut to "Smultz's Cabin," and notified Ford of his peril. When Sheriff Kinney and his posse, reached the cabin, Ford was gone. As the posse entered the doubly deserted cabin, Abraham Kitchel remarked to Kinney: "There, sheriff, is where Ford has been secreted, and you would rather give your horse, saddle and bridle than to find him here now."

By the Privy Council of New Jersey Sheriff Kinney was subsequently declared "blameable for negligence in his office, respecting the escape of Ford;" and the same body advised the Governor "to prosecute the said indictment at the next court." But the writer has neither seen nor heard of any record of his trial. A well known, and much read poet, has said: "Where there is a mystery, it is generally supposed that there must also be evil." That there is mystery, on the surface, at least, in the failure of the county officials, "to prosecute the said indictment at the next court," must be patent to all readers of this story.

Ford fled southward, paying his way with money of his own manufacture. He settled among the mountains of Green Brier County, Va., now a part of West Virginia, where he assumed the name of Baldwin, his mother's maiden name. There, with a partner, he engaged in the business of a silversmith. During a serious illness, when death was anticipated, he made a full confession of his former crimes to his partner's wife. Upon his recovery and after the decease of his partner, he married the widow. He acquired considerable property. Several children were the result of his latest matrimonial venture. The Virginia Baldwins, who became prominent in State affairs, may have been descendants of the man who is said to have "left his country for his country's good."

When the whereabouts of Ford became known to the New Jersey authorities he was, legally speaking, beyond the reach of the law, so far as arrest for the robbery of the treasury at Perth Amboy was concerned; owing to the fact that he had left the province before the confessions of his accomplices had been made. He was visited, after the lapse of a few years, by his eldest son by Grace Kitchel. The young man's name was William. He was accompanied by Stephen Halsey, who subsequently married one of William's sisters. To these visitors Samuel Ford appeared to be in a most melancholy frame of mind. He professed repentance for his past sins, and declared his intentions to lead a good life. To New Jersey he never returned. When informed of the confessions of Budd, Cooper and Haynes, in which they declared him to be the prime mover of the Perth Amboy robbery, Ford strenuously denied it. In a letter to Benjamin Cooper, written while he was in hiding near Hibernia, he berated him for his "atrocious falsehood" in charging him with the robbery of the provincial treasury, and added: "You describe me as being the chiefest promoter and first introducer of the money-making affair," by which he means the counterfeiting operations. He continues: "Did you not in the time of our depressed circumstances at the furnace (Hibernia) first move such a scheme to me?"

Ford's property at the "Hammock." what little there was left, was sold by Sheriff Kinney even to a tin cup containing milk for the babe. During the sale, Ford's son (probably William), said to the sheriff: "I have seen you in my father's shop." Dr. Joseph F. Tuttle's "The Early History of Morris County, New Jersey," in connection with his statements of the career of Samuel Ford, Jr., says: "And I cannot refrain from expressing the feeling, which an examination of all the accessible records, as well as traditions, leave on my mind, that whilst Samuel Ford was a great villain, he was acting his villainy in very respectable company, a part of which did not get to court and scaffold, as some others did." And finally, quotes the present writer:

> "Good nature and good sense must ever join;
> To err is human, to forgive, divine."

CHAPTER VII.

"Slaves, who once conceived the glowing thought
Of freedom, in that hope itself possess
All that the contest calls for;—spirit, strength,
The scorn of danger, and united hearts,
The surest presage of the good they seek."

OR nearly a score of years prior to the commencement of the Revolution, the policy of Great Britain, with respect to the American colonies, had been anything but just. During the period mentioned there were enacted by the British Parliament no ss than twenty-nine laws in restriction of infant col- iial industries. The mere mention of a few of these ws, as illustrative of the blind tyranny of the mother)untry, makes them, in the light of the twentieth cen- ıry, appear little less than ludicrous. Among them 'ere the prohibition of the use of waterfalls, of the :tting up of machinery for manufacturing purposes, ıch as looms and spindles, and of working of iron

and wood in certain forms specified. Markets for boards and fish were shut out, sugar and molasses, and the American vessels in which they were carried, were seized, and the King's arrow was set upon trees which were afterward permitted to rot in the forests. In short, the attempt was made to prevent trade of any sort by the American colonies with any country, except above it floated the British flag.

To a few of the acts of the British Parliament thus, in a general way, alluded to, it seems desirable to refer specifically, and by name. And first, to what are known as the 'navigation acts,' passed in the years 1761 and 1766, which forbade colonial trade with England, and with English colonies, except in English vessels. The restrictions of these laws were made still closer by the subsequent enactment of further laws of a similar character. The American colonies should produce commodities which could not be produced in the mother country and which the mother country needed, the colonies should consume what the mother country had to sell; they should never be competitors with the mother country, and should trade with no other nation—such, in brief, was the British idea of her colonies, and of their mutual obligations. Great Britain was willing to purchase from her American colonies tobacco and naval stores, for these she was herself unprepared to produce. As soon, however, as the colonists on this side of the Atlantic, embarked in the manufacture of woolen goods, they were at once forbidden to export the wool, or the goods, into which it was made, from one colony to another. When the colonists began to manufacture hats, the exportation of this commodity from one colony to another was peremptorily forbidden, and by promptly enacted laws an attempt was made to limit the number of apprentices to hatters. Even the slow growth of the iron industry in the American colonies, excited alarm among the iron manufacturers of Great Britain. This resulted in the enactment of a law permitting pig iron and bar iron to be imported into Great Britain free of duty; but the same law sought to prohibit the erection of mills for the manufacture of slitted iron, or rolled iron, or any plating forge in which a tilt-hammer (trip-hammer is the more common name in America) should be used, or any furnace for the making of steel. An attempt was made in the British House of Commons to abolish mills existing at the time of the above-named enactment, but by a small majority this failed. The supply of a neighborhood with the coarser articles, was deemed by the mother country the limit of the endeavor of colonial manufacturers.

One of the most obnoxious features of the navigation act was what were known as "writs of assistance," conferring authority to employ British ships and officers and seamen in the capacity of custom-house officers and informers. It became lawful, therefore, for the commanders of British armed vessels to stop and examine any merchant vessel approaching the American shores, and upon suspicion alone to seize such vessels in the name of the King. These "writs of assistance" were really search warrants, without the mention of name or place, and, armed with these, the holders thereof could seize merchant vessels, and break open stores and private dwellings, in search of goods on which it had been suspected the duty had not been paid. This was a clear violation of the principle that "the Englishman's house is his castle," which the American colonists had been taught to believe by their mother across the sea. To the execution of the "writs of assistance" there was the most earnest resistance on the part of the American colonists. Remonstrances forwarded to the King were unavailing. Leading American merchants united in the adoption of a resolution to import no more British goods until the laws above mentioned should be repealed. While the right of the British Parliament to enact laws with regard to commerce between the mother country and the American colonies, and the right, therefore to lay duties on imported goods, was admitted, it was also recognized that if, without their consent, any species of direct tax could be laid on the colonies, they would be at the mercy of King George III. The principle of no taxation without representation could, therefore, as the American colonies clearly perceived, have no exceptions whatever, and to this they faithfully adhered.

'Tis true that during the French and Indian wars the navigation acts, and the law authorizing the writs of assistance, were not very strictly enforced, and as a consequence, between the American colonies and the West Indies, a trade far from insignificant was quietly developed. Dried fish and lumber were taken to the West Indies, and large quantities of sugar and rum, and of molasses, from which New England rum was made, were brought back, and this trade became lucrative.

At the close of the French and Indian wars, in the year 1763, waged for supremacy in America, Great Britain was confronted with an accumulated national debt of nearly one and a half billions of dollars. In her extremity—for such an enormous debt presented an alarming state of affairs, before which British statesmanship might well stand appalled—she very naturally looked to the American colonies for aid toward the liquidation of this immense indebtedness. This aid the mother country would doubtless have been granted but for the stubborn insistence upon her inherent right to lay upon the American colonies a direct tax, as a partial means of raising the money needed toward the liquidation of the national debt. The children on this side the Atlantic would have counted it a pleasure to come voluntarily, or upon request, to the aid of their beloved mother, despite the facts that they had already contributed their full share toward the prosecution of the wars so recently terminated, and that the mother country had also reaped her full share of the advantageous termination of those wars.

But the attempt to force aid from the American colonies, by the laying of a direct tax, while they were stubbornly refused representation in the British Parliament, was stoutly resisted by them. When, therefore, the news of the enactment by the British Parliament, in the year 1765, of the "stamp act" reached America, the indignation of the colonists knew no bounds. The provisions of this act required that stamps, to be furnished by the British Government, and paid for by the colonists, should be affixed to all deeds, bonds, warrants, notes and similar instruments, and upon newspapers, almanacs and other printed matter. "Caeser had his Brutus, Charles the First his Cromwell, and George the Third may profit by their example," were the words of young Patrick Henry in the Legislature of Virginia when the news of the enactment of the "stamp act" reached that body. They were thrilling words—words interrupted during their eloquent utterance by the shout of "Treason!"—first, by a single listener, and then from every portion of the House of Burgesses, in which this remarkable scene occurred. But the speaker did not for a moment falter; instead, he closed with the exclamation: "If this be treason, make the most of it!"

The more formidable opposition manifested in the Massachusetts Assembly to the "stamp act," took the form of a recommendation of a Colonial Congress, which was subsequently held in New York, representatives from nine colonies being present. A declaration of rights, a petition to the King and a memorial to Parliament were, after mature deliberation, adopted. In all parts of the American colonies the resistance to the enforcement of the "stamp act" was most earnest, and assumed various forms. A single instance only of individual resistance to the enforcement of his odious act can be given. This was the case of William Winds, of Morris County, New Jersey. He was a justice of the peace, residing in Rockaway. His commission had been granted by the King. He regarded the "stamp act," however, as a species of oppression, and bravely resolved to disregard it. This he did by substituting white birch bark, on which he wrote warrants, writs, bonds, executions and other legal instruments, for the ready stamped paper furnished by the King. And such was the commanding influence of Squire Winds, that no officer of the law in the county of Morris was ever known to decline serving his legal instruments inscribed on white birch bark. This was nullification in good earnest, and it has no parallel, all the circumstances considered, so far as the writer is aware, as an example of individual resistance to the unjust enactment of a powerful but tyrannical government. The repeal of the odious "stamp act," in the year 1766, was but a postponement of the armed revolt of the American colonies then brewing, and which occurred a few years later.

The enactment of the law, in the year 1767, requiring duties on glass, paper, painters' colors and tea, coupled with the persistent claim of the British Parliament of the inherent right to tax the American colonies, led to the formation of non-importation associations. With the exception of a duty of three pence per pound on tea, the act of the year 1767 was revoked; but, inasmuch as the people were not contending against the amount of taxes imposed, but against the principle of "taxation without representation," the concession was far from satisfactory. The story of the tea shipped to New York and Philadelphia, being sent back by the same vessel that brought it; of that shipped to Charleston, S. C., being stored in damp cellars, where it spoiled, and particularly of that shipped to Boston, being thrown overboard—342 chests was the quantity; of the passage of the "Boston port bill," as a punishment to Bostonians, and the sympathetic contributions of necessaries to their sufferings, on the part of sister colonies; of Lexington and Concord and Machias Bay, and other intervening events—these are too familiar to require more than casual mention in this story of Morristown's first century. Such casual mention of the causes of the Revolution as has been made, seemed to be necessary, as a most fitting prelude to the relation of the important part borne by Morristown, New Jersey, in the seven-years' war for American independence.

At the commencement of the Revolution, the village of Morristown contained not far from 250 inhabitants. From this it will be seen that during the sixty-five years since its settlement, its growth had been slow. But in this regard it was no exception to other towns in the colony—Newark, for example. This latter town was settled nearly half a century before Morristown, and yet, when the Revolution began, the town's population was but about 1,000. It would not be difficult to discover the causes of the slow growth of these, and other portions of New Jersey during the period mentioned.

Outside of the village of Morristown was a somewhat populous farming district. The village itself was chiefly grouped about what has been known as the Green; but as regards its area, as well also as its appearance, the Green of Revolutionary days was very different from the Green of the year 1905. The Morristown Green of the present day contains about two and a half acres of land, and is finely graded, and laid out in excellent paved walks. During the season of vegetation it is carpeted with a handsome green lawn, which is kept clean and well mown. When the Revolution commenced, what had for many years been called, sometimes "the Green," sometimes "the meeting-house land," and sometimes "the parsonage land," each term having reference to the same tract of land, contained many acres. It extended at one time as far southeast as the present Pine street, as far north as Spring street, and perhaps farther, and as far southwest as Maple avenue, or even beyond. We leave our readers to judge of the appearance of a portion of the Green of the period under consideration, from the map which appears in this volume. It is true this map was made, under Washington's supervision, in the year 1777, while the Continental army was encamped the first time in Morristown; but the map is nevertheless an accurate representation, so far as it is possible for a map to be a representation of such a tract of land, of the Green and of the buildings around it, as they appeared at the commencement of the Revolution. The irregular contour of the central portion of the Green, as it appeared in Revolutionary days, cannot escape the reader's notice. The road running through it from the head of the road coming up the hill from the east (now Morris street). and passing into the Jockey Hollow road on the west (now Washington street), will also be noticed. Not only irregularity of shape marked the Green as to its contour, but its surface was also irregular. As late as about the year 1840, there was a deep depression near the centre of the tract, resembling, in form, an upturned bowl; and the writer has been informed by a gentleman now nearly eighty-five years of age, that the latter, when a boy, had seen seven feet of water in this bowl, and in this body of water he had many times taken a bath.

The writer has been asked how the First Presbyterian Church, of Morristown, came into the possession of the large and extensive tracts of land which it once owned. The present opportunity is improved in the attempt to answer this very natural query, by saying that, some time prior to the year 1740, Jonathan Lindsley and Benjamin Hathaway gave to the church a piece of land for a parsonage and burying ground; suitable reference has already been made to this timely gift. On this tract of land the original house of worship was erected, about the year 1740. A few years later Joseph Prudden deeded to the church a larger tract of land, including what is now the Green. In the year 1773 the church purchased of Shadrach Hathaway a large tract of land, which may have been situated at a considerable distance from the meeting-house. Again, in the year 1774, the church made a second purchase of land of Charles Howell. This was situated on the southwest side of the Green, between the present Market and Bank streets, and extended down nearly, if not quite, to the present Maple avenue. This purchase was made for the purpose of enlarging the parade ground, or of having a suitable parade ground, since the tract of land now known as the Green was not, in consequence of its shape and the irregularity of its surface, suitable for that purpose. This last purchase seems to have been made in anticipation of the necessity of organizing and training men for participation in impending war. The large tracts of land once owned by the First Presbyterian Church were gradually sold off in lots, until its possession consisted of the burying ground, the land ocupied by the house of worship and the parsonage, and the two and a half acres contained in what is now known as the Green.

Of some of the more important buildings grouped around the Green at the commencement of the Revolution, we shall have occasion to speak at a later stage of our story. For the present, however, let us turn for a few moments to the consideration of the stirring local incidents and scenes immediately preceding the commencement of the seven years' struggle for independence.

Among the members of the New Jersey House of Assembly, of the year 1772, from Morris County, were Jacob Ford and William Winds, the former a resident of Morristown; both of whom had freely imbibed the spirit of protest against the encroachments of Great Britain upon the rights and liberties of the American colonies.

At the session of the House of Assembly, held on the eighth day of February, in the year 1774, a standing committee of nine members was appointed, and designated as the Committee of Correspondence. This committee was instructed to inform the House of Assembly of the other twelve colonies of their appointment.

To Essex County, New Jersey, must be accorded the honor of having held the first popular meeting on behalf of the movement of protest against the tyranny of the mother country, already inaugurated in some of the progressive colonies. This meeting was held in Newark, on the eleventh day of June, in the year 1774, when resolutions were adopted requesting the other counties of the province to hold similar meetings, at which county committees should be appointed to meet in a State convention, to elect delegates to a general convention, or congress. The call for the meeting of this general congress had already been isued, and September 5, of the year 1774, was the date fixed upon, and Philadelphia the place of meeting. The object of this general congress was the formulation of a general plan of union among the thirteen colonies. To such a plan, when it should be adopted, the inhabitants of Essex County, at the meeting of June 11, pledged their support and adherence. All honor to the brave stand taken by those patriotic Newarkers!

The ripeness of the people of New Jersey for the

movement of united action against the tyrannous policy of Great Britain toward the American colonies, was unmistakably evidenced by the fact of the prompt and general response to the request to send delegates to the Provincial Congress. Morris County's response was given on the twenty-seventh day of June in the year 1774, when a popular meeting was held in Morristown, in the courthouse on the Green; this was the one-story structure erected in the year 1770. The chairman of this initial meeting of the freeholders and inhabitants of Morris County, was Jacob Ford. The resolutions adopted breathed a spirit of wisdom seldom surpassed in the deliberations of popular gatherings. Of these resolutions, too lengthy for complete reproduction here, only a resume can be given. Expressions of loyalty to the King of Great Britain were given. Willingness to be governed by British laws, so far as such obedience was consistent with constitutional liberty, was also expressed, and so was the opinion as to the unwisdom of the acts of the British Parliament, imposing revenue taxes upon the colonies. The resolutions also expressed sympathy with Boston in her sufferings in consequence of unjust restrictions upon her commerce. In them there were also expressions of confidence in the efficacy of unanimity and firmness, on the part of the colonies, for the preservation of their rights and liberties; of confidence also in the efficacy of reliance upon home productions as a means to the end above mentioned; of readiness to join with other counties of the New Jersey Province in the endeavor to form a

General Congress of the thirteen colonies; of opinion as to the propriety of contributing to the relief of Boston; of purpose to adhere faithfully to the regulations and restrictions deemed expedient by the General Congress, and opinion as to the expediency of unity of action on the part of the New Jersey county committees in Provincial Congress assembled, in the appointment of deputies to the General Congress of the following September.

The committee for Morris County, appointed at the meeting of June 27, in the year 1774, in the court-house on the Morristown Green, for the purposes above mentioned, was as follows: Jacob Ford, William Winds, Abraham Ogden, William De Hart, Samuel Tuthill, Jonathan Stiles, John Carle, Philip V. Cortland and Samuel Ogden. These gentlemen represented various portions of the county, in which they were recognized as leaders in the affairs of their respective sections.

Only to such members of this committee as were residents of Morristown, can brief allusion here be made. Concerning Jacob Ford, no little has already been said in connection with the account of the settlement and growth of Morristown. There is one fact, however, which deserves mention here; a fact which augments the significance of his appointment to the important committee just mentioned. He was, at the time of his appointment, an old man, and might justly have declined to assume the grave and arduous responsibilities placed upon him by his fellow-citizens. Owing to his advanced age, he had for some time been gradually transferring the responsibilities of his private business interests to his son and namesake, the latter of whom was also beginning to occupy his aged father's place in the confidence and affections of the people of Morristown, and Morris County. But Jacob Ford was too keenly alive to the exigencies of the hour to permit even the growing infirmities of old age to deter him from participating, up to the full measure of his ability, in the revolt against the long series of tyrannous aggressions of the mother country upon the liberties of the American colonists. As a man of business, and more especially as an extensive manufacturer of iron, his grievance against the policy of the mother country was not alone sentimental, it was decidedly practical, also, since his material interests were seriously involved.

William De Hart was a young Morristown lawyer, at the time of his appointment to the Morris County Committee of Correspondence and Consultation, and he brought to the momentous task assigned him, the vigor and enthusiasm of youth; as well, also, as the legal acumen which could be advantageously utilized in the adjustment of difficulties involving questions of law. He was at the time under consideration, but twenty-eight years of age, having been licensed as a counselor-at-law only about three years previously. As the opportunity will not again occur to speak further concerning this young patriot, it should here be said that subsequently to the stirring meeting held in the old courthouse, on the twenty-seventh day of June of the year preceding the opening of the Revolution, William De Hart became a major in the First Battalion, first and second establishments, and later, lieutenant-colonel of the Second Regiment of the Continental Army. Nor should the writer omit mentioning the fact, that two of the sons of Matthias De Hart, M. D., the father of Colonel William De Hart, were slain during the struggle for American independence. One of the streets of the Morristown of the year 1905, bears the name of the young resident lawyer of Revolutionary days, who rendered faithful service in the cause of freedom. He died on the sixteenth day of June, in the year 1801, and his remains now lie in the burying grounds of the First Presbyterian Church of the town he assisted in making famous. The other members of this committee of correspondence and consultation, who were residents of Morristown, were Jonathan Stiles, Jr., and Samuel Tuthill. Mr. Stiles was at the time of his appointment one of the county judges. He had previously held the office of sheriff of Morris County. During the Revolution he seems to have served as a recruiting officer, and mention is made of his having paid bounties to soldiers.

Samuel Tuthill is by name, no stranger to the readers of our story, nor are they wholly unaware of his public career as a county judge and sheriff. It may be added, however, to what has already been said, that he was a son-in-law of Jacob Ford, Sr., having married on the third day of November, in the year 1751, Sarah Kenny, widow of John Kenny, and daughter of the elder Ford.

On the twenty-first day of July, in the year 1774, the New Jersey county committees met at New Brunswick, when five delegates were appointed to the General Congress to be held in Philadelphia, in the coming September. It is only for the purpose of connecting the General Congress, so far as its proceedings are concerned, with the subsequent course of New Jersey, but particularly of Morris County and Morristown, in their relation to said proceedings, that anything more than a casual reference is made to the meeting in Philadelphia. Pursuant to call, the General Congress of the American colonies met in Philadelphia, on the fifth day of September, in the year 1774. Peyton Randolph, of Virginia, was chosen president of the Congress. Among the delegates were Washington, Patrick Henry and John Adams. We would fain linger in the attempt to speak at length upon the superb personnel of this, one of the most important public gatherings of history; but this would be inconsistent with the main purpose of our story. It can only be said that various resolutions were presented, which opened the way, and furnished the inspiration, also, for the free and general interchange of views, which followed, upon the grave questions then agitating the minds and hearts of the American colonists. The unanimity of sentiment there manifested amply warranted the resolution recommending the call for a second General Congress, to be held on the tenth day of May of the following year—1775.

Pursuant to a call issued by the Morris County Committee of Correspondence, a second meeting of the inhabitants of the county was held in Morristown (and almost certainly in the courthouse on the Green) on the ninth day of January, in the year 1775. The object of this meeting was the indorsement of the action of the General Congress of the preceding September. Of this meeting William Winds was the chairman. The County Committee of Correspondence read the proceedings of the General Congress at Philadelphia, after which they were carefully considered by the people assembled, and unanimously approved. The means and methods of resistance to the tyrannical and oppressive acts of the British Parliament, recommended by the General Congress, were declared wise, prudent and constitutional. It was also unanimously resolved to abide strictly by these recommendations.

A vote of thanks was extended to the delegates of the New Jersey province for the faithful manner in which they had looked after the rights and liberties of their constituents, and discharged the important trust reposed in them. The inhabitants of each township in the county, were unanimously recommended by the meeting to elect, on the twenty-third day of the current month, a committee of observation, in accordance with the recommendation of the General Congress. The County Committee of Correspondence voluntarily dissolved itself, to afford their constituents the opportunity of a new choice. The committee, as reappointed, was composed as follows: Jacob Ford, William Winds, Jonathan Stiles, Jacob Drake, Peter Dickerson, Ellis Cook, Samuel Tuthill, Dr. William Hart and Abraham

Ogden. John Carle and Philip Van Cortland, were for some reason, left off the new committee, and Jacob Drake and Peter Dickerson substituted. This committee was authorized to instruct the Morris County representatives, in General Assembly convened, to join in the appointment of delegates to the General Congress, called to meet in Philadelphia in May following. If such delegates should not be appointed by the General Assembly, the several county committees in joint meeting were to make the appointments.

James Rivington, a printer in New York, was declared to be, in the judgment of the meeting, an enemy to his country, as indicated by the publication of certain pamphlets, the effect of whose teachings was to encourage submission to the tyrannous policy of the mother country. To make use of a modern term, James Rivington was "boycotted" by the people of Morris County; they would refrain from subscribing for his papers, and by all lawful means discourage others from doing so. The nails in the timbers of the Old Morris County Jail, driven in thickly to hinder the escape of prisoners by cutting out, doubtless rattled in their holes by reason of the vociferous cheering and other demonstrations of enthusiasm, of the people assembled in the old courthouse on the occasions to which reference has been made. At one public meeting of the patriots of Morris County, held in Morristown, some of Rivington's pamphlets and papers were consigned to the flames "before the courthouse, with the universal approbation of a numerous concourse of people." One of his publications, at another meeting, was given a coat of tar and feathers, and the pamphlet in "its gorgeous attire," was nailed firmly to the pillory post on the Green, "there to remain as a monument of the indignation of a free and loyal people against the author and vendor of a publication so evidently tending both to subvert the liberties of America and the constitution of the British Empire."

It was at this latter meeting that one of those who joined in the work of applying the coat of tar and feathers to Rivington's publication, wished—and the wish was unanimous—that the author himself were present, that he might be fitted with a similar suit.

Concerning Peter Dickerson, one of the new members added at the above-mentioned meeting, to the Morris County Committee of Correspondence, there is much to be said—most of which, however, will be said at a later stage of our story.

With the exception of Hanover Township, there is no record, so far as the writer is aware, of the names of the gentlemen appointed to serve on the township committees of observation, as recommended by the meeting of January 9, in the year 1775. It is known, however, that these committees, elected on the twenty-third day of January, in the year last mentioned, were active and alert in the procurement of signatures of inhabitants of Morris County, who pledged themselves to sustain the Provincial and General Congresses; and the voters for representatives to the Provincial Congress to meet in the coming May at Trenton, were to consist of those whose signatures were procured. The lines must be tightened.

Pursuant to a call issued by the Morris County Committee of Correspondence a meeting of the inhabitants of the county was held on the first day of May, in the year 1775, in Morristown, and presumably in the courthouse. The chairman of this meeting was Jacob Ford, and the clerk William De Hart. In consequence of the sifting process to which allusion has been made, this meeting was composed of the cream of Morris County's inhabitants, so far as loyalty to the growing cause of freedom was concerned. To look in upon the throng of ardent patriots who filled the quaint courthouse of those stirring times, is a privilege which, except in imagination, is denied the present generation. The meager account of the proceedings of the meeting of May 1, in the year 1775, which has descended to us, furnishes a brilliant illustration, if the personnel and action of the meeting is the criterion, of the saying of Emerson, that "every great and commanding movement in the annals of the world is the triumph of enthusiasm."

CHAPTER IX

"War is honorable
In those who do their native rights maintain,
In those whose swords an iron barrier are
Between the lawless spoiler and the weak."

HEN the news of the encounter of the American colonists with the British regulars on the Lexington Green, and at the Concord bridge, reached New Jersey, the people were at once aroused to the highest pitch of righteous indignation. War between the colonies and the mother country had actually commenced, and the colonists were not slow in recognizing the necessity of prompt and energetic action in the work of preparation for the impending struggle. They were soon, as in due time will be seen, to verify the words:

True courage scorns
To vent her prowess in a storm of words,
And to the valiant action speaks alone.

Enough is known concerning the proceedings of the public meeting of May 1, in the year 1775, to which allusion was made in the preceding chapter, to authorize the statement that nine delegates were chosen as representatives of Morris County, in the important work of devising means and methods of preparation for the struggle for liberty which was then inevitable. These delegates were also, in accordance with instructions, to meet in the Provincial Congress, to be held at Trenton, on the twenty-third day of May, approaching. William Winds, of Pequannock Township; William De Hart, of Morristown; Silas Condict, of Morristown; Peter Dickerson, of Morristown; Jacob Drake, of Drakesville; Ellis Cook, of Hanover Township; Jonathan Stiles, of Morristown; David Thompson, of Mendham, and Abraham Kitchel, of Pequannock Township, were the delegates chosen.

The rapid progress made in the movement of revolt against the tyranny of the mother country, and in preparation for the impending struggle, may be seen in the fact that these delegates, four of whom were residents of the county seat, were vested, by the people legally assembled, with the power of legislation on behalf of the county of Morris and of the Province of New Jersey, also. They were specifically authorized to raise men, money and arms for the defense, primarily, of the county, but also of any portion of the province or the colonies in which their service might in future be required. Power was conferred upon them to devise ways and means for raising, appointing and paying the men and their officers, necessary for defense. Their action, however, was to be subject to the control and direction of the Provincial and General, or Continental, Congresses. In this circumstance we see how clearly the people of Morris County realized the necessity of unanimity of action in the struuggle which lay before them. When these delegates should have made provisions for the proper defense of the county, they were afterward to meet in the Provincial Congress, already called to assemble at Trenton, on the twenty- third day of May, where, with such other counties as should join with them, they were to levy taxes upon the province as a means of providing for the common defense. These delegates from the various counties of the New Jersey Province were to be vested with legislative authority, and if the exigencies of the hour required it, this authority was to be properly exercised. A still further evidence of the generally recognized need of unanimity of action, may be seen in the explicit understanding that the action of the Provincial Congress should be subject to the control and direction of the General, or Continental, Congress.

The initiative taken by the inhabitants of Morris County, in the meeting of May 1, in the year 1775, for the defense of the county against possible invasion, and for providing for the common defense, furnishes a fine illustration of the sturdy independence of the portion of the inhabitants who then dominated county affairs, and makes their New England origin and training to stand out in bold relief. The men of Morris County who dominated, by the influence of their character, the series of public meetings held in Morristown, preliminary to the commencement of the Revolution, as well also as during its progress, were, for the most part, at least, of the same stock as Samuel Adams and John Hancock and Joseph Warren, of Boston, and others in the Massachusetts Province whose names cannot, for lack of space, be mentioned; and they were as richly imbued with the spirit of freedom as the patriots who, on the green at Lexington, and at the bridge at Concord, faced the flower of the British army on the eighteenth and nineteenth days of April (preceding the public meeting in Morristown last mentioned), where were fired "the shots heard round the world."

On the same day of the above mentioned meeting, but apparently at a later hour, and perhaps after its adjournment, a meeting of the delegates already named was held at Dickerson's, sometimes improperly called Norris's, tavern, on what is now Spring street, at the corner of Water street. The picture of this famous building, as it appeared in Revolutionary days, which may be seen in this volume, was sketched from a description given by a lady who, as a child, had for several years played about the building, and who was, therefore, so familiar with its general appearance, interior and exterior, as to be able to remember even the peculiarity of the old-fashioned knocker on the front door (with a bell attached), as well also as the location of the principal rooms inside.

At the meeting held in Dickerson's tavern there were present, William Winds, Silas Condict, Peter Dickerson (the owner and proprietor of the tavern), Jacob Drake, Ellis Cook, Jonathan Stiles, David Thompson and Abraham Kitchel. The only chosen delegate absent was William De Hart, and the presumption is that his clerical duties in connection with the public meeting of the inhabitants of the county, on the same day, detained him. William Winds was chairman of the meeting, and Archibald Dallas clerk. The proceedings of this meeting strongly impress the careful observer with the fearless initiative of its members; and the hand of the bold William Winds, of Pequannock Township, who had served in the French and Indian wars, is plainly visible, even to him who runs, in the significant action then taken. Preliminary to the more important business to be transacted, it was first resolved that any five of the delegates chosen, should constitute a quorum at subsequent meetings, and that of these five delegates three should constitute a majority, or controlling vote, in the transaction of such business as might come before them. The next action of this meeting makes one's blood tingle with unalloyed admiration as he carefully considers it. It was resolved, and unanimously, that military forces should be raised for the pending struggle with the mother country. Of each of those eight delegates who assumed, on behalf of Morris County, the grave responsibilities implied by their heroic resolution, it may be said, and truly:

He holds no parley with unmanly fears,
Where duty bids he confident steers,
Faces a thousand dangers at her call,
And, trusting to his God, surmounts them all.

After the deliberate adoption of the resolution alluded to, the meeting was adjourned until the following day, at 9 o'clock in the morning, at the same place. If the action of the first meeting was of a general and preliminary character, that of May 2 was sufficiently definite and progressive to satisfy the most exacting. With their lives, not in their hands, as it is so frequently phrased, but in their votes, these delegates resolved that 300 volunteers be recruited for the defense of the county of Morris against invasion by former friends, now transformed into foes. What strikes one the more forcibly, as he contemplates the fearless initiative of these American colonists up among the beautiful hills of Morris County, is the fact that, while they were formulating and casting their votes for the prompt recruiting of volunteers, an army of British regulars occupied Boston, and ample reinforcements from Great Britain were even then contemplated.

The 300 volunteers to be recruited, so it was voted, were to be divided into companies of sixty men each; each company, except the two first, to be officered by a captain and two lieutenants: the two first companies to be commanded by field officers. These field officers, as named at the meeting under consideration, were to be Colonel William Winds and Major William De Hart. The captains of the three remaining companies, as named at the same meeting, were to be Samuel Ball, Joseph Morris and Daniel Budd. John Huntington was to be captain-lieutenant in Colonel Wind's company, and Silas Howell captain-lieutenant in Major De Hart's company. These companies, it was ordered, were to be disciplined or trained one day each week, the time and place of training to be determined by the respective commanding officers. Nor was provision for the supply of the sinews of war neglected, for it was voted that the pay of captains should be seven shillings, proclamation money, per day; of first lieutenants, six shillings per day: of second lieutenants, five shillings per day; of sergeants, three shillings and six pence per day, and of private men, three shillings per day, with provisions furnished, also arms and ammunition. These wages were to be paid every two months.

It was very evident, from the action of the meeting in Dickerson's tavern, that hitherto peaceful Morristown was soon to assume a decidedly warlike aspect. The land which seems to have been purchased the year preceding, for the enlargement of the village parade ground, was by no means, as daily developments were demonstrating, a premature movement. The quiet hamlet grouped mainly around the Green, which had known no disturbing sounds, save the melodious clang of the imported church bell, were ere long to resound with the stirring notes of martial music, and the steady tramp of soldiery. Before the lapse of many months, the horrors of actual war would be realized, in forms never dreamed of by their heart-rended witnesses; but the veil must not be further lifted. It is enough to know the future when it shall have become the present, with its weal or with its woe, with its victory or with its defeat, with its exultation or with its depression.

It should not be forgotten that at the commencement of the Revolution, the inhabitants of Morris County were, with few exceptions, in anything but a prosperous condition. British oppressions, long continued, had slackened the wheels of industry and partially paralyzed agriculture. The financial obligations assumed by the people, in connection with the inauguration and prosecution of the revolt against the mother country, therefore, greatly enhanced the value of the inflexible determination with which they grappled with the herculean task confronting them. The significance of their action was this: that at all hazards the revolt against persistent tyranny and oppression must be prosecuted, even to the expenditure of the last dollar they were worth, or to the sacrifice of the last man among them.

One of the most interesting features of the second meeting at Dickerson's tavern, was the vote passed to purchase 500 pounds of powder, and a ton of lead, to be kept in a magazine for the use of the regiment of 300 men soon to be organized. It would be gratifying to the student of local history to know where this magazine was situated. Inasmuch as Major William De Hart was appointed to make the purchase of the powder and lead in question, it is not improbable that the magazine was somewhere on his premises, near the corner of the present De Hart and South streets. Realizing, no doubt, that the action of the two meetings at Dickerson's tavern was, in a sense, premature (as, indeed, it was), and recognizing also the possibility that this action might be modified, or even wholly set aside, by the Provincial and General Congresses soon to convene, it was wisely provided by supplementary vote that the resolutions and votes of these meetings should be considered subject to the control and direction of the last mentioned bodies, and, that after due notice from them, any portion of the action disapproved, should be reconsidered and adjusted to the wishes of the higher authorities. The exigencies of the hour being fully realized, the possibility of an invasion of Morris County by British forces in the near future, was a matter requiring prompt attention; hence, by way of provision against such a contingency, it was by vote recommended that the inhabitants of the county, capable of bearing arms, who should not become identified with the regiment to be raised, provide themselves with arms and ammunition for self-defense. The meeting was then adjourned till May 9 at 9 o'clock in the morning at Dickerson's tavern.

> "To hallow'd duty
> Here with a loyal and heroic heart,
> Bind we our lives."

If ever these words were applicable to living men, it was to the eight sturdy Morris County patriots whose action at the famous hostelry "under the hill," on behalf of their constituents, has just been reviewed.

Let us pause here and briefly examine the personnel of the meeting adjourned from Captain Peter Dickerson's tavern, where, on behalf of Morris County, the gauntlet had been bravely thrown down to a powerful government, with a well disciplined army, and a navy amply equal to its support. We must, however, of necessity, confine ourselves to those individuals composing the meeting, whose place of residence was Morristown. Of Major William De Hart we have already spoken, and of Jonathan Stiles we have spoken also. Silas Condict shall, therefore, first engage our attention. He was the son of Peter Condict, who died in the year 1768, and whose remains now lie in the burying grounds of the First Presbyterian Church of Morristown.

Silas Condict was born in Morristown, in the year 1738. He was, through his father, of Welsh descent. At the age of five years he began attending the district school, after leaving which he continued to study under his own tutorship. Mr. Condict could, therefore, justly have claimed to be self-educated. In addition to following agricultural pursuits, he engaged during the greater part of his life, in surveying. For this avocation he fitted himself. When a young man, Mr. Condict, in compliance with the wishes of several young men in the vicinity of his house, opened a night school. Some of his pupils were disposed to be disorderly; indeed, they attempted to have "a little fun" in school. The teacher firmly insisted upon having order, and reminded the disorderly pupils that it was for their benefit the school had been opened. This had the desired effect, and thereafter order reigned in the school. This incident is related as an illustration of the strength of character with which Mr. Condict was endowed, and which, with other qualifications, made him one of the most valuable men in the State of New Jersey, particularly in connection with the Revolution. For his first wife he married Phebe Day, daughter of Captain Samuel Day. One child, Elizabeth Phebe, was the result of this union. She married James Cook, and, like her mother, dying in early life, she left one child, Elizabeth. Upon the death of her mother, Elizabeth was taken into the family of Silas Condict, and by him and Mrs. Condict was tenderly reared, and trained in genuine Christian fashion. This daughter, upon reaching maturity, married General Joseph Cutler, one of whose sons was the late Hon. Augustus W. Cutler, of Morristown. The Augustus W. Cutler farm included a portion of the land consisting of several hundred acres, formerly owned by Silas Condict. Mr. Condict's second wife was Abigail, the daughter of Ebenezer Byram, who was a descendant of John Alden, who came over in the Mayflower. In the year 1772, Silas Condict was elected trustee of the Morristown Presbyterian Church, and as clerk of the board of trustees, and as a member of several important committees, he exhibited business capacity, sagacity and sound judgment, which rendered his services to that organization invaluable. In the year 1774, he was directed by the board of trustees of the Presbyterian Church to make a trip to Perth Amboy, where he was to have the society's charter recorded; and he was also requested to make a copy of the charter for common use as a means of preserving in good condition the original. Mr. Condict also served for several years as president of the above mentioned board of trustees. In the more public affairs of Morristown, Morris County, New Jersey, and the American colonies in general, he was prominent and highly influential. In addition to his services as one of the Morris County delegates, chosen at the public meeting of May 1, in the year 1775, he was a member of the State Council of New Jersey from the year 1776 till the year 1780. From the year 1781 till the year 1784 he was a member of the Continental Congress. From the year 1791 till the year 1800, two years excepted, he was a member of the State Legislature, and during three consecutive sessions—those of 1792, 1793, 1794, he was Speaker of the House. In the year 1797 he was again reëlected to the Speakership of the same body.

Twice he was appointed one of the judges of the county court. In the work of drafting the first State consittution he served on the committee appointed for that purpose. "In whatever position he was placed he secured that loving respect, that great confidence, which could only be rendered to one who had the rare combination in his nature of the greatest integrity, of true justice, of kindness of heart, of an intuitive perception of right and wrong, and of an inherent judgment of human nature"—such is the most fitting tribute by one amply qualified to speak of the Hon. Silas Condict. The writer would fain linger upon the further contemplation of the excellencies of such a character, but this cannot consistently be done.

Peter Dickerson was the son of Thomas Dickerson, and was born at Southold, Long Island, (northeastern end) in the year 1724. He came to New Jersey during the year 1745, settling in Morris County. In the same year he married, for his first wife, Ruth, the daughter of Joseph Coe, Sr. Jonathan Dickerson, one of the eight children by the above mentioned marriage, was the father of Mahlon Dickerson, who was Governor of New Jersey. For his second wife, Peter Dickerson married, in the year 1763, Sarah A., the widow of "John Oharrow;" as a result of this union there were four children born to them. Peter Dickerson was an ardent patriot, and his tavern was, from the commencement of the difficulties with the mother country, one of the popular rendezvous of those of kindred sentiments. So far as extant historical records indicate, he first came into public notice in connection with his appointment, on May 1, in the year 1775, as one of the Morris County delegates. His presence at the meetings of the Morris County delegates, held in the Dickerson tavern, on May 1 and May 2 of the above mentioned year, has already been noted. Although no record of the adjourned meeting of the above mentioned delegates, to be held on May 9, and at the place last named, has, so far as the writer is aware, come down to the present century, it is safe to say that Captain Peter Dickerson was one of the active participants in its important proceedings. Of his presence at a meeting of the county committee held at his tavern on the fourteenth day of September, 1775, there is no question, since it is a matter of record. The business transacted was of vital importance. In the year 1776, he was a member of the Provincial Congress. Nothing, perhaps, more amply justifies the application of the term "ardent patriot" to Captain Dickerson, than the well-known fact that he personally bore the entire expense of the equipment of the company commanded by him in the opening years of the Revolution—it was the Fifth Company, Third Battalion, and first establishment of the Continental army. The amount advanced by Captain Dickerson for the purpose mentioned, which was never repaid by the government, now stands to his credit at the National Capital. Captain Dickerson's popularity as a military officer may be inferred from the fact that when, near the close of the year 1776, many men whose term of enlistment had expired, declined to reënlist, his company seems to have reënlisted in a body. While it would be inconsistent with the main purpose of our story to devote further space to the public career of Captain Peter Dickerson, we shall be justified in giving, at a later stage of this history, no little attention to the famous tavern of which he was the owner and proprietor.

It has previously been remarked that the resolutions of the Morris County delegates at Dickerson's tavern, on May 1 and May 2, in the year 1775, in regard to the raising, equipping and training of men, was in a sense premature. In confirmation of this remark it may be said that it was not till the third day of June following, that the Provincial Congress made provisions for the regulation of the militia. But the proceedings of the two meetings mentioned, received virtual indorsement by the direction of the Provincial Congress of June 3, in the year 1775, that "where companies and regiments were already formed and officers chosen and appointed, the same were to be continued."

"To obey our officers in such service as they shall appoint us, agreeable to the rules and orders of the Provincial Congress"—such was the promise made by the 300 volunteers recruited in Morris County, in accordance with the action of the meetings held in Morristown at Dickerson's tavern, on the first and second days of May, of the eventful year of 1775.

CHAPTER X

"To do is to succeed—our fight
Is wag'd in Heaven's approving sight—
The smile of God is victory."

XCEPT by the application of some mechanical force, "water has never been known to run up hill," and so obviously true is this saying that it may well be considered an axiom, which term by the lexicographer is defined as "a self-evident and necessary truth, or a proposition whose truth is so evident at first sight that no process of reasoning or demonstration can make it plainer." There is one thing, however, which possesses the inherent force enabling it to ascend even a hill, and an almost perpendicular one at that; the allusion here made is to the warlike spirit. Of this our readers are about to witness a most interesting illustration.

The series of truly stirring meetings of the Morris County delegates, held on the first, second and ninth days of the month of May, in the year 1775, at Dickerson's tavern, "under the hill," had scarcely closed, ere an independent company of mounted soldiery, which was subsequently to become famous in State history, was organized, as the writer surmises, somewhere in the vicinity of the Morristown Green; and as the writer also conjectures, at the Arnold tavern, situated on the northwest side of this tract of land, with only a narrow country road running between.

"We the subscribers do voluntarily inlist ourselves in the company of Light Horse belonging to the county of Morris, Thomas Kinney, Esq., captain, and do promise to obey our officers in such service as they shall appoint, as agreeable to the rules of the Provincial and Continental Congress. Witness our hands May 10th, 1775. Jacob Arnold, James Searing, Epenetus Beach, James Smith, Silas Stiles, Patrick Darcy, John Lasey, Benjamin Freeman, Jr., Samuel Allen, Stephen Baldwin, Elijah Freeman, Daniel Edmiston, John Crane, Adam Bests, Conrad hapler, John Mintus, Jacber Beach, George harah, Silas Hand, John Tichener, John Vanwinker, Aaron Parson, Robert Gould, Jr., James Ford, Samuel Denman, Peter Parset, George Minthorn, John Cooke, Samuel Boldsbury, John Milen, Abraham Hathaway, Saml. Wigton."

The enlistment paper just given, is copied verbatim from originals brought from Virginia; and with other papers are now known as the "Boteler Papers."

The sense of propriety, of which ex-Sheriff Kinney could not have been wholly devoid, forbids the thought that he could have been the draftsman of the enlistment roll of which the foregoing is a faithful transcript; since to have deliberately written himself down (assuming the roll to have been the product of his own hand) as "Thomas Kinney, Esq.," would have constituted a notorious example of egotism. From the peculiar phraseology of a portion of a paper written by Colonel Jacob Arnold, in the year 1788, and bearing his bold signature, a facsimile of which paper is now in the possession of the writer, the latter ventures to infer that the enlistment roll in question was drawn up by none other than Jacob Arnold; and the mere circumstance of his name being the first in the list of subscribers is in no small measure corroborative of the opinion just expressed. The writer is also of the opinion that this enlistment roll, so fortunately preserved was for a time at least kept at the tavern, in Morristown, then kept by "Thomas Kinney, Esq.," and at that prominent public rendezvous received many and possibly all of the signatures which appear upon it.

It is a matter of no small interest that of the thirty-two signatures appearing upon this enlistment roll, twelve at least, or about thirty per cent., were of residents of Morristown. And of scarcely less interest is the fact, that the average age of the twelve residents of Morristown alluded to, was but about twenty-six years. If the average age of the remaining persons whose names are on the roll was about the same, the Light Horse Troop must have been a youthful and decidedly energetic body.

To the original number of recruits, as already given, many others were subsequently added, among whom only the following names, so far as the writer is aware, have come down to us: John Blowers, Ephraim Carnes, J. C. Canfield, Josiah Butler, John Canfield, John Ester and Jacob Johnson.

The Rev. Baker Johnson, of Wisconsin, is one of the authorities for the statement that Jacob Johnson his paternal grandfather was a member of Arnold's Light Horse Troop. He also states that while serving with this Troop he contracted the disease which terminated his life. From an article which appeared in the New York Observer several years ago, written by the Rev. Dr. Joseph Tuttle, the following extracts will give our readers additional information concerning Jacob Johnson:

"On Morris Plains, three miles from Morristown, when the Revolutionary war began, lived a very respectable farmer in good circumstances named Jacob Johnson. He was very fond of good horses, one of which he rode in Captain Jacob Arnold's troop of light horse, a company which rendered invaluable service to their country. * * * Mr. Johnson was on duty a very considerable portion of the time till the year 1779. when hardship and exposure brought on consumption. His great business then was to prepare for death, in which duty Pastor Johnes rendered him unwearied assistance. Mahlon Johnson, a son of the sick man, and who yet survives at the venerable age of fourscore, remembers Dr. Johnes—how often he visited his father, how long he tarried, how earnestly he instructed, and how earnestly he prayed, until the dying soldier was ready to say: 'Lord, now lettest thou thy servant depart in peace, for mine eyes have seen my salvation.' Indeed, Dr. Johnes must have been a model pastor, in his dignified yet winning demeanor. * * * In visiting Jacob Johnson, Dr. Johnes sought also the salvation of his wife, so soon to be a widow. Anna Vail was a Quakeress, but the Spirit blessed the pastor's counsels and example, and the dying husband's quiet resignation, so that she, too, became partaker of the same grace, and not long after her husband's death Dr. Johnes had a meeting at her house, when she presented all her children to be baptized. Surely the pastor's reward is seen in the fact that Mahlon, the oldest of those children, still speaks of the pastor's gentle fervor, as he not only baptized him, but besought the Lord to be a father to these fatherless ones.

"Mr. Johnson died on the twenty-fifth day of April, in the year 1780, and his funeral drew together a great concourse of people. The son to whom reference has been made remembers that in the long procession which followed the remains of his father to the Morristown graveyard, there was only one vehicle on wheels, and this was used for carrying the corpse. Dr. Johnes and the attending physician, each with a linen scarf around the shoulders, according to the custom of the times, led the procession on horseback. The simplicity of the scene stands in singular contrast with the pomp and circumstance of a funeral in our day."

Three sons of Henry Wick, the owner of the extensive Wick farm, situated on the Jockey Hollow road, are said by some writers of local history to have belonged to this now famous company of soldiery. A recent author, however, says that "the John, William and Moses Wick, who are mentioned as serving in the Light Horse, were probably relatives of the family, living in Hanover." It is a most interesting fact, apparently corroborative of the opinion expressed by this author, that in the issue of The New Jersey Gazette, of October 28, in the year 1778, there appeared an advertisement offering for sale by "John and William Wick," a "farm and cyder mill in Hanover." Moses Wick, according to a census of the freeholders, or property holders of Morris County, taken in the year 1776 was also a resident of Hanover Township at that time.

From the enlistment roll we have learned that the first captain of this independent company of "Light Horse" was Thomas Kinney, ex-sheriff of Morris County, who is no stranger to our readers.

While in command of the Light Horse Troop, Captain Kinney with his company, escorted Governor William Franklin, the notorious royalist, to Connecticut, where, in accordance with instructions, he delivered him into the hands of Governor Trumbull for safe keeping. For this hazardous service Captain Kinney was suitably rewarded by the provincial authorities. The sum received was "105 pounds, one shilling and seven pence for himself and guard." After the resignation of Captain Kinney, which seems to have taken place soon after its organization, Jacob Arnold was appointed to the command of the Light Horse Troop, which thereafter became known as "Arnold's Light Horse Troop."

Besides other arms, each member of Arnold's Troop carried a spear, or pike (either term seems to be applicable) similar to that once borne by English heavy armed troops. This spear was about five feet in length. It consisted of a steel spearhead about eight inches in length and two in width at the widest part, with a cutting edge on one end, and at the other end a pointed steel ferrule about four inches in length. The body of the spear consisted of a smooth round oak stick, about an inch and a quarter in diameter. This weapon was carried, when not in use in action, on the right side of the mounted trooper. The pointed ferrule at the lower end of the weapon rested in an iron socket, firmly attached to the stirrup strap, the upper end of the spear being supported by a strap, which passed around the right arm thus leaving this arm free for use in driving, or in handling other weapons. When used in close action this spear was a most effective weapon, and, wielded by young men, must have been greatly dreaded by the enemy. When about twenty years ago, the Arnold tavern was moved from its original site, on the northwest side of the Green, to make way for the erection of a more modern structure, (the Hoffman building), one of these spears was found in the cellar. It was subsequently loaned by the late Joseph R. Hoffman, M. D., to the Washington Association, and is now in the highly valuable collection to be seen at the "Headquarters." Each member of Arnold's Light Horse Troop was required to furnish his own horse and equipments. The troop, as we are reliably informed, was seldom all together, but were usually divided into details of from two to twelve men, or even more sometimes, and were employed as videttes, or mounted sentinels, to watch the movements of the British forces, to convey intelligence of such movements to headquarters and to carry orders. Whenever the entire troop was together it was for the purposes of training and discipline; or, in case of alarm from the apprehended approach of the enemy in force. They were in continuous service during the Revolution. The State infantry, on the other hand, performed duty by what was known as "monthly turns." A portion at least of this troop performed service at different times at Millstone, Second River, on Raritan River, at Springfield, Connecticut Farms, Elizabethtown (frequently), Newark and Aquacknunk.

In the battles of Springfield and Monmouth, this ubiquitous troop seems to have been represented. A portion of it must also have been at Hackensack, since it is a matter of record that one of its members as he himself afterward declared, "had like to have been taken prisoner near a British fort" in the vicinity. In "Genealogical Notes, &c.," collected by Lewis Condict, M. D., now known as the "Condict Papers," is the following entry: "In John Esler's witness for John Blowers, he says, John Canfield was with Blowers and Esler at New York and Amboy;" from which it is a fair inference that a portion of Arnold's Light Horse Troop performed service at New York and Amboy, during the Revolution.

When General Charles Lee was captured in White's tavern at Basking Ridge, the Arnold Troop lay at Morristown, in a body. The messenger who brought the intelligence of Lee's capture to the county seat rode a horse which, it was ascertained, had been stolen from a member of Arnold's Troop while it lay at Parsippany, and to his delight he recovered the lost animal. It is no ordinary pleasure, as the writer conceives, to be permitted to look upon and handle the watch carried by Colonel Jacob Arnold during the Revolution, and while in command of his famous Light Horse Troop; and the next best thing to seeing and handling the watch, is the pleasure of looking upon a photographic representation of it. This pleasure is given the readers of this volume. The watch, like its owner during the Revolutionary period, has a history, which should not be hidden "under a bushel." It originally belonged to Samuel Arnold, the father of the redoubtable colonel. From Samuel Arnold the watch, at his decease, descended to his son Jacob; from Jacob it descended to his son Edward, and naturally would have descended next in order to Isaac G. Arnold, recently deceased.

But one day, during his brief illness, Edward Arnold gave explicit instructions to have the watch given to Howard Baylies Arnold, the only son of Isaac G., whose property it now is. The seal, a representation of a rattlesnake, is symbolic of the motto, never to strike till warning has been duly given. The works in this watch are of English make, the escapement being known as the "verge," both of which facts the writer ascertained from a Morristown jeweler. The chain is of steel, and from long usage some of its links are nearly worn through, necessitating careful handling.

At the session of the Provincial Congress, which on the twenty-third day of May, in the year 1775, convened at Trenton, the Morris county delegatess were present of whom William DeHart, Silas Tuttle, Peter

Dickerson and Jonathan Stiles, were from Morristown. Assuming by common consent the powers of legislation, the Provincial Congress supplanted the former Legislature, continuing its session through the months of June and August. On the third day of June, in the year 1775, the Provincial Congress passed an Act for the regulation of the militia, one of the provisions of which was, that the muster roll to be signed by recruits, should contain only the promise "to obey our officers in such service as they shall appoint us, agreeable to the rules and orders of the Provincial Congress." Two regiments and one battalion of militia were, according to the Act above mentioned, to be recruited in Morris County, the two former of which were to be designated as the "eastern" and "western battalions." That these bodies of militia were promptly recruited, and organized, is a most natural inference.

Of the eastern battalion, Jacob Ford, Jr., of Morristown, then about thirty-seven years of age, was appointed colonel. For this battalion Morristown furnished, at different times during the continuance of its organization, the following officers: Eleazer Lindsley, thirty-eight years of age, major and afterward lieutenant-colonel; Benoni Hathaway, thirty-two years of age, captain and afterward lieutenant-colonel; Richard Johnson, twenty-seven years of age, major; Henry Axtell (sometimes spelled Axtil), thirty-seven years of age, major; Joseph Lindsley, forty years of age, major; John Doughty, twenty-four years of age, adjutant; Frederick King, thirty-seven years of age, quartermaster, and Timothy Johnes, twenty-seven years of age, surgeon. Jacob Arnold, twenty-six years of age, and Jonathan Stiles, Jr., twenty years of age, and both of Morristown, served in the militia as paymasters; and Barnabas Budd, thirty-seven years of age, of the same place, was a surgeon in the same arm of the service. In the same battalion to which the above-named officers were attached, as well also as in the Second Battalion, many other Morristown residents served as commissioned officers during the Revolution.

The Act of the Provincial Congress, regulating the militia, passed on the sixteenth day of August, in the year 1775, also recommended that minute men be raised in all the counties of the province. Morris County was to have six companies of minute men. They were to furnish themselves with "a good musket or firelock and bayonet, sword or tomahawk, a steel ramrod, worm, priming wire and brush fitted thereto, a cartouch box to contain 23 rounds of cartridges, twelve flints and a knapsack." Each man was to keep one pound of powder and three pounds of lead at his house. As the term "minute men" suggests, they were to hold themselves in constant readiness to march, on the shortest notice, to any point where their services might be needed.

At a meeting of the Morris County delegates held at the Dickerson tavern on the fourteenth day of September, in the year 1775, it having been ascertained that the full number of minute men, required of the county had been enlisted, it was recommended to the Provincial Congress that a number of officers be commissioned for the command of these soldiers. Among the names recommended were those of the following residents of Morristown: Timothy Johnes, (son of "Parson Johnes"), for surgeon; Silas Howell, for captain; Joseph Lindsley, for first lieutenant; Richard Johnston, for second lieutenant; Ebenezer Condict, for captain; Benoni Hathaway, for first lieutenant: Moses Prudden, for second lieutenant; Joseph Beach, for ensign.

At a late hour on the same day a meeting of the officers of the battalion, about twenty-five in number, was held at some place in Morristown not now ascertainable. At this meeting nearly a score of the battalion officers were present. William DeHart was the moderator, and Jacob Drum the clerk of this meeting. The officers present were: William DeHart, Captain Ebenezer Condict, Lieutenant Moses Prudden, Ensign Caleb Horton, Ensign Richard Johnston, Ensign Samuel Day, Lieutenant Noadiah Wade, Captain Samuel Ball, Lieutenant Moses Keepore (probably meant for Kitchel), Captain Jacob Drum, Lieutenant Josiah Hall, Lieutenant Daniel Baldwin, Lieutenant Joseph Lindsley, Captain Silas Howell, Ensign David Tuttle, Lieutenant Benoni Hathaway. It was unanimously voted to recommend to the Provincial Congress, or Committee of Safety of New Jersey, the following gentlemen for field officers: Colonel, William Winds; lieutenant-colonel, William DeHart; major, David Bates, and adjutant, Joseph Morris. Faithful service to these field officers, should they be commissioned, was pledged by the officers recommending them. The meeting was then adjourned.

The first call of the Continental Congress upon New Jersey for troops, was made on the ninth day of October, in the year 1775. Two battalions, consisting of eight companies each, each company to have sixty-eight privates, one captain, one lieutenant, one ensign, four sergeants and four corporals, was the quota recommended to the Provincial Congress, then in session at Trenton, to be furnished by New Jersey. The privates were to be enlisted for the period of one year, liable however, to be discharged in the meantime. They were to receive $5 per month, and if discharged before the expiration of the year, were to be allowed one month's pay extra. One felt hat, one pair of yarn stockings and a pair of shoes were to be allowed the men, instead of a bounty. Each man was to furnish his own arms.

The officers were to receive, until further orders, the same pay as the officers of the Continental army then in service, and any increase in favor of the latter, should apply also to the former. The recommendations of the Continental Congress having on the thirteenth day of October, of the year 1775, been received and adopted by the Provincial Congress, the latter body on the twenty-sixth day of the month above mentioned, provided for the issuance of warrants to suitable persons to recruit the two battalions called for by the Continental army. Mustering officers were also appointed, whose duty it should be to review the companies to be recruited.

"I ——, have this day voluntarily enlisted myself as a soldier in the American Continental army for one year, unless sooner discharged, and do bind myself to conform in all instances to such rules and regulations as are or shall be established for the government of the said army."

Such was the form of enlistment under which these men were to be recruited. These battalions were promptly raised and mustered. The officers were appointed by the Provincial Congress, and the appointments thus made were subsequently confirmed by the Continental Congress. Of the two battalions designated as the "eastern" and "western," the eastern was raised largely in Morris County. Morristown furnished the following officers for the eastern battalion: William DeHart, major; Silas Howell, captain, and Richard Johnson, second lieutenant.

Again on January 10, in the year 1776, the Continental Congress called for another battalion from New Jersey; and in accordance with the recommendation of the Provincial Congress this command was organized at once. Of one of the companies of this battalion, Peter Dickerson, of Morristown, was the captain; and of the privates Morristown seems to have furnished the following: Luke De Voir (sometimes spelled Devour), Jeremiah Guard (or Gard), Thomas Hathaway, John Hill and Timothy Losey.

As the commanding officer of the eastern battalion of militia, comprising about 800 officers and men, Jacob Ford, Jr., had doubtless awakened to the realization of the need of gunpowder as an indispensable means to its efficiency as a fighting force. Hence, early in the year 1776, he caused to be erected a mill for the manufacture of this necessity. In this enterprise he seems to have been assisted by his father; indeed, such is the statement of Silas B. Condict, in a series of articles on the "Genealogical History of the Ford Family of Morris County." Mr. Condict's words are: "Col. Jacob Ford Jun. took a very active part with his father, and we find them engaged in building a powder mill on the Whippany river near Morristown." That reliance is to be placed upon this statement the writer does not for a moment question.

Major Joseph Lindsley seems to have supervised the erection of this building, and, inasmuch as this officer was subsequently spoken of as the "Blind Major," it is the opinion of some students of local history, that in consequence of having assisted in the manufacture of gunpowder in Ford's mill, his eyesight had been impaired. Ford's powder mill, as it came to be known, was erected on the Whippanong River, in the rear of what is now the residence of Augustus Crane, which is situated on the left of the road leading from Morristown to Whippany, and nearly opposite the commencement of the road leading to Columbia, formerly Afton. Or, with reference to the "Headquarters," the Crane residence is about the fifth or sixth house beyond, in the direction of Whippany, and on the same side of the road. The path leading to Ford's powder mill was through an almost impenetrable thicket, and was so completely surrounded by trees as to render it very difficult of discovery by the enemy; indeed, a more isolated spot could scarcely have been chosen. Through the courtesy of Philip H. Hoffman, of Morristown, a picture of this interesting building is to be seen in this volume. The sketch from which the picture herein published is made, was drawn under the supervision of Mr. Hoffman, from a description furnished indirectly by persons who had themselves seen the building before its removal, and it may, therefore, be relied upon as a practically accurate representation of the mill where saltpeter, sulphur and charcoal, mixed and afterward granulated, were chemically transformed into gunpowder under the supervision of Colonel Jacob Ford, Jr.

The provincial authorities, having ascertained that Colonel Ford was engaged in the manufacture of gunpowder, were desirous of having him increase the output of his mill. As an inducement to him to accede to their wishes, they offered to loan him £2,000, without interest, on condition of his giving good security for the loan. They also offered to receive the payment of the loan in gunpowder, at the rate of one ton each month, until the entire amount should be paid. This offer was accepted by Colonel Ford, and the loan was in due course of time paid as per agreement.

The writer has somewhere seen the statement that most of the gunpowder used in the Revolution was made in this mill, hidden away so completely among the trees and thicket on the banks of the placid Whippanong, that the eyes of no redcoat ever had the pleasure of looking upon it. It may, however, be more in accordance with the facts in the case, to say that most of the gunpowder used in New Jersey during the Revolution, was manufactured in Ford's mill. This old mill was removed about a hundred feet from its original site, in the year 1815, and made into a dwelling. About this time Joseph M. Lindsley, a son of Major Joseph Lindsley, of Revolutionary fame, secured a piece of one of the timbers of the mill, about two inches in thickness, twelve inches in length and ten inches in width. It was highly polished, and on one side an excellent representation of the old mill of Revolutionary days was made. It is now to be seen at the "Headquarters."

Colonel Benoni Hathaway had personal charge of the Ford Powder Mill, and supervised the removal of the powder from the isolated manufactory on the Whippanong, to the magazine in the vicinity of the Green, where it was stored for future use. There is an apparently well-founded tradition to the effect, that when the output of the mill ran low, the resourceful colonel was wont to substitute sand for gunpowder, and with barrels well filled with this substitute for the genuine article, would transport it with special demonstrations of sufficiency, from mill to magazine. Not a few British spies and resident Tories were deceived as to the actual output of the mill by this ingenious ruse of the resourceful colonel.

The writer paid a visit a few weeks since to the Revolutionary residence of Colonel Benoni Hathaway, still standing in Morristown, and by his escort, the present owner of the building, had his attention directed to several ground depressions in the rear of the house. It is the opinion of the owner, who for many years has been familiar with the premises, that these depressions mark the former resting place of small cannon, placed there by Colonel Hathaway during the Revolution, for the purpose of commanding the approach to the Ford Powder Mill, situated about half a mile to the eastward. This theory has no little support in the fact that several cannon balls have been found near the Hathaway house, some of which the writer has seen; and by the more significant fact that a few years since what seemed to be the remains of a gun carriage wheel, was also found on the premises.

Near the Ford powder mill, and standing on the left of the road leading from Morristown to what, in Revolutionary times, was still known as Whippanong, was the Major Joseph Lindsley house. A large old-fashioned oven was attached to this house, in which the women of the family were accustomed to baking generous quantities of bread for the American soldiers stationed during the Revolution as guards about the Ford mansion, then the headquarters of Washington. The men of the household, at the period to which we are about to allude, were all absent in the army. Fears of a raid by the British were constantly entertained, not only by the women of the Lindsley household, but by the men employed in the powder mill nearby. Hearing one night the tramp of horses, the women were startled on looking out, at the sight of a company of horsemen in full uniform, near the house. The women were greatly relieved in mind when they ascertained that the soldiers were in search of the powder mill, and that they had been sent by Washington to guard the mill and house from an anticipated British raid. After some urging, one of the patriotic women consented to guide the horsemen to the powder mill, and, on foot, and going ahead of them, she led the way through the dense thicket to the mill by the river. These horsemen, as was soon ascertained, were a portion of the Arnold Light Horse Troop, which were then acting as a bodyguard to Washington.

Reference has already been made to the inhabitants of the village of Morris Town, and of the outlying country included in the township, at the opening of the Revolution. It is fortunate for the lovers of local history, that a list of the freeholders of Morris Town entitled to vote for deputies, or representatives, to the Provincial Congress which was to meet at Burlington, on the tenth day of June, in the year 1776, has been preserved. The election, it should be said, occurred in Morris Town, on the fourth Monday in May, 1776. This list is now to be presented. That it will be found of great interest there is no question. Following are the names of the freeholders:

"John Allen, Jacob Arnold, John Ayres, Moses Allen, Gilbert Allen, Nathaniel Bonnell, Daniel Bishop, James Brookfield, Joseph Beach, John Beach, Samuel Broadwell, Joseph Bruen, Epenetus Beach, James Bollen, Jabez Beach,

John Brookfield, Augustine Bayles, Uriah Cutler, Enoch Conger, Jabez Condict, Wood Cammer, William Cherry, Philip Condict, William Connot, Edward Cornell, Jabez Campfields, Philemon Dickerson, David Dalglass, Jesse Dickerson, Jeduthum Day, George Day, Ezekiel Day, Benjamin Day, Stephen Easton, Daniel Freeman, Phineas Fairchild, Zopher Freeman, Stephen Funhill, Jacob Frazey, Seth Gregory, Josiah Goldsmith, Ezekiel Goble, Joshua Guerin, Benjamin Goble, Henry Gardner, William Gardner, Jonas Goble, Christopher Gardner, William Gray, John Gwinnup, Levi Holloway, Philip Hathaway, Silas Hallsey, John Holloway, William Hayware, (Hayward?) Daniel Hayward, Caleb Howell, Benoni Hathaway, Ichabod Johnson, Richard Johnson, Elisha Johnson, William Johnes, Joseph Kitchell, Frederick King, Abraham Ludlum, Daniel Layton, Joseph Lewis, Joshua Lambert, Abraham Ludlum (Jr.?), Daniel Lickamore, David Leonard, Matthias Lum, David Muir, Philip Minton, Samuel Miller, Wartshill Monson, Moses Morrison, Peter Mackie, John Masco, Timothy Mills, Jr., Jacob Morrell, Jedediah Mills, Robert McElee, Abraham Monson, Solomon Monson, Shadows Mahan, Stephen Moore, Samuel Oliver, Jonathan Ogden, David Ogden, Benjamin Pierson, Jr., Abraham Pierson, Jr., Joseph Prudden, Moses Prudden, Peter Parsels, Isaac Pierson, Peter Pruden, Timothy Peck. Isaac Prudden, William Pierson, George Phillips, John Roberts, Jedediah Rodgers, Richard Runyon, Samuel Roberts, John Roberts, Jr., Robert Rolf, John Stewart, Daniel Smith, Joseph Stiles, Silas Stiles, Jonathan Stiles, Jr., Ezekiel Thoss, William Templeton, H. D. Tripp, Isaac Whitehead, David Ward, Jr., Isaac Whitehead (Jr.?), Nathaniel Woodhull, Joseph Winger, Jonathan Wood, Robert Young."

According to an ordinance passed by the Provincial Congress, which met at New Brunswick, in the months of February and March, of the year 1776, those freeholders were qualified to vote for representatives in General Assembly "who had signed the general association recommended by this Congress," and all other persons of full age who had resided for one year preceding the election in any county of the colony, and was worth at least fifty pounds proc. money in personal estate, and had signed the association aforesaid, should be admitted to vote. The deputies of representatives, were to be freeholders, with at least 500 pounds proc. money.

CHAPTER XI.

"Hail! independence, hail! heaven's next best gift,
To that of life and an immortal soul!
The life of life, and to the banquet high
And sober meal gives taste; to the bow'd roof
Fair dreams, repose, and to the cottage charms."

HAT these colonies are, and of right, ought to be, free and independent States; and that all political connection between us and the State of Great Britain is, and ought to be, totally dissolved"—such was the bold resolution presented by Richard Henry Lee, of Virginia, in the Continental Congress, in session at Philadelphia, on the seventh day of June, in the year 1776. Owing to the momentousness of the matter, its formal discussion was deferred until the month of July following. A committee, of which Thomas Jefferson was chairman, was meanwhile appointed to prepare the form of a Declaration for presentation to Congress as a basis of discussion. Such a Declaration was, on the second day of July, presented to Congress. The opening sentence was:

> "When, in the course of human events, it becomes necessary for one people to dissolve the political bands which have connected them with another, and to assume, among the powers of the earth, the separate and equal station to which the laws of nature and of nature's God entitle them, a decent respect to the opinions of mankind requires that they should declare the causes which impel them to the separation."

Following these words was a detailed statement of the wrongs which had induced the people of the American colonies to thus declare themselves free and independent to the mother country. Surpassing in thrilling effect the opening sentence of the immortal document whose presentation to Congress has just been noted, were its closing words, which were:

> "For the support of this declaration, with a firm reliance on the protection of Divine Providence, we mutually pledge to each other our lives, our fortunes, and our sacred honor."

At 2 o'clock in the afternoon of July 4, after its serious consideration, paragraph by paragraph, for nearly four days, the Declaration of American Independence was adopted by a unanimous vote of the Continental Congress, assembled in the old State House, at Philadelphia. With a hundred animated strokes of the iron-tongue of the old bell in the tower of what is now known as "Independence Hall," this epoch-making and far-reaching act was proclaimed, the prompt response to which were the enthusiastic acclamations of the people, followed by cannon peals, bonfires and illuminations, not in the Quaker City only, but through the united colonies.

That Morristown joined in these demonstrations of exuberant joyfulness, it would be superfluous to add. Animated and supported in spirit by the consciousness that they were then, and thenceforth were to be, the United States of America, the people bravely renewed their determination to prosecute the pending war to a successful issue.

Early in the month of July, of the year 1776, Washington was in New York and vicinity, with an army whose numbers did not exceed 17,000 men. With a combined force of 35,000 men, including a large body of Hessian troops, General Howe took possession of Staten Island. Landing soon afterward on the western end of Long Island, the British forces surrounded and captured 2,000 of the American troops, under General Putnam; less the killed and wounded. Washington, under cover of a dense fog, quietly withdrew his entire force from Brooklyn, across the East River, to New York. Acting upon the advice of his officers, he retreated to White Plains, where an engagement occurred with the enemy, the result of which was disadvantageous to the American forces. Again the American army fell back, this time upon North Castle. The enemy did not pursue. Leaving one detachment at North Castle, a second at Fort Washington and a third at Peekskill, Washington crossed the Hudson, and, by way of Hackensack, Newark, Elizabethtown, New Brunswick, Princeton and Trenton, retreated through that portion of the State, crossing the Delaware with his diminished and disheartened army, at the point last named on December 8.

With the foregoing necessary, and meager review of events transpiring since the opening of the year 1776, we must return with our readers to the consideration of occurrences in Morristown. The presence at the county seat of Morris of a powder mill, whose monthly output was a ton of first-class gunpowder, a due proportion of which was made into cartridges under the supervision of bustling Benoni Hathaway, was no ordinary allurement to the enemy, then in undisputed possession of New York and vicinity. Through information furnished by spies, or resident tories, or perhaps by both, the enemy was aware of the local circumstances mentioned. It is very doubtful, however, that either spy, or enemy knew the exact whereabouts of the mill, whose product was in future to be used in propelling bullet and ball against the ranks of British redcoats, and Hessian mercenaries.

The first attempt upon the part of the enemy to reach Morristown, with a view of destroying Ford's powder mill, by blowing it up with its own product, was made soon after its erection. Through the vigilance of Colonel Jacob Ford, Jr., and the efficiency of his battalion of Morris County militia, the attempt was successfully thwarted. Hitherto the attempts of the British to reach

Morristown, for the destruction of the powder mill, had been made by small detachments of horsemen, but during the month of December, in the year 1776, General Leslie, with a considerable force, was sent out on the same important errand. Intelligence of this movement of the enemy having in some way been conveyed to Colonel Ford, he, with his battalion of militia, marched to Springfield, where on the fourteenth day of the month last mentioned, a sharp engagement took place with the force commanded by General Leslie. The British commander received so convincing a demonstration of the high quality of Morristown gunpowder, and of the corresponding efficiency of Morris County militia, that he unceremoniously retreated toward Spanktown, now Rahway. Withdrawing his battalion from Springfield, Colonel Ford encamped at Chatham, to watch the further movements of the enemy. It is said that "when the French Government heard of the battle of Springfield, fought as it was, by militia alone, they made up their minds to assist our struggling forefathers. I mention this to you as important historically, and also as a tribute to the patriotism of the Morris County men, who were mainly the force employed on that occasion. There is another important fact. The French Government supposed the war of the Revolution was got up by selfish, designing men, and that they hired the soldiers who fought the battles. But when they saw the earnestness of the farmers and country people of our county and State,they made up their minds that it would be a long, earnest and truly patriotic fight, and they resolved to help."

Retracing our steps somewhat, chronologically, it will be ascertained that Colonel Ford's battalion of militia had, previously to the engagement at Springfield, demonstrated its efficiency. Anticipating his retreat through New Jersey, after the disastrous campaign in New York State, Washington called upon New Jersey for troops to cover his rear against Cornwallis, who, with an ample force, was in pursuit of the American army. This important service was, in part, performed by the Morris County men, with credit alike to the State and to Colonel Ford and his battalion, which had been detailed for that object. The "mud rounds" is the significant term by which the campaign including the movements above mentioned has since been known.

On the fourteenth day of December, in the year 1776, Morristown was visited by an American officer of high rank, General Alexander McDougall, whose presence at the county seat, at that period of local history, was an occurrence of no ordinary interest.. The arrival, on the seventeenth day of the same month, only three days after the date above mentioned, of three regiments of eastern troops from Ticonderoga, seems to indicate that General McDougall was in Morristown under instructions from Washington, for the purpose, perhaps, of arranging for an encampment. And, as the arrival of Washington himself, with his decimated army, in Morristown, occurred only about three weeks later, it may be inferred that the presence of General

McDougall at the county seat was also in some way connected with that interesting event. The three regiments of eastern troops, which, as we have seen, arrived in Morristown on the seventeenth of December, were in command of Colonel Vose, and comprised Greaton's regiment of about 250 men, Bond's regiment of about 100 men and Porter's regiment of about 170 men: a force aggregating about 520 men. On the twentieth day of December, following the arrival of the regiments in command of Colonel Vose, Washington in a letter to the president of the United States Congress, said:

> "I have directed the three regiments from Ticonderoga to halt at Morristown, in Jersey (where, I understand, about 800 militia have collected), in order to inspirit the inhabitants, and, as far as possible, to cover that part of the country."

In view, however, of all the circumstances, as now understood, it is almost certain, notwithstanding the reasons given in the letter above mentioned, for the presence of "the three regiments from Ticonderoga," that the force in command of Colonel Vose was in Morristown chiefly for the protection of Ford's powder mill, which the enemy, in spite of repeated but futile attempts to reach and blow up, were still determined to destroy. In war, no less than in diplomacy, language is not infrequently employed with the design of hiding the real intent and Washington was no stranger to this art of concealment. Morris County troops would unquestionably have been fully equal to the protection of the invaluable powder manufactory at Morristown, particularly in conjunction with Colonel Ford's battalion, but for the absence in the regular service of a county regiment in command of the brave Colonel Winds.

It was not until the twenty-second day of December, five days after the arrival of the three regiments from Ticonderoga, that Colonel Ford arrived in Morristown with his battalion from Chatham, where they had been watching in vain for a second opportunity to demonstrate their efficiency as soldiers. Nine days after the arrival home of Colonel Ford's battalion—that is to say, on the thirty-first day of December, they were on parade, presumably on the grounds to the south of the village Green, between the present site of the national bank and Bank street, and including a portion also of the South street of the year 1905. Doubtless the battalion of militia, which had returned so recently from its highly creditable engagement with the red coats at Springfield, was disbanded soon after the parade above mentioned. It was a parade which was proudly witnessed, the writer ventures to suggest, by the assembled patriots of the county seat and vicinity.

Before the parade closed, Colonel Ford, to employ the quaint language of his day, was seized "with a delirium in his head and was borne off by a couple of soldiers, after which he never rose from his bed." On the tenth day of January, in the year 1776, he died of inflammation of the lungs—lung fever, as it was then termed, or pneumonia, as the medical profession would now call it. His illness was without doubt induced by the exposure and hardships of his recent services in the field. His body, by order of Washington, was buried with the honors of war, Captain Rodney's light infantry company acting as an escort to the remains.

In the midst of exceptional usefulness, and in the full vigor of young manhood, there thus passed away one of the most promising men ever produced in Morristown. In view of the brilliancy exhibited by this early martyr to freedom, during his brief public career, it would have been safe to predict for him almost unlimited achievement as a military officer, in the war which, at his untimely disease, had been in progress but little more than a year.

Born on the nineteenth day of February, in the year 1738, Colonel Ford had, therefore, at the time of his decease, scarcely attained the thirty-ninth year of his age. On the twenty-seventh day of January, in the year 1762, he married Theodocia, the accomplished daughter of the Rev. Timothy Johnes. Five children were the result of this union of hearts, namely: Timothy, Gabriel H., Elizabeth, Jacob and Phebe. Colonel Ford's remains now lie in the older portion of the burial grounds of the First Presbyterian Church, of Morristown. The inscription upon his monument, as carefully transcribed by the writer, is as follows:

Sacred
To the Memory of
Colo. Jacob Ford Jun'r,
Son of
Colo. Jacob Ford Sen'r.
He was Born
February the 19th, Anno Domini 1738,
And departed this life
January the 10th, Anno Domini 1777,
And Being then
In the Service of his Country,
Was Interred in this place
With Military Honors.

In vain we strive by human skill
  To avoid the Shaft of Death;
Heav'n's high Decree it must fulfil
  And we resign our Breath.
The friends who read our Tomb and mourn
  And weep our Early Fall,
Must be lamented in their day
  And share the fate of all.

On the sixth day of January, in the year 1777, there arrived in Morristown one whose presence has from that hour to this, rendered sacred the ground he trod, and the very atmosphere he breathed. It was none other than Washington. He came fresh from the brilliant and decisive victories of Trenton and Princeton. For his headquarters he promptly selected the Arnold tavern. This tavern, the exceptionally interesting story of which would of itself make a volume of rare value, was erected, as nearly as can now be ascertained, by Samuel Arnold, the father of Colonel Jacob Arnold, about the year 1740, and by the father it was subsequently conveyed to the son. A necessarily brief description of the building will in due time be given.

Prior to the commencement of the Revolution this tavern was kept by Thomas Kinney, a prominent man in county affairs, and the owner of no little landed property. Jacob Arnold, however, had resided in Morristown village since the year 1772. It seems to have been about the month of June, in the year 1775, that Jacob Arnold assumed the proprietorship of what is now known as the Arnold tavern. From the commencement of the difficulty between the American colonies and the mother country, the name of Jacob Arnold had been the synonym of intense patriotism; and that his large and well kept hostelry should have become the favorite rendezvous of the patriots of Morristown and Morris County, was but an almost inevitable sequence. Washington was doubtless in some measure influenced in the selection of headquarters by the reputation of the tavern, and its proprietor, for their well-known loyalty to the growing cause of freedom. Either prior to, or closely following, the arrival in Morristown of the commander-in-chief, Jacob Arnold was appointed aide and paymaster. That the unique personality of this patriot was an additional attraction to the distinguished guest who sought the hospitality of his ample roof, is the writer's opinion. From a descendant of Mr. Arnold, the writer has learned, that in height he was about five feet and eight inches. He was a thick set, broad shouldered man, with a large head and neck. His eyes were blue, and his hair dark.

Attached to this tavern, and running back to the Jockey Hollow road (now Western avenue), extending also northeastward as far as the present Speedwell avenue, was a farm of considerable area, the products of whose soil contributed in no small measure to the bountifully prepared table of this famous hostelry. The Arnold tavern was a three-story building, with a large chimney at either end. Running back from the main portion of the building, which was 43 feet in length and 25 feet in depth, was a two-story L or wing, which did not extend entirely across the rear of the structure. This wing was about 20 feet in depth by 25 feet in width, and two stories in height.

The main portion of the building was divided by a wide hallway running from front to rear, through the centre. Access to the second floor was by means of a broad, winding stairway leading out of the hallway mentioned. On the southern end of the building were a front and back parlor, while on the opposite end were a bar-room, dining-room and kitchen. Over the dining-room and kitchen, both of which seem to have been in the rear extension, was a commodious hall, in which assembly balls were not infrequently held. In this hall, the army Masonic lodge held its meetings during the winters of 1777 and 1780. During his winter's sojourn at this famous tavern, Washington occupied the two rooms on the second floor, over the bar-room (the bar-room was at the northeast of the building, to the right of the main front entrance); the front room being used as an office, and the one directly back of the office as a sleeping room. "The commander-in-chief appointed the light infantry to be his personal body-guard, requiring 26 men to mount sentry around the Arnold tavern. That this guard might always be within a more convenient distance than was the general camp (at Lowantica Valley) the entire regiment was installed about one mile away, in the large Ford mansion, now the well known 'Headquarters.' General Green quartered with a Mr. Hoffman, whom tradition mentions as a good-natured man, whose charming wife was a great lover of the clergy. * * * A few days after the army reached Morristown, Colonel Daniel Hitchcock, of Rhode Island, who had fought and marched under Washington from the outset, fell a victim to the fatigues and exposures of the campaign. At Assunpink and Princeton he had commanded a brigade of five regiments and was congratulated by his Chief after the battles."

On the eleventh day of January, smallpox (said by some to have been deliberately introduced by the British authorities) broke out in Morristown, the first victim being Martha, the widow of Joshua Ball. During the same month two more deaths occurred from this disease, and within the period of one year the list was increased to sixty-eight, including old and middle-aged and young. Nor were sex or condition regarded by this dire disease. Putrid sore throat, dysentery and other maladies swelled the number of deaths in the village to 205.

Among the soldiers, the ravages of the smallpox became so prevalent, that establishments for inoculation were provided near Morristown, some of which were in private houses. So numerous did smallpox cases become, that the Presbyterian and Baptist churches in Morristown, were used as hospitals. The use of the Presbyterian church as a smallpox hospital, necessitated the holding of divine services on Sunday in private houses, and when the weather was suitable, in the open air. A favorite place for these open air services was in a somewhat secluded dell in the rear of the residence of Rev. Timothy Johnes, which was also partially protected from the elements by a copse of trees, and by the ground elevation between the meeting place and the Whippanong River beyond.

It was on the thirteenth day of January, one week after his arrival in Morristown, that Washington opened a brief, but notable correspondence with Lord Howe, the subject of which was the inhuman treatment of captured American soldiers and sailors. Against this Washington vigorously protested. If tradition from two distinct sources may be relied upon, and in this particular case there seems to be ample ground for reliance, the serious phase of the correspondence between the two distinguished gentlemen alluded to, was relieved by the employment of a vein of humor on both sides. It is said that Lord Howe sent to Washington, while the correspondence was in progress, a copy of Watt's version of the 120th Psalm, which reads:

"Thou God of love, thou ever blest,
  Pity my suffering state;
When wilt Thou set my soul at rest
  From lips that love deceit?

Hard lot of mine! my days are cast
  Among the sons of strife,
Whose never ceasing brawlings waste
  My golden hours of life.

O! might I change my place,
  How would I choose to dwell
In some wide, lonesome wilderness,
  And leave these gates of hell!"

Washington, so it is said, returned to Howe Watts's version of the 101st Psalm, of which two stanzas are quoted:

"In vain shall sinners strive to rise
By flattering and malicious lies;
And while the innocent I guard
The bold offender sha'n't be spared.

The impious crew, that factious band,
Shall hide their heads, or quit the land;
And all who break the public rest,
Where I have power shall be supprest."

On the nineteenth day of January, in the year 1777, Colonel Jacob Ford, Sr., died of fever, at the age of seventy-three years. Immediately to one side of the monument of his son now lie the remains of Colonel Jacob Ford, Sr.

"Sacred
To the Memory
of
Colo. Jacob Ford
He was born
April the 13th, Anno Domini 1704
And departed this Life
January the 19th, Anno Domini 1777,"

is the simple inscription upon his monument. His memory will be cherished so long as the freedom for which he toiled is appreciated.

CHAPTER XII

"They pitched their camp and through it made
A main street passing wide;
And in the midst a flagstaff set
For all the country side."
Ballads of New Jersey in the Revolution.

T was on the sixth day of January, in the year 1777, that Washington, with his patriot army, reached Morris County and went into. winter quarters. Washington's army was encamped chiefly at Lowantica Valley; or Spring Valley as it is now called, about three miles east of the Morristown Green. Not a few of his soldiers were, however, quartered, or "billeted," in private houses in various portions of the county. Some of the officers were quartered at the Arnold tavern in Morristown, and at other houses in the village, and outlying country.

The condition of this army is well described by the Rev. William Gordon, D. D., in "The History of the American Revolution." He says:

"The army under General Washington marched on to Pluckamin in their way to Morristown, pulling up the bridges as they proceeded, thereby to incommode the enemy and secure themselves. By the time they got there (Morristown), the men were so excessively fatigued, that a fresh and resolute body of five hundred might have demolished the whole. Numbers lay down in the woods and fell asleep, without regarding the coldness of the weather. The royal army was still under such alarming impressions, that it continued its march from Trenton to Brunswick, thirty miles, without halting longer at least than was necessary to make the bridges over Stony Brook and Millstone passable."

There is but a single flaw in Historian Gordon's estimate of the efficiency of Washington's "excessively fatigued" army, and it is this: His understanding of the stuff of which they were made, differed radically from that of the British commander, who had so recently received a practical demonstration of the fact on several battle-fields in New Jersey. From a letter written by Washington from Morristown to General Philip Schuyler, on the eighteenth day of January, of the year 1777, the following extract is given:

"The enemy by two lucky strokes, at Trenton and Princeton, have been obliged to abandon every part of Jersey except Brunswic and Amboy, and the small tract of country between them, which is so entirely exhausted of supplies of every kind, that I hope, by preventing them from sending their foraging parties to any great distance, to reduce them to the utmost distress, in the course of this winter."

Fourteen days after his arrival in Morristown, Washington wrote Governor Livingston, of New Jersey, a most cheering letter, in which, among other things of importance, he said: "Our affairs here are in a very prosperous train. Within a month past, in several engagements with the enemy"—he evidently refers to the battles at Trenton, Assunpink and Princeton—"we have killed, wounded and taken prisoners between two and three thousand men. I am very confident that the enemy's loss here will oblige them to recall their force from your State. If I am properly supported, I shall hope to close the campaign gloriously for America."

Washington's army, on his arrival at Morristown, as Gordon rightly estimated, did not exceed in number 4,000 men, and by some historians, 3,000 is the estimate given. The British force in New Jersey at the time numbered fully 10,000 men. The short term of enlistment—one year—of most of the soldiers in the American army, would, as the commander-in-chief was well aware, soon expire, and how to replenish the ranks of his army, so soon to be depleted, became to him a matter of deep solicitude. In his endeavor to meet the grave exigency which confronted him, Washington dispatched letters to the New Jersey Council of Safety, to the Governors of the thirteen newly constituted States and to the President of the United States Congress, urgently calling upon these official bodies for recruits, and for the munitions of war necessary for the conduct of the prospective campaign. In response to these appeals for recruits they in due course of time began to arrive at the various army camps, in what numbers, and with what degree of promptitude, may be learned from a communication written by Washington on the twenty-sixth day of January, in the year 1777, in which he said:

> "Reinforcements come up so extremely slow that I am afraid I shall be left without any men before they arrive. The enemy must be ignorant of our numbers or they have not horses to move their artillery, or they would not suffer us to remain undisturbed."

Unwilling to await the expiration of their term of enlistment, not a few of the soldiers of Washington's army, prior to their arrival at Morristown, and even afterward, deserted. The number of desertions became so large that Washington awoke to the necessity of prompt and energetic action to check the growing evil. Since his army was not only daily diminishing in numbers, and hence in efficiency, but those who remained would, it was apprehended by the sagacious commander, soon become demoralized in spirit, Washington, therefore, wrote letters to the United States Congress, earnestly requesting that body to recommend to the different States the enactment of stringent laws against deserters, and against such persons also as should harbor and protect them. He wrote also to the Governors of the States, pressing the same important matters upon their attention. His letter addressed to the representatives of New Jersey closes with the words: "Desertion must of course cease when the offenders find they have no shelter." The punishment inflicted upon deserters apprehended and brought back to camp was diverse, and, in not a few instances, severe. "Running the gauntlet," as it was termed, was a mode of punishment sometimes inflicted upon deserters. The entire battalion of six or seven hundred men to which the apprehended deserter was attached, would be drawn up in two lines, about four feet apart on the parade ground. The deserter, who had been stripped of all clothing, save his pantaloons, was then compelled to run between the ranks, while the soldiers on either side applied their whips to his bared back. Three times the deserter was required to thus run through the open ranks of his battalion, while officers near at hand, compelled the men who shrunk from the performance of the disagreeable duty to apply the whip, until sometimes the punished soldier would fall to the ground from sheer exhaustion, with the blood running from his lacerated body. This mode of punishment was usually effectual with the victim, and acted also as a deterrent to further desertions. Hanging was also occasionally resorted to as the penalty for desertion. It is said that two deserters who were shot at the Lowantica encampment, are buried there.

The smallpox, of whose beginning we spoke in the previous chapter, was proving so fatal in Morristown, and the vicinity, that on the fifth day of February, in the year 1777, Washington was impelled to address a letter to the United States Congress upon the subject in which he said:

"The smallpox has made such a head in every quarter that I find it impossible to keep it from spreading through the whole army, in the natural way. I have, therefore, determined not only to inoculate all the troops, now here, that have not had it, but I shall order Doctor Shippen to inoculate the recruits, also, as fast as they come to Philadelphia."

Many of the people seriously objected to submitting themselves to inoculation; and in the work of persuading his parishioners of the efficacy of this operation, Rev. Timothy Johnes, by reason of his great personal influence, materially aided Washington in his effort to thus stay the ravages of the terrible disease. The smallpox, which, as we have seen, began with Martha Ball, on the eleventh day of January, in the year 1777, extended through the First Presbyterian Church parish with truly alarming strides. On the twenty-fourth, and also on the thirty-first day of January, of the year above mentioned, there occurred a death from the dire disease. Rev. Mr. Johnes, during the month of February, attended in his parish eleven funerals of residents of Morristown who had succumbed to the smallpox; this was an average of nearly three each week in the month. In the month of March, the number of deaths fell to nine. During the month of April, there were twenty-one deaths, an average of nearly one death for each weekday. In the months of May, June, July and August there were, respectively, eleven, six, eight and one deaths, from the same disease. The unfaltering faithfulness of "Parson Johnes" may, with some measure of adequacy, at least, be emphasized by the statement that on the second, seventh and eighth days of the month of April he officiated at two funerals of the victims of the prevalent disease, and on the fourteenth and thirty-first days of the same month, he officiated at the funerals of three of his parishioners. This was an aggregate of sixty-eight in his own parish alone, not to mention the deaths in the Baptist parish. It is said that it was no uncommon occurrence during the prevalence of smallpox in Morristown, to find, in the morning, several bodies of victims who had succumbed to the disease during the previous night, lying under the pews in the Presbyterian Church. Among the smallpox patients in the Presbyterian Church, was Nehemiah Smith, a soldier in Washington's army, who was the maternal grandfather of the Rev. Rufus S. Green, recently pastor of the First Presbyterian Church, of Morristown.

There is an apparently well-grounded tradition, which, so far as the writer is aware, has never been questioned, that in the winter of 1777, and during the prevalence of small-pox, Washington was ill with quinsy sore throat. Intelligence of his illness being conveyed to Martha Washington, she hastened to the bedside of her illustrious husband, and in the modest sleeping-room on the second floor of the Arnold tavern, then occupied by Washington, nursed him back to health. At a time during the illness of Washington, when his decease was apprehended, he was asked by a friend at his bedside, whom he could designate as being suitably qualified to succeed him as commander of the American army; and, being unable to speak in audible tones, he pointed, without a moment's hesitation, to General Nathanael Greene, the quartermaster-general of the army, who was among the anxious watchers at the couch of his beloved chief.

The winter of 1777 was an extremely cold one, and there was much suffering among the soldiers of the American army. A scarcity of food was also experienced by the patriot army at Morristown and vicinity.

"There was a time," said a surgeon who was with Washington's army during the winter just mentioned "when all our rations were but a single gill of wheat a day."

Washington was not unmindful of the sufferings and sacrifices of his soldiers, and frequently rode to the various points where they were encamped, and billeted, to look after their welfare, and to speak words of cheer to them.

"Washington used to come 'round and look into our tents" (we quote again from the surgeon above alluded to), "and he looked so kind and he said so tenderly: 'Men, can you bear it?' 'Yes, general, yes, we can,' was the reply; 'if you wish us to act, give us the word and we are ready.' " Than this incident, none in the public career of Washington brings out more clearly the better side of his splendid all-round character. In the light of such incidents, as illustrative of his character, it should be no matter of wonder that Washington's influence over his soldiers was so great and that during the seven years' struggle for independence he should have succeeded in holding his army together under circumstances the most trying. In a letter written by Washington to General Irvine, Commissary, on Saturday, the twenty-second day of February, in the year 1777, he says:

> "The cry of want of Provisions comes to me from all Quarters—Genl. Maxwell writes word that his men are starving—Genl. Johnston, of Maryland, yesterday informed me that his people could draw none—this difficulty I understand prevails also at Chatham—What Sir is the meaning of this?—and why were you so desirous of excluding others from this business when you are unable to accomplish it yourself? Consider, I beseech you, the consequences of this neglect."

On the sixth day of March, in the year 1777, Washington wrote from Morristown as follows, to Governor Trumbull, of Connecticut:

> "I tell you in confidence, that, after the fifteenth of this month, when the time of General Lincoln's militia expires, I shall be left with the remains of five Virginia regiments, not amounting to more than as many hundred men, and parts of two or three other Continental battalions, all very weak. The remainder of the army will be composed of small parties of militia from this State and Pennsylvania, on which little dependence can be put, as they come and go as they please."

From the Journal of Colonel Timothy Pickering, the following entry under date of March twenty-second, in the year 1777, will be found of no ordinary interest:

"Went to Morristown. Finished my business with the Paymaster, and drank tea at headquarters (Arnold's tavern), General Washington and his lady being of the company, and then took leave of the General."

It was on the second day of March, in the year 1777, that Washington wrote from Morristown: "General Howe cannot have less than 10,000 men in the Jerseys. Our number does not exceed 4,000. His are well disciplined, well officered and well appointed; ours raw militia, badly officered and under no government." If Washington knew the condition and numbers of Howe's army, Howe was far from acquainted with the status of the American army at Morristown and vicinity; and it was by resort to such ingenious means and methods as the following, that General Howe was deceived. A certain man had been employed by Washington as a spy upon the British army. It was, however, surmised by some of the more vigilant of Washington's officers, Colonel Alexander Hamilton among them, that this spy was "playing double," in other words, that he was taking information to the British commander, while in the service of Washington. Quartermaster-General Greene's office was at the time in a small building which stood on the present site of Henry M. Smith's store, at the northwest corner of South and Morris streets. Colonel Hamilton was one day at Greene's office when the suspected spy entered. Hamilton, having previously resolved to make use of this spy, had commenced what purported to be a careful statement of the condition of the American army at Morristown and vicinity. Both as to numbers and munitions of war, this report was a deliberate exaggeration of the actual facts; in short, the American army and its resources were made to appear four times as great as they really were. This report Hamilton was apparently at work upon as the spy entered Greene's office. Pretending to have some errand outside, Colonel Hamilton excused himself, remarking that he would return soon. As if by accident, in consequence of seeming haste, Hamilton left the report on the table where he had been writing and passed out of the office. Glancing hastily over the pages of Hamilton's report, and assured in his own mind that he had an invaluable piece of information for the enemy, the spy quickly folded and thrust into his pocket the precious document. In a few moments the spy was on his way to the British commander. On returning to the office of the quartermaster-general, and finding the fictitious report missing, Hamilton's suspicions of the spy were satisfactorily established. General John Doughty, by whom, after the close of the Revolution, the above incident was related, said that it was the opinion of Colonel Hamilton that the fictitious report of the condition of Washington's army, so eagerly conveyed by the spy to the British commander, was in no small measure the means of preserving the American army at Morristown from attack by the enemy, at a time when it was in poor condition to repel it.

On the twenty-third day of March, in the year 1777,

Colonel Elias Dayton's regiment of Morris County soldiers, arrived in Morristown, and were there mustered out of service. On the same day, Silas Condict was appointed, by Governor Livingston, a member of the New Jersey Council of Safety. This committee subsequently met several times at Mr. Condict's house, situated about a mile north of the Morristown Green, and a little off the main road now known as Sussex Avenue. With the New Jersey Council of Safety Washington met not a few times at the house of Mr. Condict. This house had no door (as the writer has been informed by a descendant of the Condicts) on what was naturally the front; on, that is to say, the side facing the crossroad on which it was situated. If there were windows on that side of the house they were covered by wooden shutters, always closed during the occupancy of Morristown and vicinity by the American army. The door was on what would naturally be considered the back of the house, and from this rear door entrance was had to the interior, with its wide hallway running from front to rear of the building, and with two rooms on either side. The reason for the rear entrance, and for the closed windows, was the privacy desired for the meetings of the Council of Safety, before whom matters of grave importance were brought, the consideration of which necessitated the greatest possible precaution against ascertainment by outsiders.

During the Revolution, Mr. Condict, being fully aware that his capture by the British was devoutly wished, was accustomed to sleeping with a gun and a spear at his bedside, as a means of protection against British marauders and Tories. He often declared he would never be captured alive by the enemy. After the battle of Princeton, several British officers (captured probably at the battle mentioned), in charge of a detachment of American soldiers, were brought to Morristown, as prisoners of war. For some reason, perhaps because there was no room for them in the old jail on the Green, these officers were for a time at least quartered in the house of Mr. Condict. The British officers, so the writer has been informed by a descendant of Mr. Condict, occupied a front room, and the American soldiers a rear room. The British officers brought with them a dog, which for a while they kept in their room. To this, for some reason, Mr. Condict objected; and at length he ordered the canine to be removed from the house. With a volley of oaths the British officers declared the dog should remain; but Mr. Condict firmly insisted upon his removal; and he was, thereby, removed. The officers became very angry; and in unmistakable manner gave expression to their feelings. Mr. Condict afterward remarked, that he "expected the enraged British officers would run me through with their swords." The American soldiers in the adjoining room, on hearing "the rumpus," opened their door to ascertain the cause. They came, of course, to the support of Mr. Condict, and thereafter peace reigned in the temporary jail.

While Washington was in Morristown with his

ırmy—this incident has come to the writer from a ource whose reliability he sees no reason to question —James Pitney, familiarly called "Jim Pitney," of Mendham, just returned from service as a soldier in he patriot army, called on the Hon. Silas Condict, or the purpose of ascertaining where the commander-n-chief could be found, as he wished to call upon him. Mr. Pitney was without a hat, and his clothes were agged and torn. Accompanied by Mr. Condict, who vas glad to serve a man of Mr. Pitney's standing in the ommunity, the latter called upon Washington at his eadquarters. He was introduced, by Mr. Condict, to he commander-in-chief, as "a man of property and inluence at his home in Mendham." Washington must, y his courtesy on the occasion, have made a very faorable impression upon Mr. Pitney, for the latter requently remarked, as he subsequently recalled the nterview, that "Washington is a very fine man."

This house was occupied by Mr. Condict until the ear 1798, when he built the house on Cutler street, ıow occupied by Mrs. Julia R. Cutler, widow of the ate Hon. Augustus W. Cutler. After the completion of his new residence in the year above mentioned, Mr. Condict removed into it, and here he passed the closng years of his life. During Mr. Condict's occupancy of his new home, Colonel Joseph W. Cutler, who, as ve have seen, married his only granddaughter, lived or a time in the family. He subsequently removed to he old Condict house, where he resided until the decease of Mr. Condict. He died in the year 1801, in his new home, on what is now Cutler Street. This house is practically unaltered since the Hon. Silas Condict occupied it. There may still be seen the same spacious hallway extending from front to rear of the house with the wide stairway leading from the hallway to the second floor. After the decease of Mr. Condict, Colonel Cutler returned to the new house built by the former, where he resided during the remainder of his life. Mrs. Silas Condict continued to reside in her home in the family of her granddaughter, until her decease several years subsequent to that of her husband.

The old Condict house, on the road leading to Brant's paper mill, after a somewhat "checkered career," was torn down a few years since, and a club house erected on its site. This club house was burned. The site of what was without question one of the most famous houses in the State, and the preservation of which would have been an act of practical patriotism, may still (1905) be discerned, particularly by a clump of lilac bushes still standing, which marks the southwest corner of the old house.

One of the possessions, in the way of a relic, upon which the writer congratulates himself, is a piece of a timber from the famous Silas Condict house of Revolutionary times.

There is scarcely a letter of which a transcript has appeared in our story of more interest to Morristonians than the following:

"Morristown, April 7, 1777.

"Dear Sir—This day I received your favor of the twenty-third ultimo, wherein you acquaint me that I have been appointed one of the Council of Safety. I am much concerned that you have so few members attending at this critical season, and, although it is extremely difficult at present for me to leave home (my family being inoculated and not yet through the smallpox), yet I will come at any time rather than public busines should suffer, on notice being given me that it is necessary. Colonel DeHart told me to-day that the battalion had arranged its officers, and only wanted an opportunity to present it for commission. The colonel says that he has, at General Washington's request, examined several of the prisoners now in jail here, and that it will be best for the Council of Safety to sit in this county soon; and if this is thought proper I think it will be best to sit either at Mendham or at Captain Dunn's, in Roxbury, as the army is still at Morristown, and it will be inconvenient to sit there. I am, with great respect, your most obedient and humble servant, SILAS CONDICT.

"His Excellency, Governor Livingston."

As we learn from the foregoing, the county jail on the Morristown Green was full of prisoners, many of whom were Tories. In the jail there were also spies and dangerous characters. To the credit of Morris County it should be said, that most of its inhabitants were, during the Revolutionary period, warmly attached to the cause of freedom; and the intense patriotism of the county was chief among the considerations which attracted Washington with his army to this portion of the State, where for two winters they were encamped. Many incidents illustrative of the experiences of Morris County Tories are related. Of these only two or three can be given. The threat of the application of a coat of tar and feathers to an English emigrant, by some of the hot-blooded Morristown patriots, forced from this incipient Tory a public confession in the Hanover Presbyterian Church, of the sin of toryism. So thorough was his conversion to the cause of freedom, that he made application to Parson Johnes, of Morristown, for the privilege of a similar confession before his influential congregation. This, he was informed, was superfluous, as one confession was sufficient to save him from the enforcement of the "repent or perish" rule adopted by Morris County vigilantes.

Less fortunate, however, was one Thomas Milledge, a leading Hanoverian. Just before the commencement of the Revolution, he was elected sheriff of the county. Having scruples against taking the oath to support the cause of freedom, he declined to be sworn. From this negative attitude toward the popular cause, there was but a step to avowed toryism, and, consistently with his sentiments, he took that step. Hoping to save his large estate from confiscation to the uses of the New Jersey Province, he joined the enemy. His estate was, however, confiscated and he became an exile from his home. He was commissioned as major in the British army, and in that capacity served through the Revolution. After the close of the war he settled in Nova Scotia. Several years afterward, Milledge visited Morris County, and, during his brief stay he was waited upon by a committee of citizens to ascertain his business. To their inquiries he boldly replied:

"When my business here is finished I will leave the country, but not before." He received no further molestation.

One of the most important personages in Morris County, prior to the commencement of the Revolution, if indeed, he were not the most important, was Peter Kemble, "the Honorable Peter Kemble, Esq.," as he was sometimes spoken of. He removed from New Brunswick, to Morris County, as early probably as the year 1760, and settled in Morristown, his residence being situated on the Basking Ridge road, about four miles south of the Green. He became the owner of several hundred acres of land, which extended northward along the Basking Ridge road to a point within about a mile of the village of Morristown. Under the Provincial Governor he held for several years important offices. Socially, he stood very high; in proof of which statement it may be said that one of his daughters was the wife of General Gage, commander successively of the British troops in Boston and New York. His eldest son, Samuel, was the collector of the port of New York, under British appointment. Peter Kemble was a Tory, as might naturally be expected. To save the Kemble estate from confiscation, his son and heir, Richard Kemble, took the oath of allegiance to the United States, although he, too, was without doubt a Tory at heart. During the Revolution—it was in the 1777, while Washington was in Morristown—Peter Kemble, then old and infirm, was cited before the Court of Quarter Sessions, by order of the commander-in-chief, to answer the charge of aiding the enemy; his alleged offense being the circulation of the proclamations of the brothers Howe. These proclamations of the British commanders, it will be remembered, offered a free pardon to all rebels who should lay down their arms, and complete protection of person and property to those who should take the oath of allegiance to Great Britain.

For some reason, Peter Kemble was discharged, presumably because his son, Richard, who was technically, at least, an adherent of the cause of freedom (and was legally so regarded), became responsible for the future conduct of his father. Passing over many facts of deep interest connected with the Kembles, it may be remarked, that the last survivor of the family, Elizabeth, the daughter of the original Peter Kemble, was among the organizers of St. Peter's Episcopal Church of Morristown. She died on the homestead in the year 1836. Four years later what then remained of the extensive Kemble estate, passed into other hands. The Kemble mansion stood somewhat farther down the lawn than the McAlpin house of the present. The slaves' quarters were a little to the rear of the house above mentioned.

The entire family of Peter Kemble are buried on the grounds between the Basking Ridge road and the McAlpin house. A copse of trees indicates the location of the large stone lying horizontally on the ground, and only slightly elevated above its surface.

From the stone, now broken in five pieces, the writer recently copied the following inscription.

Within this enclosure
Rest the remains of the following persons
Let no one disturb their ashes
PETER KEMBLE
Born on the 12th of December, 1701
Died the 23d of February, 1789
ELIZABETH KEMBLE
His wife, born the 12th day of April, 1711
Died the 30th of March, 1804
ANN EDWARDS
Born in Smyrna, in Asia Minor
and died in July, 1808
in the 80th year of her age
RICHARD KEMBLE
Son of Peter Kemble, born in August, 1733
Died 13th of September, 1815
ROBERT T. KEMBLE
Son of Peter Kemble, born April 1, 1735
and died 1st January, 1820
ANN KEMBLE
Daughter of Peter Kemble
Born 9th of June, 1757
Died 2d of September, 1820
ELIZABETH KEMBLE
Daughter of Peter Kemble
Born 18th of December, 1753
Died 16th of June, 1836.

Among the large number of Tories and other prisoners confined in the Morris County Jail, during the year 1777, was a minister of the Gospel, Rev. Isaac Brown. In the year 1747 Mr. Brown became the rector of Trinity Episcopal Church, in Newark. In addition to preaching, Mr. Brown practised medicine, a common thing for ministers to do at that period. Some of his parishioners objected to his presentation of bills for medical services rendered by him, on the ground that such services should have been included in his spiritual administrations. During the Revolution Mr. Brown continued a loyal adherent of the King of Great Britain, and in consequence of his avowed toryism he was taken to Morristown and there confined in the county jail. After his release he went over to New York, then occupied by the British army. In the year 1784 Mr. Brown removed to Nova Scotia, where three years later he died.

In obedience to a summons from Washington, there arrived in Morristown about the middle of April, in the year 1777, an American officer of no inconsiderable note; it was Captain Daniel Morgan. During the preceding winter, Washington, by special solicitation from the United States Congress, had secured the promotion of Morgan to a colonelcy. This he had done with a view to the gathering and organization, by Captain Morgan, of a body of 500 picked men from the different regiments composing the army, active, hardy men, accustomed to the woods and skilful in the use of the rifle. These men were to constitute a select corps of sharp-shooters. The early military experience of the commander-in-chief had taught him the value of such a corps, in frequently turning the tide of battle. In pursuance of orders from Washington, the requisite number of men were gathered and organized for the purpose named. The command of this corps was given to Colonel Morgan, his lieutenant-colonel and major being, respectively, Richard Butler and Joseph Morris, both of whom were promoted from captaincies. Under date of June 13, in the year 1777, Washington wrote Colonel Morgan: "The corps of Rangers, newly formed and under your command, are to be considered as a body of light infantry, and are to act as such, for which reason they will be exempted from the common duties of the line." In his official reports and correspondence the commander-in-chief bore frequent testimony to the great value of Morgan's sharpshooters in several engagements in New Jersey and elsewhere. "They constantly advanced upon an enemy far superior to them in numbers and well secured behind strong redoubts," was Washington's report to Congress concerning this corps in one of the engagements in New Jersey.

In a communication to General Gage, an American officer, to whom Washington had sent Morgan's corps for special service, the commander-in-chief said: "This corps I have great dependence on, and have no doubt they will be exceedingly useful to you as a check given to the savages, and keeping them within proper bounds, etc."

"I can get away easily enough if I wanted to," remarked a stout, rugged-looking fellow, who had been arrested in Rockaway on suspicion of being a spy. He was on his way to the Morris County Jail, in charge of James Kitchel, who was then about twenty years of age. "If he (the suspected spy) attempts to run, or to come toward you, shoot him down," had been the instructions of Squire Abraham Kitchel to his son, before the latter started for Morristown with the prisoner. James Kitchel was mounted on a good horse, and, in accordance with instructions, he compelled the supposed spy to walk a certain distance in advance of him. Young Kitchel, as his father knew, was one of the best shots in the county. The prisoner had gone submissively enough until Morris Plains, only two miles distant from Morristown, was reached, when the conversation between the two above alluded to began.

"Well, try it then," was Kitchell's reply to the prisoner's remark about escaping.

"But I don't want to get away," said the suspected spy. "Let me walk alongside of you. I don't like to be driven along this way.

"Keep your distance, or I'll blaze away," declared Kitchel, instantly poising his gun to suit the action to the word; and the prisoner prudently kept his distance until he was under lock and key in the jail on the Green at Morristown.

CHAPTER XIII.

"Come then, religion, holy, heaven-born maid,
Thou surest refuge in our day of trouble."

T was evidently in the early part of the year 1777 that about eighty Hessians, and ten or more Tories were brought, as prisoners of war, under a strong guard of state militia, to Morristown. They had been captured a few days previously at Connecticut Farms, by two or three companies of New Jersey soldiers; not, however, until, in consequence of their stubborn resistance, several of the enemy had been killed and wounded. These prisoners of war, a portion of them, at least, were placed in the county jail, on the Green. As these Hessians and Tories were all mounted when captured, their horses proved an important acquisition to the resources of the patriots of Morris County.

It has often been said that during the Revolution, the foot of no Britisher, except he were a spy, or belonged to some mounted marauding detachment, ever pressed the soil of Morris County; and this is true, with some modification, however. A British officer visited the county seat of Morris in the year 1777, while Washington and his army were encamped there. With other redcoats he had been captured at the battle of Princeton, and brought as a prisoner of war, by the American army, to the camp at Lowantica Valley, where he and the other captives were confined under guard, either in private houses in the vicinity, or in cabins erected in the midst of the camp for that particular purpose. The officer of whom we are speaking was confined in the house of a resident by the name of Munson. His antipathy to the army of Washington, and the American people in general, was of the rankest sort, and this was the cause of no little trouble between him and his captors. Suspicion that his captors would administer poison to him in his food, was one of the forms this Britisher's antipathy assumed, and as a means of circumventing the imaginary designs for his untimely removel, it was his habit to wipe with the skirt of his coat the plate on which his meals were served. He seems, however, to have had no fear of being poisoned in consequence of the use of applejack, for on the occasion of this visit to Morristown he imbibed so freely, and became so completely intoxicated, as to be irresistibly possessed with the desire to make his escape from the single guard who attended him.

The writer is at present unaware at which of the

famous hostelries in Morristown, Arnold's or Dickerson's (the latter of which was then kept by Robert Norris, Captain Peter Dickerson, the owner, being absent, engaged in the service of his country), the thirsty redcoat procured his applejack; the effect, no doubt would have been the same wherever the liquor was imbibed. As a punishment for his attempt to escape, the British officer, after returning to camp, was flogged by American soldiers. This called forth from the irate Britisher a perfect storm of curses upon his enemies, supplemented by the words: "As to the flogging part of it, I did not mind that; but to be put through the operation by these —— rebels, that is more than flesh and blood can bear."

Reference has been made in a previous chapter to the circumstance that while, in the year 1777, the Presbyterian and Baptist churches (and the courthouse, also, it should be added) were used as hospitals, "Parson Johnes's" congregation worshiped in private houses, and, when the weather was suitable, in the open air. In the orchard to the rear of the parsonage, where these open-air Sunday services were held, the benches were placed in semi-circular form, Dr. Johnes occupying a central position from which he could be advantageously heard by his devout listeners. That Washington and other American officers and soldiers occasionally attended the open-air services, held in the orchard to the rear of the Presbyterian parsonage, is now too well authenticated to question. It is related that while the general, seated one Sunday in his camp chair, conveyed by his orderly from the Arnold tavern to the place of worship in the orchard, a woman with a small child in her arms entered the grove. There being no available seat for her, Washington rose, and with the quiet dignity which invariably characterized his deportment, offered his camp chair to the encumbered young mother. This is a simple incident, but it nevertheless most clearly exhibits the better side of Washington's character, and increases rather than diminishes admiration of the true greatness of "the Father of his Country."

In a variety of ways Washington during his sojourn in Morristown, in the winter of the year 1777, had been severely tried. The privations and sufferings of his beloved soldiers, which he was powerless to ameliorate; the loss of valuable officers and private citizens; the awful scourge of smallpox in the army and among the people, scores of whom were succumbing to the dire disease; the prevalence of other diseases scarcely less fatal in their consequences; the decimation of the ranks of his army by expiration of the term of enlistment of his men, and by frequent desertions; the perplexities invariably incident to the command of a military force, engaged, as in this instance, in a palpably unequal struggle—these were the causes of a depression of spirit on the part of the commander-in-chief, which only appeal, (as he came at last to realize) to a higher than merely human power could adequately relieve. To that higher power, Washington, like many before and since, turned in his extremity for support and consolation.

It was presumably, while experiencing the depression of spirit consequent upon the suggested multiplicity of difficulties confronting him, that the commander-in-chief, one morning, after his accustomed daily inspection of camp at Lowantica Valley, called upon "Parson Johnes," at his home. These two men were no strangers to each other; neither was this the initial visit to the Presbyterian parsonage of the commander of the American army, encamped at the county seat of Morris. Association in the work of devising means and methods for the control of the smallpox and other diseases in the army and in the village; occasional, and perhaps frequent, attendance upon religious services conducted on Sunday by the beloved pastor of the only Presbyterian church then in Morristown; and association, also, in the important deliberations at the Presbyterian parsonage of the New Jersey Council of Safety, in which both Washington and Dr. Johnes had participated, had doubtless resulted in a mutual acquaintance of these two men, which had ripened into a friendship of no ordinary character. It was on a morning of the week previous to the semiannual celebration of the Lord's Supper in the Presbyterian church, that Washington drove up to the home of Dr. Johnes. He left his handsome bay horse in the charge of his mounted orderly, and with stately but heavy tread, ascended the steps of the front veranda and lifted the old fashioned brass knocker on the door, whose short, distinct rap would gain him admission. The usual preliminaries attended to by hostess and host, the following conversation ensued between them:

> "Doctor," said Washington, "I understand that the Lord's Supper is to be celebrated with you next Sunday. I would learn if it accords with the canons of your church to admit communicants of another denomination?"
>
> "Most certainly," replied the clergyman. "Ours is not the Presbyterian table, general, but the Lord's table, and we hence give the Lord's invitation to all his followers, of whatever name."
>
> "I am glad of it," declared Washington; "that is as it ought to be; but as I was not quite sure of the fact, I thought I would ascertain it from yourself, as I propose to join with you on that occasion. Though a member of the Church of England, I have no exclusive partialities."

Having been assured by Dr. Johnes of a most cordial welcome, Washington was among the participants in the memorial service of the following Sunday, observed under the trees of the orchard in the rear of the parsonage. Who that has experienced the soothing, sustaining and inspiring effects of the sincere commemoration of the sacrificial love of Jesus, can for a moment doubt that the commander of the patriot army returned to headquarters with a heart relieved of its burdens, because those burdens had been deliberately, and in response to Divine invitation, rolled upon the heart of the Infinite Burden Bearer? This commemoration of the Lord's death was probably the only ocasion on which Washington, during his public career, participated, outside of his own church, in such a service.

The gambling evil became so prevalent among the officers and soldiers of the American army while encamped in Morristown and vicinity, that Washington issued a general order, prohibiting playing with cards and dice, even for amusement; since, if this were permitted, it would be next to impossible to distinguish between playing for diversion and playing for gain.

"Officers attentive to their duty will find abundant employment in training and disciplining their men, providing for them and seeing that they appear neat, clean and soldierlike. Nor will anything redound more to their honor, afford them more solid amusement, or better answer the end of their appointment, than to devote the vacant moments they may have to the study of military authors."

If ever the practical wisdom of the American commander in the management of men was exhibited, it was in this paragraph of his general order, in which, as a substitute for the pernicious gambling he sought to prevent, he recommended something alike interesting and essential. The closing words of this general order were:

"The adjutant-general is to transmit copies of this order to the different departments of the army. Also, to execute the same to be immediately published in the gazettes of each State, for the information of officers dispersed on the recruiting service.

"By his excellency's command,

"MORGAN CONNOR, Adj. pro tem."

This order was dated: "Headquarters, Morristown, 8th May, 1777."

It must not for a moment be supposed by the readers of this story, that the attention of Washington, during the sojourn at the Arnold Tavern, in the winter of the year 1777, was wholly occupied with the adjustment of the local difficulties already mentioned. Military movements of no insignificant character were meanwhile devised and conducted under the supervision of the alert commander-in-chief. In confirmation of this statement the following extract from a letter of Washington is presented; it was written soon after his arrival in Morristown:

> "I have the satisfaction to say that General Philemon Dickerson's behaviour, in an action that happened near Somerset Courthouse, on Mill Stone River, reflected the highest credit on him; for, though his troops were all raw, he led them through the river, middle deep, and gave the enemy so severe a charge that, although supported by three field pieces, they gave way and left their convoy of forty wagons and upward of one hundred horses, most of them of the English draft breed, and a number of sheep and cattle which they had collected."

It may have been some time in the month of February, after the arrival of Washington in Morristown, that he stationed strong detachments of Continental troops and State militia in the vicinity of Pluckemin and Quibbletown, in Somerset County. The militia were in command of General William Winds, of Morris County. These troops, who were quartered in New

Brunswick, were designed to keep close watch of the movements of the enemy and to protect that portion of the state. Several severe skirmishes occurred between the American and British forces, in which the militia, under the bold and impetuous Winds, behaved with great bravery. Of one of these engagements, an American officer gave an interesting account in the New Jersey Gazette, of March the eighteenth, in the year 1777.

The engagement took place "near Quibble or Squabbletown," and the officer commanding 2,000 of the enemy "is under arrest, for undertaking, like Don Quixote, to do impossibilities. He. instead of marching directly to Brunswick, which he might have done, must needs go fourteen miles out of the direct road to take prisoners General Maxwell and his party at Sparktown, and to make his triumphant entry into Brunswick, leading his captives in chains, like an old Roman general, in which he found his fatal mistake when too late to remedy it, for he found that he had surrounded a nest of American hornets, who soon put his whole body to flight."

On Sunday, the eighteenth day of May, in the year 1777, Rev. Timothy Johnes preached what was undoubtedly a stirring sermon from the text: "But my servant Caleb, because he had another spirit with him, and hath followed me fully, him will I bring into the land wherein he went; and his seed shall possess it." These words are found in the fourteenth chapter and twenty-fourth verse of the Book of Numbers. That the text and the sermon based on it, as delivered by

Dr. Johnes in the orchard to the rear of his residence, were suggested by existing local circumstances, is the opinion of the writer. That our readers may judge for themselves in the matter, the first page of the sermon notes used by Dr. Johnes, on the occasion alluded to, are herewith given, with abbreviations as employed in them, completed by the writer, except where the writing of Dr. Johnes is illegible:

> "First, what is to follow the Lord fully?" Second, "What spirit is it which will dispose us to follow the Lord fully?" Third, "We are to follow the Lord fully in times of general apostacy. God will own and honor us in times of general calamity. Premise—it does not imply sinless perfection—sincere endeavor in gospel sense to follow the Lord fully is to follow him universally, not divided between ourselves and ——— or between more mortification and less mortification. But regard the whole will, commandments and government, not partially, when it suits our ease or interest. We are not to be ashamed; in all the relations and stations of life, under all trials, as Caleb here, though threatened to be stoned, we should follow the Lord fully. We should follow the Lord boldly, courageously, public-spiritedly. Caleb knew of the giants and Anakims, of the cities great and fenced about, in the Land of Canaan—but he spoke public-spiritedly in opposition to the ten cowardly, dastardly spies, and in behalf of the public good, etc."

Among the most illustrious foreign officers who came to this country, and applied for service in the patriot army, was the Polish general, Thaddews Kosciusko. He brought with him a letter from Benjamin Franklin to Washington. He probably, and almost certainly, found Washington at the Arnold Tavern, in Morristown; it was during the early part of the year 1777. "What do you seek here," inquired the Commander-in-Chief. "To fight for American independence," was the noble reply. "What can you do," said Washington. "Try me," was the simple response of the Polish patriot. There was something in the bearing and deportment of Kosciusko, which won the confidence of Washington; and he was appointed an aide-de-camp on the staff of the commanding general. Kosciusko proved a most trustworthy and efficient ally in the Revolution. It is said that Kosciusko taught the American officers the science of engineering, by reason of which the efficiency of the patriot army was greatly augmented.

"Alexander Hamilton, speaking of the close of the campaign of 1777, and of the way in which Washington held the greatly superior forces of Cornwallis in severe check, says: 'There was persented the extraordinary spectacle of a powerful army straightened within narrow limits by the phantom of a military force, and never permitted to transgress those limits with impunity.' Irving speaks of the British army as 'held in check by Washington and his handful of men, castled among the heights of Morristown'; and in closing his account of these memorable days, writes thus:

'These ineffectual attempts of a veteran general to penetrate these fastnesses, though at the head of a veteran force, which would once have been deemed capable of sweeping the whole continent before it, were a lasting theme of triumph to the inhabitants; and it is still the honest boast among the people of Morris County that 'the enemy were never able to get a footing among our hills.' "

Near the close of the month of May, in the year 1777, the American army, which for about five months had been encamped in Morristown and vicinity, broke camp and marched away over the same route taken on its entrance into Morris County, at the opening of the year. For an account of the disastrous campaign following the departure of Washington and his patriot army from Morris County, we refer our readers to the pages of United States history.

On the seventh day of August following the departure of the American army from Morris County, the New Jersey Council of Safety held a meeting at Morristown, perhaps in the courthouse on the village Green. Of the members of the council there were five present, including Governor Livingston and Silas Condict. The doorkeeper was John Martin. At this meeting Colonel John Munson was ordered to at once arrest and bring before the Council of Safety, John Troop, Peter Saunders and James Moody. These men had for some time been engaged in northern New Jersey in recruiting men for the British army. Moody alone, according to his own statement, had recruited 100 men for the King's service, good pay and plenty to do, being the inducements held out to the recruits. Prompt action on the part of Colonel Munson and his regiment of militia, resulted in the speedy apprehension of Troop and Saunders, and more than fifty Tory recruits. Moody made his escape and subsequently emigrated to Nova Scotia.

On the eleventh day of August, Troop and Saunders were before the Council of Safety, at Morristown. It being ascertained that Troop was a lieutenant of the British Volunteers, he was sent under guard to General Washington, for further examination. The choice between enlisting in the American navy, or standing trial upon the charge of aiding the enemy, was given to Saunders. Nine days of confinement and serious meditation in the county jail, on the part of this latter prisoner, resulted in his decision to enlist, and he was therefore sent under guard to Philadelphia, where he would be received into the naval service. The Tory recruits captured with Troop and Saunders were placed in irons and marched under a strong guard of county militia to Burlington, by way of Trenton.

In the months of September and October, in the year 1777, the New Jersey Council of Safety was in session at Princeton. On the fifth of October, this body ordered eleven prisoners to be sent to the Morris County Jail, where they were to be kept in close confinement; and this was accordingly done. Among this batch of prisoners were James Iliff and John Mee. By authority of the Council of Safety, the Court of Oyer and Terminer for Morris County, tried a large number of cases (nearly a hundred, it is said) for offenses committed outside the county. The trial of these cases occupied nearly three weeks. Of the number tried, thirty-five were sentenced to death and thirty were pardoned on condition of their enlistment in the American army. On the second day of December following the trial of their cases, Iliff and Mee were hanged on the Morristown Green. Not far from the present soldiers' monument probably stood the gallows on which these two men were "hanged until they were dead." Before their execution, Iliff and Mee were earnestly exhorted by Sheriff Carmichael to make a confession of their crimes, to which they in substance replied:

> "We are guilty of no crime, save loyalty to the King of Great Britain; hence we have no confession to make."

Governor Livingston, in a letter under date of January 7, in the year 1778, addressed to the British general in command of the King's troops in New Jersey, said:

> "Iliff was executed after a trial by jury for enlisting our subjects, himself being one, as recruits in the British army, and he was apprehended on his way with them to Staten Island. Had he never been a subject to this State he would have forfeited his life as a spy. Mee was one of his company and had also procured our subjects to enlist in the service of the enemy."

From a Morristown militiaman, who was on duty at the county jail when the thirty-five Tory prisoners previously spoken of were sentenced, we learn that orders were given by the officer in command of the guard, that the wives of the condemned Tories, who might so desire, should be admitted into the jail to take a farewell of their husbands. Among those who did this was one devoted wife, who polished her husband's shoe, knee and stock buckles, and also his shoes. She washed his linen and his white pantaloons, and brushed his coat and hat, that he might present a gentlemanly appearance on the gallows. All honor to the noble wife! Truly she was loyal to her matrimonial promise to take him "for better or for worse." The officer in command of the jail guard came to the jail on the morning appointed for the execution of the thirty-five Tory prisoners above mentioned, and said to them:

> "With two exceptions (those were Iliff and Mee), I offer you all a reprieve from the gallows if you will enlist in the American army for the remainder of the war. As fast as you say you will enlist you will be conducted under guard to the upper room of the jail, to remain there until your proper officer comes to enroll you and have you sworn."

One by one, after a little hesitation, the entire batch of condemned prisoners said, "I will enlist," and they were all placed under guard in the upper room. The father of one of the men reprieved—he was a Tory Dutchman from Bergen County—came up to the jail, and the son, catching sight of him, put his head out of the window and said:

"How do you do, father?"

"What are doing up dere, my poy?" was the father's interrogative.

"I am reprieved," said the son.

"How's dat?" asked the father.

"I had the offer, if I would enlist for the rest of the war, and I have enlisted," was the son's answer.

"Listed among the rebels! I would rather have followed you to the gallows," was the old Dutchman's sturdy remark.

"Take care, you old rebel," exclaimed one of the jail guard, as he leveled his musket at the father, "or we will hang you up where your son was to go."

Upon this the Bergen County Dutchman beat a hasty retreat from the Green, much to the amusement of those who witnessed the scene.

Another important case tried in the courthouse on the Green at Morristown, in the month of December, of the year 1777, was that of Alexander Worth, who was charged with "coming out of and going into the enemy's lines without the license required by law." He had been captured in Woodbridge, and was taken before the Council of Safety, then in session at Trenton. Careful examination of the prisoner disclosed the fact that he was a tory soldier of the British army, found within the American lines. By order of the Council of Safety, Worth was sent under guard to Morristown, where he was tried on suspicion of being a spy. He was found guilty, and was given the choice of being burnt in the hand or enlisting in the Continental army to fight against the King.

"Death is preferable to fighting against the King,"

was the heroic reply. He was, therefore, branded in the hand. The painful operation was performed by Sheriff Carmichael, of Morris County. The prisoner's hand and arm were securely fastened to a block of wood expressly prepared for the purpose, and the hot iron was then applied by the county official. Worth afterward returned to Staten Island.

Some of the more responsible Tories confined in the Morris County Jail at the period under consideration, were released from custody, on condition that they would remain within a mile of the courthouse, and return to jail when wanted by the authorities. Other prisoners from Bergen County were permitted, in compliance with their petition to the county court, to reside in Morris Township on parole; not, however, until they had given bonds that they would remain within one mile from the county jail. In response to their petition to the court, three prisoners from Essex County, were permitted to go to their own county jail, on condition that they should bear the expense. Several prisoners escaped from the old jail on the Morristown Green: three in the month of December, of the year 1778, who were advertised by the sheriff.

CHAPTER XIV.

"All desp'rate hazards courage do create,
As he plays frankly who has least estate;
Presence of mind, and courage in distress,
Are more than armies, to procure success."

THE New Jersey Council of Safety, composed of his excellency the Governor, and twelve or more representative citizens, selected from various sections of the State, was a migratory body, so to speak, moving about from place to place as local exigencies seemed to require. During the years 1777 and 1778, this important official body sat several times in Morristown. The mention of some of the local matters brought before the Council of Safety, while sitting at the county seat of Morris, may very appropriately be prefaced by a few words quoted from a local historian, and appearing in connection with his account of the counterfeiting operations in Morris County by Samuel Ford, and his highly respectable accomplices, just prior to the commencement of the Revolution. "We would fain pass by it, but truth is inexorable and the historian has no choice."

From the historically invaluable minutes of the Council of Safety, the following extracts are selected and presented, with their respective dates affixed:

June 18, 1777—"John Drummond, a prisoner committed by Captain O'Harra, was discharged upon taking the oath of abjuration and allegiance, there being no evidence against him."

June 21, 1777—"Benjamin Morgan, Esq., a prisoner in Morris County (committed by order of his excellency, General Washington), petitioned to be removed from prison to some private house. Ordered that the said Benjamin Morgan be removed to the house of the widow (second wife of Matthew Lum) Jemima Lum, in Morristown, and there to remain or within one hundred yards thereof until further order of the Governor and Council of Safety or otherways discharged by due course of law; on his giving bond of two thousand pounds to remain there till discharged as above, which bond was executed accordingly."

June 21, 1777, afternoon session—"Mr. Peter Mackie being summoned before the Governor and Council as suspected of being disaffected to the State, and was offered the oaths of Abjuration and Allegiance and refusing the same, and appearing to be too dangerous to be suffered to go at large, was ordered to be committed to Gaol. * * *

"Peter Mackie offering to take the oaths after the warrant of commitment was made out, was sworn accordingly and discharged." This was evidently the identical Peter Mackee from whose land a Morristown "school hous" was removed in the year 1771, by order of the trustees of the Presbyterian church.

June 28, 1777—"Robert Norris appeared before the board pursuant to citation and took the oaths of Abjuration and Allegiance to the government, as established by the Legislature of the State." Mr. Norris, it may be remarked, kept the Dickerson tavern while Captain Peter Dickerson, its owner, was absent in the military service of his country.

July 3, 1777—"The petition of Ben-Jamin Morgan, now in confinement in Morristown, was read, setting forth that he is desirous to take the oaths of abjuration and allegiance agreeably to law, and is willing to be circumscribed in his boundaries, and laid under such penalties as the board may think necessary; and praying that he may be permitted to return home. Agreed. that as the petitioner was apprehended by order of his Excellency General Washington, he is to be considered as a military prisoner, and therefore that the said petition be referred to the General."

August 21, 1777, afternoon session—"Agreed, that the Governor direct Major Benoni Hathaway to deliver the field-pieces and appurtenances, and also the powder you are to receive for the public use, to the commanding officer of the militia stationed along the frontiers near Staten Island, or to his order, taking his receipt or the receipt of the person by him authorized to receive it. * * *

"Mr. Kimble having been cited to appear before the board, informed the Governor by letter that he was, through indisposition of body, unable to attend. Ordered, that Justice (Benjamin) Halsey calling to his assistance another of the magistrates of the county of Morris, do wait upon the said Peter Kimble and take his recognizance to appear at the next Court of General Quarter Sessions of the Peace, to be held for the said county, and in the mean time to be of good behaviour."

With the gradual approach of autumn, in the year of 1777, with its more bracing air, the smallpox epidemic, which for a period of nearly six months had raged uncontrolled among the inhabitants of Morristown, began to subside, and by September 1 had so far ceased from its ravages that all fear of its continuance had passed away.

That some of the sick and wounded soldiers of the departed American army were, however, still in Morristown, is evidenced by the following extract from the minutes of the trustees' book of the Presbyterian Church, under date of September 16, 1777:

> "Agreed that Mr. Conklin, Mr. Tuthill, Mr. Lindsly and Mr. Stiles, or any two of them, wait upon some of the Doctors of the Hospital in Morristown and apply for a resignation of the meeting-house. and if obtained, then to apply to the Commanding Officer at this post to remove the troops thence, and at their discretion to proceed further in cleansing and refitting the house for Public Worship and to make report of their progress in the premises at their next meeting."

There is considerable evidence, which will appear to the reader as he progresses, that the "Commanding Officer" at Morristown, at the period now passing under review, was none other than Colonel Benoni Hathaway. He seems to have had under his command at the time, a regiment of militia.

The first meeting of the New Jersey Council of Safety held in Morristown, in the year 1778, occurred on January 9. Of this meeting, however, there is no record, so far as the writer is aware. On January 17, at a meeting of the Council of Safety, held at the county seat of Morris, it was "agreed that Mr. Kinney (ex-Sheriff Thomas Kinney, probably) be allowed the sum of forty shillings for providing the Council of Safety with firewood, candles and so forth, while they sat at his house." If ex-Sheriff Thomas Kinney be the "Mr. Kinney" referred to in the above cited minute (and it is almost certain he is), then the meeting of the Council of Safety alluded to was perhaps held in the house now known as the "Dr. Lewis Condict place," situated nearly opposite the Lyceum, on South street, which, at the period under consideration, seems to have been owned and occupied by ex-Sheriff Kinney.

Students of State history are aware of the enactment, soon after the commencement of the Revolution, of a law fixing the prices at which certain specified commodities should be sold by those engaged in trade. By not a few of the good citizens of New Jersey this law was regarded as arbitrary and unjust, because, as they conceived, it was a plain violation of the natural law of trade, based upon the more fundamental principle of personal liberty. It is very evident to one who carefully reviews the matter, that only as a temporary expedient, "a war measure," we would now term it, was the law in question justifiable. The independence of character exhibited by some of the Morris County remonstrants against this law, is truly refreshing to contemplate, however one may be inclined to the opinion that they should have loyally acquiesced in its enforcement, as a temporary expedient.

The Council of Safety while in session at Morristown, in the year 1778, was called upon to deal with several cases of the violation of the law alluded to. For example it was:

> "Ordered that Benjamin Pitney be summoned to attend this board, on Tuesday morning next at 10 o'clock. * * * Agreed that his excellency draw upon Mr. Jonathan Ballwin for 500 pounds weight of bullets of different sizes, if so many can be spared, to make up the deficiency in lead to be run into bullets at this place."
>
> "On the twenty-seventh of January, in the year 1778, Benjamin Pitney being called before the board, and it being proved upon oath that he had spoken disrespectfully of an act of the Legislature lately passed for regulating the prices of produce, and so forth; agreed, that he be bound for his appearance at the next Court of General Quarter Sessions of the Peace for the County of Morris, which he accordingly was, with James Puff Locey, his surety, in £300 each. Agreed, further, that the said Pitney be fined £6.0.0 for the breach of the said law in selling shoes for more than the stipulated price, and also that he forfeit the sum of four dollars and a half, the price the said shoes were sold at."

If any reader of local history, not conversant with original sources of information, has ever doubted the oft-repeated statement of the meeting, during the Revolution, of the Council of Safety at the Presbyterian parsonage, he need doubt no longer; for at a meeting of the above mentioned body, held in Morristown, on the thirty-first day of January, in the year 1778, it was "Agreed that there be paid to the Rev. Mr. Jones for firewood and candles provided for the Council of

Safety, during their sitting at his house, the sum of £4.00."

In a communication from the Rev. Theodore L. Cuyler, D. D., published a few years since in the Christian Advocate, appear the words: "General Washington spent many an hour with my old ancestor (Rev. Timothy Johnes) in that house (the Presbyterian parsonage) while he was quartered in Morristown."

It was not alone with local matters that the Council of Safety was required to deal, for under date of February twenty-sixth, in the year 1778, the following minute of one of their meetings held at the county seat of Morris is recorded:

> "Four deserters from the British army were * * * brought before the board. Whereupon, Agreed that they be delivered over to the disposal of General Pulaski, and that they be allowed sixty dollars for four stand of arms brought with them from the enemy."

On the tenth of March, in the same year last mentioned,

> "Samuel Titus was called before the board, and it being proved that he had asked for five pounds of butter more than the law allows, agreed that he be fined the sum of £6.0.0 for the breach of the law in so doing and forfeit the sum of thirteen shillings and nine pence, the price asked for the butter aforesaid." "Agreed that Gerardus Duychinck for certain goods sold to Joseph Lindly, upon his own confession, incur the following fines and forfeitures, viz., etc."

Such is a portion of the minutes of the meeting of the Council of Safety, held in Morristown on the first day of May, in the year 1778. A list of the fines and forfeitures imposed upon Mr. Duyckinck is also annexed, the aggregate amount of which must have impressed this Morristown merchant with the fact of the unprofitableness of violating a law legally enacted and with public sentiment supporting it.

"Ordered that there be paid to Benoni Hathaway, for repairing carriages and moving field pieces by the order of the Council of Safety, the sum of £4.18.3."

In the light of the foregoing extract from the minutes of the body whose deliberations we are reviewing, it is evident that "bustling Benoni Hathaway" was a very useful man in the cause of freedom, at home no less than, as will in due time be seen, on the field of battle. That he was also a responsible man, the following minutes of the meeting of the same body held at Trenton on the seventeenth of March, in the year 1778, amply proves:

"Agreed that Colonel Hathaway receive from Mr. Ogden, at Boontown, the 20,000 flints sent or to be sent into this State, by Mr. Archibald Mercer, from Boston (first paying to Ogden at Boontown for the cartage) and to be accountable for them when properly called upon."

On the thirtieth day of April the Council of Safety was in session at Morristown again, and among the delicate matters disposed of was this:

"That Mrs. Esther Troup, the wife of John Troup, together with her child have leave to pass to her husband in the enemy's lines, upon condition that she do not return into this State during the present war, and that she take with her, her own and her child's wearing apparel."

Commencing with May 6, and closing with August 26, in the year 1778, the Council of Safety held no less than seven different meetings at Morristown. From the minutes of these meetings the following extracts arranged in chronological order, are presented:

"Agreed that there be paid to Captain John Lindley the sum of £7.10.6 for the amount of what he paid to Doctor Jones for the cure of a wound his son John received in the service."

"Agreed that Captain Arnold be allowed 40s. for the use of his room for the Council of Safety." So the New Jersey Council of Safety evidently sat within the walls of the famous Arnold Tavern.

"Agreed that Captain Morrison for enlisting as substitutes certain convicts whom he knew to have been before enlisted in their own right, be summoned to attend this board." In the light of this fact, which is only illustrative, how apt are the words: "Say not thou, What is the cause that the former days were better than these? for thou dost not enquire wisely concerning this."

"Agreed that Colonel Hathaway be desired to furnish a Sergeant and five men to guard a number of prisoners from this place to Gloucester, and that he direct them to draw rations where they can and keep a regular account of their expenses, to be laid before the Council of Safety on their return."

"Ordered that 15,000 of the Flints, now in the posession

of Major Kelsey, in Princeton, be sent for and lodged in the care of Colonel Hathaway at this place."

"Agreed that the Gaol Guard at Morristown be increased with twelve additional men, and that Colonel Hathaway be ordered to detach so many men from his regiment for that purpose."

"Agreed that Colonel Hathaway be authorized to deliver to General Winds, or his order, any number of the 15,000 flints belonging to this State and lately lodged in his hands by order of this board."

"July 13th, 1778, the Trustees (of the Presbyterian Church) met at Docr. Tuthill's; present, Mr. Conklin, Mr. Tuthill, Mr. Stiles, Mr. Lindsley, Mr. Mills and the President; agreed that Mr. Tuthill, Mr. Stiles and Mr. Mills be a committee to wait on Doct. Draper and inform him of the Law of this State Relative to Billeting of Soldiers, and that the committee or either of them be Impowered to prosecute such Person or Persons who may take possession of the meeting house or other property of the Trustees contrary to the said Law, and that they make report what they have done in the premise to this Board at their next meeting."

From the foregoing extract from the minutes of the Trustees' book of the Presbyterian Church of Morristown, it is a fair inference that while the members of the "Old First Church" were second to none in ardent patriotism, and in devotion to the cause of freedom, they were not unaware of their legal rights. While necessity required it, they were willing to worship God under the blue canopy; but when that necessity ceased they preferred using a house of worship with a shingled roof, and comfortable seats and protection from the elements.

Not alone from the minutes of the Council of Safety, held in Morristown, do we glean information concerning the affairs of the county seat of Morris during the years of 1777 and 1778. In the New Jersey Gazette, also, through the medium of advertisements and announcements therein appearing, is light thrown upon the condition of affairs in the patriot hamlet nestled among the hills of northern New Jersey. Under the date of February 21, in the year 1778, the following announcement appeared:

> "Any person properly recommended who understands the business of a riding-chair maker and would be willing to act in the capacity of a journeyman may meet with good encouragement by applying to Frederick King at the postoffice in Morris-Town, who carries on the business. Said King would also be willing to take a young lad of a good character as an apprentice."

Frederick King, who removed to Morris County from Long Island, in the year 1762, was the first postmaster of Morristown, his son Henry succeeding him in the office. Frederick King seems, from the press announcement just quoted, to have been postmaster at Morristown in the year 1778, although a local historian states that he was appointed to the office in the year 1782, by Postmaster-General Ebenezer Hazard. The building in which the postoffice was located stood about on the site of the present (1905) Methodist Episcopal Church.

As early as the year 1778, Morristown, with its population of about 250 souls, had two silversmiths, or jewelers, as they are now called. They were Cary Dunn and John Dickerson. The latter was the son of Captain Peter Dickerson, and the following advertisement, in the New Jersey Gazette, which appeared under date of August 24, in the year 1778, will prove of interest:

> "Any person that understands the silversmith's business, or that of repairing watches, and inclines to work journey-work at either. will find good encouragement by applying to John Dickerson, at Morris-Town."

The battle of Monmouth occurred on the twenty-eighth day of June, in the year 1778. Morristown was honorably represented in this battle of Moll Pitcher renown. An interesting reminder of this circumstance has survived in the form of the following announcement in the State press, under the date of July 24, of the year last mentioned:

> "Lost by Colonel Lindsley on the ground at Monmouth, in the action of the twenty-eighth of June, a light coloured bay mare, near 15 hands high, a small star in her forehead, three of her feet mostly white, paces and trots, is branded with a 9 on the left shoulder, shod all around, is 5 or 6 years old, has a bright eye and good courage. Whoever will deliver said mare to the subscriber living near Morristown, shall have twenty dollars reward and all reasonable charges paid by Eleazar Lindsley."

Eleazar Lindsley, of Morristown, was second major and lieutenant-colonel of the Eastern Batalion of Morris County. In the Continental line he was lieutenant-colonel of Spenser's regiment.

"Good encouragement will be given to any man who will hire as a journeyman for one, two, three or six months or a year. The person will be exempted from military duty. Enquire of Daniel Smith, saddler, Morris-Town," is another advertisement which appeared during the year 1778, as also the following:

"Strayed or stolen from the house of Captain Arnold in Morristown, on the 9th of August, a bay horse about 14 hands and an inch high, branded with W E on the near thigh about 12 or 13 years old, trots and paces a small travel. Whoever takes up said horse and brings him to Captain Arnold, in Morristown, or Israel Woodward living in Upper Freehold, Monmouth County, shall have twenty dollars reward, and reasonable charges."

During the same year, 1778, there appeared in the newspaper last mentioned, the following announcements and advertisements, the dates of which are omitted by the present writer:

"Bond and Pain, of Morristown, advertise a quantity of dry goods and a few barrels of brimstone for sale. Persons indebted to the estate of Dr. Bern Budd, of Morris County, are notified to pay up. Anthony L. Bleeker, of Morristown, notifies the public that he has indigo and Scotch snuff for sale, and John Van Court, of the same place, advertises a stolen horse. Ogden & Curtis, of Morristown, advertise a shop for the sale of dry goods, etc., next door to the Court House. Geradus Duyckinck, advertises a drug store in Morristown. We hear from Morristown that his Excellency, the Governor, upon intelligence that a number of people in Schooley's Mountain had enlisted in the enemy's service, had several of them apprehended and committed to gaol. At the funeral of the widow of the Rev. Azariah Horton, in Chatham, the Rev. Timothy Johnes, of Morristown, officiated, preaching the sermon. Inquisitions against the following persons in Morris County, who had absconded and gone over to the enemy, were published: Thos. Milledge, Wm. Demayne, Anthony Hollinshead, Stephen Skinner, Ashur Dunham, Ezekiel Beach, Adam Boyle, John Thorborn, Hugh Gain, Nicholas Hoffman, Joseph Conlife, John Stewart and John Throp. The publication is authorized by Alexander Carmichael, Commissioner. In the same paper, Aaron Kitchell, Commissioner, published the following additional list: Philip Van Cortlandt, Edward, Charles and Richard Bowlby, Jacob Hylor, Humphrey Devenport, William Howard, George Beaty, Thomas Huske, Lawrence Buskirk, Jacob Demarest, Samuel Ryerson, Isaac Hornbeck and Nicholas Vreeland. Stephenson & Canfield, advertise a store in Morristown, opposite Captain Peter Dickerson's. Mary Moore, of Morristown, advertises rock salt. Nathaniel Lewis, of the county seat, announces a horse strayed or stolen. Arnold, Kenny and Co., announce the opening of a store in Morristown, next door to Col. Henry Remsen's. Jacob Arnold offers for sale a farm between Mendham and Morristown. John Dickerson, offered a reward of $200 for the arrest of thieves who robbed his silversmith shop in Morristown."

Of one meeting of the New Jersey Council of Safety, it is highly desirable, owing to the intimate relation of a portion of its transactions to local interests, to speak particularly. This meeting was held at Springfield, about ten miles southeast of Morristown, on Wednesday, the seventh day of January, in the year 1778. There were present on this interesting occasion the following members: His excellency the Governor, Colonel Jacob Drake, Colonel Edward Fleming, Silas Condict, William P. Smith and Benjamin Manning. From the minutes of this meeting the following extract is presented:

> "Ordered, that in addition to the orders already given to Mr. Caldwell, with respect to the erection of Beacons for the purpose of alarming the county in the case of invasion, he be further desired to direct that one be set up at Morristown and another at Longhill, and one or two to the northward of New Ark, and that he be requested to appoint proper persons to take the care of and attend them and that the person so provided, shall be exempted, when known, from military duty."

As a proof of the fact that the orders of the Council of Safety promulgated at their meeting at Springfield, on the date above mentioned, were promptly executed; and as an illustration, also, of the enterprise of the New Jersey press of the Revolutionary period, the following extract from the New Jersey Gazette of January 28, in the year 1778, will be found of special interest:

> "That near Morris Town a beacon forty feet high has lately been erected in form of a block house (with a six-pounder on the top) filled with dry wood and other combustible stuff, for the purpose of catching fire soon, in order to the more quick discharge of the cannon, on the report of which, and the light from the building, the country is to take the alarm, and those who do not turn out may, by their laws, be instantly put to death by their next neighbor, and escape

with impunity. Buildings of a similar construction are also erected at Long Hill and on the heights at Bound Brook."

From a life-long resident of Morristown, the present writer learns that for many years he has understood from information derived from an aged person, that in Revolutionary days there was a beacon station on the summit of what is now popularly known as "Fort Nonsense." This is mentioned as a corroboration of the foregoing statement concerning the establishment of a beacon station in Morristown, during the Revolution.

Soon after the close of the Revolution, one Jonathan Ruchman, who had served in the State militia, made application for a pension, the grounds upon which his claims were based being that, as he personally testified, he had "performed one month's duty near Morristown, at Fort Nonsense, Captain Cory, in May (1778). Was very loth to go on account of planting corn. Before Monmouth battle." In view of the circumstance that during the Revolution the various companies of State militia were accustomed to render one month's service, alternately (as Ruchman's testimony implies), it is at least probable that other companies besides Captain Cory's performed their allotted month's service "near Morristown at Fort Nonsense" during the spring and summer of the year 1778.

"Lossing in his "Field Book of the American Revolution" says that while in Morristown, in the year 1848, he visited Fort Nonsense, where he saw the remains of what he terms "block houses;" and of "earthworks and ditches" also. The block houses of whose remains this famous author speaks were, as he surmises, large enough to accommodate a company of soldiers, and a company, as during the Revolution companies were composed, consisted of from fifteen to fifty men as circumstances required. Concerning the appearance of Fort Nonsense hill, in the year 1848, Lossing says: "The embankments and ditches, and the remains of the blockhouses of Fort Nonsense, are very prominent."

Only one or two men, as may be reasonably inferred from the order of the New Jersey Council of Safety with regard to the establishment of a signal station "near Morristown," were required to "take the care and attend" to said station. From the testimony of John Ruchman, just quoted, taken in conjunction with the statement of Lossing, the reader will do no violence to his reason, if he concludes, that there were on duty on Fort Nonsense hill, in the month of May, certainly of the year 1778, an entire company of militia, composed of from fifteen to fifty men. This company, say of twenty-five men, it is very evident, was not required at that point to attend to the signal station there established. What then was this company of State militia there for, except for the protection of the county seat of Morris against British attack, daily anticipated by the inhabitants? And if that were the object of the presence of this company of militia and probably of other companies, during the spring and summer of the year 1778, on Fort Nonsense hill, is it not a most natural conclusion that as a means of repelling the apprehended British attack, rude earthworks were thrown up either by Captain Cory's company, or by one of the other companies which seem to have "performed one month's duty" there?

On the northernmost and highest point of the mountain range terminating above and to the rear of the present Morris County Courthouse, at Morristown, may still (1905) be seen the gradually disappearing traces of what are generally conceded to have been earthworks, evidently "thrown up" or, more scientifically expressed, constructed, for military purposes. A picture of a section—the southwesterly—of these earthworks may be seen in this volume. The photograph from which the accompanying picture was made was taken at about 7 o'clock on the morning of May 8, of the present year.

Two theories as to the origin of the earthworks on Fort Nonsense hill are entertained. One is, briefly stated, that they were constructed during the second encampment of the American army in Morristown, by order of Washington, to divert the attention of his soldiers from the privations and sufferings and homesickness incident to that terrible winter. The other is, that they were constructed by the State militia during the spring and summer of the year 1778, for protection against anticipated British invasion of Morris County. The writer frankly confesses that he is inclined toward the acceptance of the latter theory; and this inclination is encouraged by facts already mentioned.

That Washington would have set his soldiers to work on the summit of the hill to the rear of the Morris County Courthouse, during one of the coldest winters ever experienced in this region, merely for their diversion, seems highly improbable. That these soldiers, half fed and poorly clad, could have survived the extreme rigors of that winter, had they been employed as above suggested, seems still more improbable; indeed, such a theory seems to border on the impossible. "Why," exclaimed a Morristonian not long since, as the popular theory concerning the origin of the earthworks on Fort Nonsense hill, was mentioned, "if Washington's soldiers had attempted to throw up earthworks on the summit of that hill in the winter of 1779-80, every rag of their scanty clothing would have been blown from their bodies."

The writer is of the opinion, however, that Fort Nonsense hill, with its rude fortifications thrown up probably by the State militia during the spring and summer of the year 1778, and its blockhouses erected probably at the same time, were utilized by Washington during the winter of 1779-80, perhaps as a picket-post, or a signal station, or both.

Mr. McClintock in "Topography of Washington's Camp of 1780 and its Neighborhood," says:

"The facts adduced (by himself) concerning the beacon station prove, however, that the supposed useless 'fort' was of genuine and constant service to the patriot cause, and furnish additional grounds for the respect paid to the spot by the monument and the annual salutes. Washington must certainly have made some use of it, if only because of the shelter afforded by the buildings. The extant records mention as having definite locations at or near Morristown, the provost guard' and the 'main guard,' the latter being the post of the detachments regularly sent from camp for picket duty in and around Morristown. Possibly one of these posts was located at Fort Nonsense."

> "Truth, in its own essence, cannot be
> But good."

"Camp Valley Forge, April 16th, 1778.

"Sir—I have desired the bearer, Lieut. Kinney, to call at Wick Hall and request Mrs. Wick to try if any of her keys will open my Father's under desk drawer but one, in order to get my Beaver hat Sold to Mr. Kinney, and to put some things in the drawer belonging to me which will be delivered by him.

"You doubtless expect to received a budget of news on the arrival of a letter from Camp, herein; at this time, however, you will be disappointed, for our Camp affords no news, and I do not expect anything extraordinary will be done till our reinforcements arrive. ,000 are expected next week from Virginia. As soon as they appear here, I expect the Jersey Brigade will be ordered to West Jersey. The Commissioners from ours and How's army met last week to settle a cartel for the exchange of Prisoners, but could not agree as the Enemy's Commissioners would not pledge the faith of the British nation for the faithful performance of the cartel but How's personal honor only, which by no means would answer, as How might be removed and then we might whistle for the performance of the exchange. This you may depend on that we have 1100 Prisoners besides Burgoyne's army more than they have, so that an exchange on their flimsy principles would never answer.

"As to our situation, etc., etc., Doct'r Leddel has seen, and I suppose already informed you of it, to whom, with his Family, I desire to be particularly remembered. You can show the Doctor my Letter, and at the same time I must desire he would write me word, as well how both your familys are, as how Politicks go on in your part of the country, and also how Independence (my horse I mean) comes on.

"I imagine you live quiet and peaceable to what you have done some time past. I reckon either you or Mrs. Wick would as soon part with your lives as to have another family as noisy as the one you was lately troubled with. However, be that as it will, I shall positively make Wick Hall my Headquarters, at any rate when I am so happy as to come into your corner of the globe, but when that will be God only knows; but if I am not killed or taken prisoner this campaign, I think it is very probable I shall have the pleasure of seeing you next Autumn.

"I have grown exceeding fat and hearty and am, I think, as well as ever, except my arm and fingers which have not yet recovered their perfect usefulness.

"Lieut. Kinney will satisfy you in any questions you

think proper to ask him about the Army and his Major.

"With my most respectful Complyments to Mrs. Wicks, Miss Tempe—Polly Wick, not forgetting little Polly, and due regards to Mrs. Spencer and her family when you have an opportunity of seeing them.

"Remain, Sir,

Your Most Obedt hble Servt.,

JOS. BLOOMFIELD."

Joseph Bloomfield, the writer of the above letter, was a major of Colonel Elias Dayton's Regiment, 3d Battalion (2d. Establishment) of New Jersey troops of the Continental Line. During the encampment of Washington's army in Morristown in the winter of the year 1777, Major Bloomfield was quartered in the family of Henry Wick. The above letter was addressed to "Mr. Henry Wick, at Wick Hall, Morris County. Favored by Lieut. Kinney." Lieut. John Kinney was Ensign, afterward Second Lieutenant of the second company of Colonel Dayton's regiment.

The following brief letter was written by Dr. Bloomfield, father of the major, and was directed to "Mr. Henry Wick, at Wick Hall, Morris Town:

"Sir—We are all well and desire to be remembered to you and Family. Let my Boy have 30 wt. of Pork. Be so kind as to take care of my Gemmons (his horse, probably). I congratulate you upon ye good news from France. We will flogg ye Rogues yet. I hope we have gone through the worst of it. I am Sr

Your humbl Servt

MOSES BLOOMFIELD.

"Princeton, May ye 7th, 1778."

Moses Bloomfield was a Surgeon in the Continental Army, and had evidently enjoyed the hospitality of Mr. Wick during the first encampment of Washington's army in Morris County. Major Joseph Bloomfield was Governor of New Jersey from the year 1801 till the year 1811.

CHAPTER XV

"Across the old Morris Green they march
  And take the 'mountain road'
To their winter quarters mid the hills
  And there make their abode.

"With beat of drums and flying flags
  And never-ending tramp
Of horse and man they pass to reach
  That bleak mid-winter camp."

Ballads of New Jersey in the Revolution.

OLLOWING the departure, in the month of May, of the year 1777, of the recuperated and inspirited American army from its comfortable winter quarters in Morristown and vicinity, event upon event, military and political, had successively crowded in the career of the newly cemented colonies. On the whole, these events had been positively favorable to the cause of freedom, and distinctly presaged its ultimate triumph upon the already consecrated soil of the Western Continent.

Passing over minor successes of, and not a few reverses to, the American arms, the surrender of the entire British army under Burgoyne at Saratoga, on the seventeenth day of October, in the year 1777, should be specially noted. The extreme privations and sufferings of the patriot army in its winter quarters at Valley Forge, were followed, in the subsequent February, by the acknowledgment on the part of France of the independence of the American colonies. An alliance between the two countries was also formed the sincerity of which was practically demonstrated by the dispatch, about the middle of the month of April, in the year 1778, of a French squadron to America, in command of Count D'Estaing. On the twenty-eighth day of June, in the year last mentioned, Washington, despite the peculiar odds against him, defeated the British army under Clinton at Monmouth, New Jersey, with great British losses in killed and wounded, augmented by many desertions from the enemy's ranks. D'Estaing failing to come to his support, General Sullivan alone repulsed the British force under General Pigot at Quaker Hill, Rhode Island, with a loss of over two hundred on either side. At Kettle Creek, Georgia, the Carolina militia, under Colonel Pickens, signally defeated a force of Tories in command of Colonel Boyd, the latter being among the slain. The capture, at midnight, on July 15, in the year 1779, of Stony Point, by "Mad Anthony" Wayne, sent a thrill of patriotic exultation through the colonies; and well it might, for with the loss in killed and wounded and prisoners on the part of the enemy, of more than six hundred, and of only fifteen killed and eighty-three wounded on the American side, this important strategic position had been recaptured, literally, at the point of the bayonet; that is to say, without the firing of a gun by Anthony's men.

Wayne's characteristic report of the victory, dispatched before daybreak of July 16, to the commander-in-chief, deserves mention; it was this:

> "The fort and garrison, with Colonel Johnson, are ours; our officers and men behaved like men who are determined to be free."
>
> "I do most sincerely declare that your assault on Stony Point is not only the most brilliant, in my opinion, throughout the whole course of the war, on either side, but that it is the most brilliant I am acquainted with in history,"

wrote General Charles Lee, to Wayne, after this memorable battle.

Less important, perhaps, from a strategical point of view, and yet a brilliant achievement, was the capture, on the nineteenth day of August, in the same year, of Paulus, New Jersey, by Major Henry Lee, with 150 of the British garrison as prisoners of war. Again was Sullivan successful, this time in western New York, in defeating a combined force of Indians and Tories at Chemung, on the twenty-ninth day of August, in the year 1779, and capturing immense quantities of much-needed corn. On the English coast, two British frigates, in the month of September of the last named year, surrendered to Paul Jones, whose remains, after more than a century's rest in French soil, thanks to the patriotic endeavors of a typical American are now interred in the soil of the land whose naval battles he helped to fight.

The following brief letter, introduced, by reason of its tardy discovery by the writer, somewhat out of chronological order, will, as he believes, be found of such particular interest as to justify its introduction at this stage of our story.

Dear Genl.

My best compliments waits on your Hounor Lets you know that I Cald at your Qutrs. last Evening but as your Hounor was Not at Home would Gladly have Cald this morning but my Horse is so Lame he Can hardly go. If aney thing Special Should be much Oblgd to your Hounor to Let me know it by a Line and I will attend imdtly.

I am Dear Sir your Most Obedient
and Humble Servt
ELEAZR LINDSLEY, Lt. Col.

Minnisink,
March 11th, 1779.
To Genl Hand.

With the close of the campaign of the year 1779, the solution of the perplexing problem of selecting winter quarters for the decimated and fatigued American army, was assigned to Washington's efficient quartermaster-General, Nathanael Greene. Late in the month of November of the year above mentioned, General Greene was in Morristown, with a view to the examination of grounds for the accommodation, in the approaching winter, of the patriot army. On the thirtieth day of the same month, and of the same year, General Greene wrote one of the New Jersey quartermasters that "we are yet like the wandering Jews in search of a Jerusalem, not having fixed upon a position for hutting the army."

It appears that Greene had previously suggested two positions to Washington, "the one near Aquacanock, the other near Mr. Kemble's" about four miles south of Morristown. On reaching Morristown, in the month of January, nearly two years previously, Washington had expressed his dissatisfaction with this locality as a position for winter quarters, in the following language, constituting a portion of one of his letters: "The situation (Morristown) is by no means favorable to our views, and as soon as the purposes are answered for which we came, I think to remove, though I confess I do not know how we shall procure covering for our men elsewhere."

From the following subsequent communication of Greene to the same State quartermaster, we learn that between the two positions for winter quarters suggested and described by the former to the commander-in-chief, Washington chose Morristown, although his quartermaster-general preferred Aquacanock.

"The general has fixed upon a place for hutting the army near Mr. Kimball's, within about four miles of this town.

His reasons for this choice are unnecessary to be explained, but, whatever they are, they will prove very distressing to the quartermaster's department. * * * I beg you will set every wheel in motion that will give dispatch to business."

If Washington had, at the opening of the year 1777, questioned the desirability of Morristown and vicinity as a suitable position for winter quarters, he was two years later in no doubt as to which of the two places suggested by his quartermaster-general, Aquacanock or Morristown, to fix upon as the resting place of his army during the winter of 1779-80. The marked demonstration he had received of the ardent patriotism, and of the devoted loyalty of Morris County, to the cause of freedom, during the first encampment of his army here, was alone sufficient to have settled in his mind the question as to which of the two positions named he should select. But to one who has carefully examined the positions of the camping grounds actually selected, there appears the following additional and scarcely less potent reasons for such selection. These camping grounds, which were sufficiently removed from the village to insure freedom from annoyance by the unrestrained portion of the soldiery, were yet near enough to general headquarters for the convenience of the commander-in-chief, and the subordinate officers who were required to be in daily communication with him. So far as protection from the severities of winter weather was concerned, finer positions for the encampment of the several brigades of the patriot army could not have been chosen. As a osition favorable for the repelling of attack by the nemy, even though with greatly preponderating numers, it could not have been surpassed by any locality n Morris County, nor in the entire State, for that natter. When to these considerations there are added he fact of the excellent facilities afforded for the prourement of water, one of the most indispensable reqisites of the camp, as well also as the excellent means f intercommunication between the eleven brigades of he American army, scattered as they were over an rea of several square miles the wisdom of the selecion finally made is most admirable to contemplate, nd exhibits military sagacity of the highest order.

The camping grounds, as already stated by the uartermaster-general, were "about four miles" from Iorristown, in a southwesterly direction. Access om the village of Morristown to the locality chosen as over the course of two roads, the Jockey Hollow oad, then commencing at the southwestern corner of he Green, and the Basking Ridge road, then comnencing a little southwest of the lower side of the reen. The latter road, was the one mostly used by he patriot army.

On the southeastern slope of Kemble's (Kimball, as ometimes spelled by General Greene) Mountain, hich strictly speaking, is the southwesterly portion of he mountain range terminating above and to the rear f the present Morris County Courthouse, Stark's briade was encamped. This camp faced the Basking idge road, and lay about two-thirds of the distance up, between the road and the summit of the mountain to the northwest. The huts composing Stark's encampment could be distinctly seen from the road below. The view from the site of Stark's brigade encampment must have been an inspiration even to cold and hungry men, especially as the spring of the year 1780 was seen approaching, with its signs of reviving nature. To the southwest as far as Bernardsville, to the northeast as far as Caldwell, and to the southeast for several miles the eye could reach, taking in with its enraptured survey, hill and valley and wooded and cleared lands, and constituting what is unsurpassed for beauty and grandeur and wide extent of varied country. The eye-witness of this magnificent scene has a feeling akin to that of the disciples of the inner circle, when they exclaimed: "Lord, it is good for us to be here; if thou wilt, let us make here three tabernacles: one for thee, and one for Moses, and one for Elias."

On the slope of the mountain mentioned, there now stands a monument marking the site of the camping ground of Stark's brigade of about (at its maximum strength) 800 men. On the bold front of this rugged monument (so strikingly symbolic of the character of the famous officer whose name it perpetuates) appears the following laconic inscription: "Stark's Brigade Occupied This Slope." By whom, and under what circumstances was this substantial monument erected, do our readers inquire? Following is the answer to such inquiry. The present owner of the land on which Stark's brigade was encamped in the Revolution, is

Emory McClintock, LL. D., who has a fine residence ı short distance to the northeast of the camping ;round. In the construction of the road now passing he Stark monument, it was necessary to disturb three ›iles of stones once included in the chimneys of Rev›lutionary soldier-huts. These stones, in accordance vith Mr. McClintock's instructions, were sacredly ;athered, and as sacredly built into the monument ıow marking the site of the encampment of the bri;ade of the New England general, who, on the eve ›f the battle of Bennington, fought on the sixteenth lay of August, in the year 1777, promised his men the ›lunder of the British camp. And, as he entered the ›attle next day, he exclaimed: "Now, my men! There ıre the redcoats! Before night they must be ours, or Molly Stark (his wife) will be a widow." Molly Stark, ıowever, was not made a widow; for "before night," he British were "ours." For his gallantry at Benıington, Congress made Stark a brigadier-general.

> "I needed a road at about that level, and laid it out :hrough the woods so as to disturb only three piles of chimıey stones—those, namely, which remained in rows where hey fell after serving in the hut-chimneys of the soldiers. All of the stones visible in the monument, except the one nscribed, came from those three piles, and all the stones in :he three piles form part of the monument,"

s Mr. McClintock's modest statement to the writer. Propriety forbids, for the present, the adequate ex›ression of the writer's admiration of the practical pariotism exhibited in the timely erection of the Stark monument, as a marker of the brigade encampment in the Revolution, of one of the most famous of its officers.

> "For as the light
> Not only serves to show, but render us
> Mutually profitable; so our lives,
> In acts exemplary, not only win
> Ourselves good names, but do to others give
> Matter for virtuous deeds, by which we live."

Fain would the writer linger much longer upon this phase of our story; but this would be to deprive other phases of the attention due them. Only this will be added to what has already been said: To the east of the Stark brigade encampment a short distance, was an excellent spring, still flowing, which furnished the soldiers with water, the spring having been enlarged by the sinking of a hogshead.

If ever the writer distinctly heard the voice of in-dwelling divinity saying to him, "Put off thy shoes from off thy feet, for the ground whereon thou standest is holy ground," it was when for the first time, a few weeks since, he looked upon the unmistakable traces, still visible, of several of the dug-outs on the mountain slope, about a hundred and fifty feet to the northeast of the Stark monument, marking the site of some of the rude huts occupied in the winter of 1779-80 by a portion of Stark's brigade. And scarcely less enthusiastic over this accidental "find" was William A. Dunn, the superintendent for a period of more than a quarter century of the Morris Aqueduct, who had previously pointed out to the writer the sacred spots.

Perhaps it should here be said that the parade ground of Stark's brigade was a somewhat level tract of land below the camping ground and between it and the Basking Ridge road. The following extract from a general order issued by Washington to his army during its encampment southwest of Morristown, will serve, among other purposes, as an indirect verification of the statement made in the present chapter concerning the traces of "dug-outs" on the mountain-side above the Basking Ridge road:

> "Where huts have been built on the declivity of Hills and are Sunk into the ground, particular care is to be taken to have the Snow removed and trenches dug Round to carry off the water, without which the Soldiers will sleep amidst Continual damps, and their Health will consequently be injured; this must be done Immediately."

This order was issued on the sixteenth day of February, in the year 1780.

A little more than half way (or about two and a half miles) from the Morristown Green, down the Jockey Hollow road, and on the left and in sight of the road, was the camping ground of Clinton's New York brigade. The camp seems to have run parallel to the Jockey Hollow road. The camping ground of this brigade may be more definitely located by the reader familiar with the neighborhood, if it be stated that its site is situated a little to the northeast of what has for many years been known as the "Tuttle House," owned at present by the Morris Aqueduct company. The level piece of ground just northeast, and in the front and rear of the "Tuttle House," seems to have been used as the parade ground of this brigade. The spring from which the soldiers of Clinton's brigade procured water for camp purposes, may still be located; it lies at the base of the hill on which the encampment was situated, and but a short distance to the rear, in a southeasterly direction. This spring is still (1905) partially open.

With regard to the camping ground of Clinton's brigade, a local author, who has made a special study of the subject, says:

> "In one way or another they made use of pretty much all the ground between the road and the hillside, which slopes down to the brook (the Primrose), but their huts were arranged in lines in view of and parallel to the road, not far from the edge of the hill, as is clearly noted in a contemporaneous map of the Wick farm now (1894) in the hands of Mr. (E. D.) Halsey. The New York huts and those used a year later by a body of troops from Pennsylvania happened to form part of a legal description and so came to be indicated on the farm map. Washington's own map, drawn by Erskine—no doubt less accurate—places the New York camp as a whole near the road. The southwestern end of it was on ground somewhat lower than the northeastern, and between that point and the road is a level field, which may well have served as the brigade parade, a word then used for what we now call parade-ground."

The Hon. Charles F. Axtell, a native, and a life-long

resident of Morristown, whose ancestor, Major Henry Axtell, rendered excellent service in the Revolution, has recently informed the writer that as a boy he spent many hours down the Jockey Hollow road, and thus became familiar with the historic Revolutionary grounds with which it abounds. "I have often seen a pile of stones, which I have always understood once composed the fireplaces and chimneys of soldier huts in the Revolution, lying just northeast of the "Tuttle House." When asked how far from the road this pile of hut chimney-stones lay, he replied: "O, about a stones-throw, and in a clump of bushes; I have played around it many an hour."

A monument to mark the site of this camping ground of the New York brigade? Alas! there is none, and the same must here be said of all the camping grounds of the eleven brigades of the patriot army, save that of Stark. The traces of these camp sites are rapidly becoming effaced, and if they are to be definitely located for the benefit of coming generations of freedom-loving Americans, the patriotic societies and public-spirited citizens of our great country should bestir themselves.

Still farther down the Jockey Hollow road, and off to the right about an eighth of a mile, approximately, and to the rear of what is still known as the "Groff house," on the hill, were the camping grounds of the two Pennsylvania brigades, the first brigade occupying the right, and the second brigade the left, of the encampment.

"The first brigade"—the writer now quotes from "Topography of Washington's Camp of 1780 and its Neighborhood," by Mr. McClintock—"had the ground between Sugar Loaf and the smaller hill west of it, and got its water from a spring northwest of Sugar Loaf, the water from which goes to join a brook which crosses the Mendham road on its way to the Whippany river. A by-road may still be traced upwards from the Mendham road near the brook, which would give access to the camp; and the Sugar Loaf road was no doubt also used. Either the by-road in question or the Sugar Loaf road must have been ascended from the Mendham road when Luzerne, the French minister, and a committee of Congress were escorted by Washington, with a brilliant cavalcade, to view the camps on April 25, 1780. The route announced from the Headquarters, by way of the Park of Artillery to the first of the camps to be visited, those of Pennsylvania, would naturally lead that way. The party came back to Morristown by way of Mr. Kemble's house and the Basking Ridge road. Washington's map indicates that the Pennsylvania lines of huts ran nearly north and south, inclining a little to the southeast. The camp of the second brigade lay south, a little southeast, of that of the first, the huts all having the same general alignment. If the map is correct, this brigade did not occupy the highest part of the ridge south of Sugar Loaf, but the sloping ground just west of the ridge."

It should be here remarked that the positions of the various brigades of Washington's army, as given in the present chapter, are those occupied by them on their arrival in Morris County, in the early part of the month of December in the year 1779. Later in the winter, some of the brigades changed their camp-grounds. Failure to recognize the fact just stated has ed, and is still likely to lead, to no little confusion regarding the position of some of the brigades of the patriot army during the winter of the years 1779-80. As an illustration of this statement, it may be said hat while upon the entrance of the American army ino the county of Morris at the opening of the above mentioned winter, the two Pennsylvania brigades established their camps in the position stated, one at least of these brigades, later in the same winter, occupied the vacated camp and huts of Hand's brigade of whose location mention will in due time be made. On at least one diagram of the camping grounds of the American army, to the south of Morristown, the Pennsylvania troops are represented as occupying a position at the southwestern corner of the Jockey Holow and Menham roads; whereas, in point of fact, this position was occupied by the Pennsylvania troops only fter its abandonment by Hand's brigade.

One of the most interesting and important features of the locality contiguous to the site of the Pennsylania encampment, is a clump of tall locust trees, covring a piece of ground about 25 by 150 feet in width nd length, respectively. If to any persons the markng of the sites of the various brigade camping rounds may at present seem impracticable, surely the rection of some suitable marker on the spot just alludd to, should receive prompt attention, for the reasons ollowing: In the vicinity of this clump of locust trees, he site of which, can still be definitely located, stood. n Revolutionary times, an hospital. A short distance to the westward of the locust grove just mentioned, may be seen an old apple tree, one among several in the same field. Under this tree, and to the southward, is the site of a spring; the spring itself, however, so far as external appearances indicate, having been obliterated, covered, indeed, in the processes of the Morris Aqueduct company in furnishing water to the growing population of Morristown and vicinity. Near this old apple tree and spring stood, in the winter of 1779-80, the division hospital of the Pennsylvania troops, and from the spring alluded to, then active, water was procured for the sick soldiers. It is the opinion of not a few persons that the old apple tree now marking the site of the Revolutionary hospital mentioned, was in its youth, and bore fruit while the Pennsylvania division were encamped in the locality a century and a quarter ago. In this hospital occurred numerous deaths during the eventful winter of 1779-80. The remains of these deceased American soldiers, at least 100, it is estimated, were interred in a double row of graves, running parallel to each other.

No mounds or other visible indication of these patriot graves now mark, or, perhaps, ever marked, the resting places of the men who sacrificed their lives in the cause of Freedom; and, except for the sacred thoughtfulness of a friend of the patriot dead, the present generation would perhaps be as totally unaware of the spot where they sleep as were the American people of the resting place of the remains, until very recently, of Paul Jones, who, like his compatriot naval officer in the Revolution, Captain Jeremiah O'Brien, "plowed the seas in search of the enemy, and hurled retaliation upon his head."

As a means of preventing in future years the desecration of the grounds holding the remains of those who now quietly sleep therein, some thoughtful person (John B. Wick, a collateral descendant of Henry Wick, the original proprietor of the Wick farm, it is said) planted in the early part of the nineteenth century, the young locusts, since grown to their present proportions. These noble locusts must, and will, in the due course of nature, disappear, leaving the resting places of our patriot dead there interred, unknown and unrecognized by succeeding generations. A granite monument bearing a suitable inscription, and including a just tribute to the planter of the perishing locusts, should be erected without delay. And if the piece of ground holding the remains of those who perished for their country were purchased, with right of way to and from the same, the commemorative deed suggested would be complete.

The failure of the Hon. Samuel B. Axtell, (a native of Morristown), Representative in Congress, at the time, from San Francisco, to secure the passage of a bill by him introduced, providing for an appropriation by the General Government, for the erection of a suitable monument to mark the resting place of the patriot dead who lie near the site of the Pennsylvania encampment, should not prevent a second attempt to rouse the slumbering sentiment of Congress to the passage of a bill having for its object the same commendable work.

As the writer, a few weeks since, in company with the long-time superintendent of the Morris Aqueduct, who, as might be expected, is thoroughly familiar with the grounds, passed over the roadway through the now dense woods, once pressed by the feet of the patriot soldiers of 1779-80, in their passage to and from the Pennsylvania camps to the main road, his kindled imagination again peopled those woods with the living forms of the men long since gone to their reward. And even as he writes these lines he can almost hear the rustling of the leaves beneath the feet of the soldiers far from home and loved ones, engaged in the unequal, but eventually successful, struggle for American independence as they wended their way to and from camp.

Returning to the Jockey Hollow road, and continuing southwestward a short distance, there may be seen on either side of, and from the road, the sites of the camping grounds of the First and Second Maryland brigades, the former on the right and the latter on the left of the road. The First Maryland Brigade was encamped on the slope of a hill facing southeast. This slope is now partially covered with stunted cedar trees. On the westerly side of the Morris Acqueduct reservoir about eastward of the camp site, was the spring, not now to be seen, however, which furnished the First Maryland Brigade with water. The site of the spring, as the writer is informed by one who saw it before its obliteration, is now marked by a certain patch of particularly green grass growing on the side of the reservoir cobblestone embankment. Nearly opposite, and on the other side of the Jockey Hollow road, and extending up the hill toward what is known as the "Harvey Loree Place," was the camping ground of the Second Maryland Brigade, which faced northwestward, but which was, however, protected from the winds by the hills and woods just beyond.

At the southeast side of a piece of meadow land, and on the edge of a piece of woods, and just behind a rude rail fence, may still (1905) be seen the remains of a stone oven, used probably by both of the Maryland brigades for bread baking purposes. The ruins mentioned consist of a circular heap of stones, which indicate that the once round oven collaped, by reason of its own weight, inward, which explains the fact just stated, that the heap of stones is circular in form. An examination of the stones shows the marks of contact with fire and smoke in the process of baking. This oven was, of course, duplicated and reduplicated, all over the various camping grounds ocupiced by the American army during the winter of 1779-80, so that to see the ruins of one is to see the ruins of the many still visible, or certainly, until quite recently, visible at various points.

Leaving unmentioned, for the present at least, a spot of great historic interest on the left, as we proceed down the Jockey Hollow road toward the Mendham road (the road running from the Basking Ridge road to the southeast, toward Mendham off to the northwestward), we reach the camping ground of Hand's Brigade, said to have been the smallest, numerically, in the patriot army at the period under consideration. This camping ground was on the slope, and extending up toward the summit of a hill facing the southwest, toward the Mendham road; its side, however, running along and parallel to the southeastern side of the Jockey Hollow road. The camp faced the Mendham road. A row of stones now lying in extended heaps along the road last mentioned, were undoubtedly utilized for some purpose by Hand's Brigade while encamped on these grounds. Rev. Dr. Joseph F. Tuttle says they were used in "the hut fireplaces and were drawn off to clear the ground for plowing" the side hill.

Up the hill slope to the northeastward of the Mendham road, a level piece of ground at the summit was cleared by the troops for the free movements of light artillery which was planted there for use in case of attack by the enemy; for from the summit of this hill, known as "Fort Hill," cannon could sweep the entire face of the surrounding locality. Two or three lines of fortifications, partly of stones and partly of logs and brushwood, were also thrown up on the summit of "Fort Hill." Traces of the former may still be seen by the careful observer.

The spring which supplied Hand's Brigade with water was on the opposite side of the Mendham road from camp

The road leading from the corner of the Jockey Hollow and Mendham roads toward the Basking Ridge road, was in Revolutionary times nearly straight in its course. The present road, however, is somewhat circuitous. Down the straight road of the Revolutionary period toward the Basking Ridge road, about half the distance, and off a little to the left, or northeast, the camping grounds of the First and Second Connecticut brigades were established. These camp grounds lay on the slope of Fort Hill; the camp of the First Connecticut brigade on the right, facing southeast, and that of the Second brigade on the left facing east. The location chosen was an almost ideal one. It was the writer's rare privilege to go over these camp grounds for the first time not long since, with one who has made a special study of the topography of Washington's camp grounds of 1779-80. The numerous heaps of hut-chimney stones, some of which lie just where they fell with the collapse of the log-huts they once made comfortable, mark with almost startling definiteness the camp-streets, once alive with the presence of the brave men who helped to achieve the independence of the American colonies. Several times during the above mentioned morning tramp over these camp grounds, did the alert guide turn to the writer, and exclaim with evident enthusiasm: "Here was a camp-street;" and the distinct alignment of the hut-chimney stones to be seen, evidently undisturbed since they fell in heaps, was a sufficient corroboration of the opinion expressed.

A large, circular heap of stones, not a few of which still show the effects of fire, was, as guide and writer agreed, the ruins of a bake oven, similar to those on the Jockey Hollow road, already spoken of

Than the camping grounds of the two Connecticut brigades none are more distinctly marked; and a personal examination, by the lover of Revolutionary history, of no other camp of the patriot army during the winter of 1779-80, furnishes greater satisfaction than those on the easterly and southeasterly slope of Fort Hill. Twice, since his initial visit to the camping grounds of the Connecticut brigades, has the writer, with growing interest and with fresh discoveries, gone over these grounds.

To locate the camping ground of the New Jersey brigade, in which many of our readers will be specially interested, we must retrace our steps, going to the northwestward along the Mendham road until we reach what is now, and what was even in Revolutionary time, known as the Wick House. The relation of the history of this very interesting house must be deferred until a later stage of our story. Off to the southwest, across the Mendham road and over fields lying beyond it a short distance, the New Jersey troops were encamped on either side of a small brook, which, to the southeast, ran into a larger one.

Thanks to the Rev. Dr. Joseph F. Tuttle; to his worthy successor, as a county historian, the late Hon. Edmund D. Halsey, and to the more recent investigator, Emory McClintock, LL.D. (whose "Topography

Washington's Camp of 1780 and Its Neighborhood" ›ntains the results of his careful investigations), the te of the camping grounds of the New Jersey brigade definitely located.

From the Cook spring, so-called, situated somewhat the northwest of the camping grounds, the New ersey soldiers procured water for brigade purposes. he brigade parade ground seems to have been on the ›rtheastern side of the brook running through the mp, comprising an almost circular piece of cleared nd.

In the spring of the year 1905, the writer, in comny with the Rev. Joseph F. Tuttle, D. D., LL.D., sited, for the first time, the site of the camping ounds of the New Jersey brigade during the winter 1779-80. Lest the reader infer from the foregoing atement that the writer is a victim of what many gard as the modern delusion of spiritualism, an exanation may be desirable; this he proceeds to give. he results of Dr. Tuttle's examination of the camping ounds of the New Jersey brigade, made in the year 352, are extant in the form of a somewhat lengthy ticle, to be found among the collections of the New ersey Historical Society. With increasing interest e writer had read and re-read this article, until the sire to verify, by a personal visit, Dr. Tuttle's excelnt description of the grounds in question, fruited in e resolution to do so. Starting early on a beautiful ay morning of the year above mentioned, with two ell-filled kodaks, a carefully prepared lunch and a bound copy of the New Jersey Historical Collections containing Dr. Tuttle's article, the writer, thanks to his favorite exploring horse, "Prince," from the stable of Charles H. McCollum, of Morristown, found himself in about an half hour's time at the famous Wick House. Leaving his conveyance at the place mentioned he set out with kodaks and lunch basket and the book alluded to, the latter under his arm, for what had to him come to seem like enchanted ground. With great difficulty, by the aid of a "big stick" employed to beat down the heavy growth of bushes, of which a liberal share were blackberry, he forced his way across the intervening meadow, through which ran the brook on either side of which Maxwell's Jersey soldiers built their huts in the winter of 1779-80. It seemed at times, so stubbornly did the blackberry bushes resist his advance, as if, like the man in the Nursery Rhymes, he would scratch out his eyes and then scratch them in again. But the objective—the slope of Blachly's hill—must be reached at all hazards; and, not to weary the reader with further reference to the obstacles surmounted, the writer, with Dr. Tuttle at his side, reached the westerly side of the piece of meadow, weary and hand-sore and hungry; but exultant. It was then near noon by the watch, and fully so, judging from gastronomical intimations. Selecting for table and chair a pile of hut-chimney stones he had eagerly sought and rejoicingly found, the writer thoughtfully partook of his lunch, with a relish such as only a genuinely hungry man experiences. As he sat there alone upon the grounds occupied, a century and a quarter ago, by men engaged in the struggle for national independence, and re-read the article of Dr. Tuttle to assist him in "getting his bearings," it seemed, at least in the realm of an awakened imagination, as if the place was once more peopled with the patriot soldiers, the remains of whose temporary habitations in the winter of 1779-80, lay all about, as almost speaking witnesses to their former presence. But of the strange workings of the writer's imagination on the occasion alluded to, he can only say, with another: "What I can fancy, but can ne'er express."

Lunch completed, and the grounds carefully examined for purposes of verification, the writer set out for Blachly's hill. Here again imagination was active, as pile after pile of hut-chimney stones, some of them apparently undisturbed since they fell with the collapse of the hut in which they had been built by patriot hands. On the slope of the hill and about one-third the distance up from its base, could be distinctly traced the former alignment of the huts which once sheltered living soldiers. Of the resuult of his examination of the camp-site of Maxwell's Jersey brigade, the writer can only say, that even after careful reading of Dr. Tuttle's excellent description of these grounds, "the half has never been told." Since that first visit in the month of May, 1905, the writer has twice gone over the grounds, each time making new discoveries indicating the presence of the patriot soldiers of 1779-80. Some of the results of these visits may be seen, by the reader, within the covers of this volume. Freedom-loving Morristonians could scarcely render a more patriotic service, to the rising generation particularly, than by organizing occasional local pilgrimages to some of the historic grounds "down the Jockey Hollow road," for the Fourth of July, including the Jersey camp-site of the winter of 1779-80. With a good band to discourse national airs, an historical address by some person acquainted with local annals, the reading of the Declaration of Independence by other than a political aspirant, the Day set apart for the celebration of the anniversary of our national independence would be much more suitably and profitably spent, than by a vain attempt, through politico-patriotic celebrations, concocted in a corner, to gather the people and galvanize them into a patriotic frame of mind. Such attempts can but remind a thoughtful American citizen of the words of Lincoln, of which the following is a substantial quotation: "You can fool all the people part of the time, and you can fool some people all the time, but you cannot fool all the people all the time."

"Then none was for a party;
  Then all were for the State;
Then the great men help'd the poor,
  And the poor men lov'd the great;

"Then lands were fairly portion'd;
  Then spoils were fairly sold;
The Romans were like brothers
  In the brave days of old."

Early in the year 1780 the New Jersey brigade removed to the vacated quarters on the Jockey Hollow road of the Maryland brigades, which had been ordered to march to the southward. The excellent diagram. showing not only the relative positions of the ten brigades of the American army during the winter of 1779-80, but the location of several Revolutionary houses and other points of great historic interest, is, by permission of Emory McClintock, LL.D., published in connection with the present chapter. To one unacquainted with the latest conclusions concerning the sites of the camping grounds of 1779-80, this diagram, as a guide, is simply invaluable, and when consulted in connection with the most admirable "Topography of Washington's Camp of 1780 and Its Neighborhood," by the same authority, it becomes luminous with reflected information concerning the locations of historic buildings and spots now justly famous in Revolutionary annals.

CHAPTER XVI.

"Ev'n to the dullest peasant standing by
Who fasten'd still on him a wondering eye
He seem'd the master spirit of the land."

ASHINGTON'S army, during its second encampment in Morristown and vicinity in the winter of 1779-80, included, in addition to the ten brigades of infantry, the locations of whose camps were given in the previous chapter, a brigade of artillery in command of General Henry Knox, one of the most brilliant officers in the Continental army.

Knox's artillery brigade was encamped about half a mile to the northwest, by direct line, from the Morristown Green, on the road then and now leading toward Mendham, and was composed of three regiments of artillery and a regiment of artificers, the latter in command of an officer named Baldwin. In addition to the light mounted field pieces composing the various batteries of his brigade, General Knox had in charge several heavier guns designed for siege purposes. As may be inferred from the fact of a regiment of artificers, or mechanics, there were in the artillery camp several forges and machine shops for the repair of disabled guns. The encampment of Knox's brigade was spoken of in the military parlance of the day as the "Park of Artillery."

On the slope of the hill, on the right as one goes toward Mendham from Morristown, and commencing at the point where the road turns abruptly to the left (this point being the terminus of the present Washington street, and the beginning of the Mendham road), and extending nearly a third of a mile parallel to the road, is the site of Knox's brigade encampment. One of Morristown's lawyers recently informed the writer that when a boy he frequently heard his father (a Revolutionary descendant), who resided near the site of the camping grounds, speak of the hill slope in question as "the park." From this same well-known lawyer it was ascertained that during his early years, bayonets, firelocks and other evidences of the years of "mad war" were found on "the park," probably on or near the sites of some of the field forges or machine shops of the brigade artificers alluded to.

To the south of the brigade camp grounds, and on the opposite side of the road, were two pieces of level ground, then in grass, where, in the spring of the year 1780, the artillery horses were turned to graze. It is probable that the tract of land, until recently dammed and covered by "Burnham's Pond," was a portion of the meadow land used as a parade ground by the artillery of Knox's brigade. A resident of Morristown, whose fondness for nature is a conspicuous trait, says: "I have picked daisies and buttercups on the meadow once, and, until quite recently, covered by 'Burnham's Pond.'" This pond, as already suggested, has been drained, and the land will once more become meadow. Whether this is in line of progression or retrogression is a debatable question.

General Knox's quarters were a short distance to the westward of the brigade encampment, in a farmhouse, a portion of which, at least, still survives as part of a modern residence, to be seen from the Mendham road. It will doubtless be interesting, more particularly to local readers of our story, to know that access to the "Park of Artillery" was chiefly, so far as foot travelers during the Revolutionary period were concerned, across intervening fields, then included in one or more farms, Washington street not then having been opened up. Mounted travelers, and travelers in the primitive vehicles of that day, could reach the "Park of Artillery," from the Morristown Green, by way of "town hill," thence up the present Spring street hill, sometimes called Sander's hill, into the present Early street, and through its former extension into what is now known as the Mendham road, all of which route, from the foot of Spring street, was, in Revolutionary days, known as the Mendham road.

The attention of the reader has already been directed to the fact that each brigade of the American army encamped in Morristown had its own parade ground, frequently in front of the respective camps. Indeed, this was the case whenever the formation of the adjacent grounds permitted. Then, for the use of the entire army, there was what has been termed the "grand parade," which was situated on the right of the Jockey Hollow road, as one goes from the Morristown Green toward the Mendham road, and within about one and one-half miles from the latter. On the "grand parade" the daily guard mountings for the army took place; the various detachments for the daily relief of the outposts, picket posts and hospital guards here rendezvoused, and here, also, military executions were performed, sometimes in the presence of the entire army, the graves of the condemned soldiers having been previously dug at the foot of the gallows.

On the southeastern slope of Sugar Loaf hill, which lies just off the Jockey Hollow road to the right as one goes from Morristown, and about three miles from the last named place, there stood, during the winter of 1779-80, a log building. This building was used by the Pennsylvania division for courts martial; and it may also have served as a guard house. From an order book kept by Colonel Francis Johnston, of the Second Pennsylvania regiment, commander of the Pennsylvania division, from February tenth, of the year 1780, until April twenty-ninth of the same year, it is ascertained that among the military trials conducted during the period referred to, which were probably held in the log building mentioned, were the following:

"On the eighteenth of February, Sergeant Mitchell, of the ninth Pennsylvania regiment, was tried and convicted for concealing stolen goods, and was sentenced to receive 100 lashes 'on his bare back well laid on.' James Hammel and Samuel Crawford, of the fifth Pennsylvania regiment, were tried on 'suspicion of robbery and found guilty of the charge.' They were sentenced to be hung on the next day, between the hours of three and four o'clock in the afternoon, on the grand parade. It was ordered that the officers of the day attend the executions; and that the corps of artillery (Knox's) 'will send a band of music to attend ye criminals to the place of execution.' The Pennsylvania Division was ordered to furnish an escort of officers, two drums and fifes and fifty privates; and each of the other divisions was to furnish two hundred men. The corps of artillery was to furnish one hundred men, properly officered. Hammel was executed; but Crawford, as the following order from Headquarters shows, was pardoned by Washington. 'The Commander-in-Chief is Pleased to remit the Sentence against Samuel Crawford. The frequent occasion the General takes to Pardon where strict Justice would compel him to Punish ought to operate in ye minds of Offenders to the Improvement of their morals.' "

"For attempting to force a falsehood on Colonel Craig, of the Pennsylvania division, respecting his attendance on the regimental parade, Lieutenant John Armstrong was tried by court-martial. He was found guilty and discharged from the service. Washington, however, restored Armstrong to his former rank and command, saying: 'From the general good character of Lieut. Armstrong he hopes what he was charged with proceeded rather from a want of Recollection than any ill design ' Incidentally it may be said that among the entries in the order book of Colonel Francis Johnston, is the following: 'On February twenty-third (1780), Colonel Craig loses a silver epaulet in the rear of the Pennsylvania encampment, and offers a reward of thirty dollars.'

"On the sixteenth of March, of the year 1780, Washington issued a general order concerning the observance of St. Patrick's Day in the army. On the next morning the following division orders were issued by Colonel Francis Johnston: 'March 17, 1780. The commanding officer desirous that the Celebration of the day should not Pass by without having a little Rum issued to the Troops, had thought proper to direct Commissary Night to send for a Hogshead which the Colonel has purchased for this Express purpose in the Vicinity of Camp. While the Troops are celebrating the anniversary of St. Patrick in Innocent Mirth and Pastime he hopes they will not forget our worthy friends in the Kingdom of Ireland, who, with the greatest unanimity, have stepped forth in Opposition to the Tyranny of Great Brittain, and who like Us, are determined to be Free. The Colonel expects the Troops will conduct themselves with the greatest sobriety and good order.'

The courts-martial general of the American army during its encampment in Morristown in the winter of 1779-80, were held at several different places, among which were Dickerson's Tavern, and the residence of Quartermaster General Joseph Lewis, on Morris street; and the log building on the slope of Sugar Loaf may also have been used for this purpose. In the early part of the month of February in the year 1780, one John Beaty, esq'r., "commissary of prisoners," was tried by general court martial on a charge of "improper intercourse with the City of New York," in having written there for and introduced sundry articles from thence contrary to the resolve of Congress. Beaty was found guilty. Washington in speaking of Beaty's offense, says: "The General thinks Mr. Beaty's Conduct in this Instance exceedingly reprehensible; in his situation he ought to have observed a peculiar Delicacy; the whole tenor of the Evidence Introduced by himself show that he was well aware of the Impropriety of the Intercourse, & though he may have generally discountenanced it, it is not an excuse from the present deviation, etc., etc." Mr. Beaty was, however, released from arrest. Lieutenant Porter, of the seventh Maryland regiment, who at the same time and place was tried for "unofficer, unsoldier, & vilainous Conduct on Staten Island, Robbing & plundering a Woman of Money," was summarily cashiered. At the intercesion of officers of the third New York regiment, Edward Burk was pardoned by Washington, the Commander-in-Chief taking occasion to say: "The case of Burk ought to be a Striking example to the Soldiery of the dangerous Excesses and Fatal Consequences to which the pernicious Crime of Drunkenness will frequently betray them."

By no means the least interesting bits of information to be gleaned from the order book of Colonel Johnston, are the following: On the sixth of March a corporal and four privates were sent to build an oven for "Mr. Ludwick the baker in Morristown." Two men were also sent to " Mr. Gamble's in Morristown" to assist in securing hides and tallow. On the fifteenth of March a sum of money, "less than 500 dollars, was found between Headquarters and the Church in Morristown."

On the twenty-second of March Lientenant-Colonel Howard was tried by court-martial, on the charge of not parading with his battalion, not having it in a state fit for action, and kindred breaches of discipline. The court condemned him; but the Commander-in-Chief came to the rescue, and after extenuating the officer's alleged misdemeanors, dissolved the court-martial. Among the causes cited by Washington for excusing Colonel Howard was "the extream severity of the weather at that period, * * * while the men were walking to keep themselves warm." It was on the twenty-third of March that Major Moore was tried by court-martial on several charges, of which the fifth was that of "speaking in a very dishonorable and disrespectful manner of his Excellency, the Commander-in-Chief, and Generals of the Army." The court, however, "fully and clearly" acquitted Major

Moore of the charge above specified. In commenting on the sentence of the court-martial Washington said he was happy in the acquittal of this officer on the fifth charge, which he was "sorry was ever made a matter of Publick discussion."

For sending out two sleighs and horses with John Van-Winkle and others to bring back some ladies from "Bergen Town," Lieutenant-Colonel Hay was sentenced by court-martial to be reprimanded in general orders. He was released from arrest by Washington, with the following comments: "Lieut. Col. Hay, not having the command on the lines in the quarter where he was, had no right to grant the permit he did, as Bergen Town was out of our lines, and within, or very contiguous to, those of the enemy. At the same time the General is Perfectly satisfied that in doing it, he was actuated merely by humane & benevolent motives, to facilitate the return home of two Ladies on their way from New York, where they had been permitted to go, & who, it appears, required assistance."

On the twenty-fourth of March, the officer commanding on the lines was directed in case of any "sudden & serious movement of the enemy in that quarter to Cause the Alarm Gun on the Height above Springfield to be fired, to be answered by the alarm guns in camp upon which the brigades are to form on their respective parades."

On March thirty-first, Ensign Spear was discharged from the service for disorderly conduct in a "publick house." "The General confirms the sentence against Ensign Spear because there was a Shameful combination of a number against a Single Person who seems to have given no provocation."

Thomas Brown, of the second New Jersey regiment, was charged with desertion. By a division court-martial convened by order of Major General Lord Sterling, Brown was declared guilty; and the court upon ascertaining that he was an old offender, having repeatedly deserted, "do unanimously sentence him to be hanged by ye neck till dead, & the commander-in-chief approves the sentence."

"Sobriety, Fidelity and a good temper are essentially necessary, as are cleanliness, genteel shape & small Size," were the qualifications mentioned by General Maxwell, in his announcement for "a servant understanding the care and management of horses."

Charged with saying he was sick, when he was only indisposed; and with attending a "Morristown ball" without leave, Lieutenant Hoops was tried by court-martial, and honorably acquitted.

General Irvine informed the troops in April that the "Honorable House of Assembly in Philadelphia had voted each officer and soldier at the expiration of the service certain quantities of land, free of taxes. The allotment was as follows: "A Major General, 2,000 acres; A Brigadier, 1,500; A Colonel, 1,000;" and so on down to the privates who were to receive 200 acres each.

On the twenty-fifth of April Washington issued the following message to the troops: "The commander-in-chief at the request of the minister of France has the pleasure to inform Major General the Baron Steuben & the officers & men of the four battalions that the appearance & manoeuvres of the troops yesterday met his entire approbation & afforded him the highest satisfaction." In the general orders from Headquarters of the twenty-sixth of the same month, appear the following words: "His excellency the minister of France was pleased to express in the warmest terms his approbation of the Troops in the review of yesterday. Applause so honorable cannot but prove a new motive to the emulous exertions of the army."

On the twenty-seventh of April, Augustine Washington was made an ensign in the second Virginia regiment, and he was to do duty in the commander-in-chief's guard "till further orders."

It is possible that the entries in the order book of Colonel

Johnston, from which the foregoing extracts and information are taken, were made at the Headquarters, and at the "small, ink-stained stand which bears the name of Gen. Washington's dispatch table."

Almost startlingly interesting is the fact, that upon "these ancient and blotted relics" of the Revolution—Colonel Johnston's order book— appear the names of Colonels William DeHart, Elias Dayton, Jacob Ford, Livingston, Ogden—"with Fullerton, Craig, Lyttle, Kinney, Kline, and the commanding officers Clinton, Stark, Sterling, Maxwell and the rest."

The officers of the patriot army, many of them at least, including even regimental and company commanders, instead of sharing quarters with the rank and file, sought more comfortable accommodations in the farmhouses surrounding the camps. As a means of protection against marauding by the soldiers, the presence of these officers was welcomed by the families in which they found a home.

The soldiers of the patriot army were quartered, after temporary use of tents immediately following their arrival in camp, in huts, those of the officers each accommodating three or four persons, while those of the rank and file accommodated ten or more soldiers each. In accordance with the orders of the commander-in-chief through Quartermaster-General Greene, the huts were of uniform construction and size, and were arranged in rows with the exactness of a well-laid-out modern city. At one end of the huts was a plastered wood chimney with spacious stone fireplace, and at the other end were bunks. In some of these huts there were apologies for windows, and in all of them facilities for ventilation. As illustrative of the extreme care of Washington for the health and comfort of his soldiers, it may be said that in his instructions for the erection of their winter quarters he explicitly ordered that "any hut not exactly conformable to the plan or the least out of the line shall be pulled down and built again." It is a most interesting circumstance, and one that merits mention, that the huts in question were constructed without the use of nails, and probably without the use of hammers, axes being about the only tool required. Mention of the fact should not be omitted that most, if not, indeed, all, the brigade camps of the American army were established upon grounds covered with trees, which were expeditiously cleared away to make room for the huts which were to furnish shelter through what proved to be one of the severest winters, as regards both the temperature which prevailed and the immense quantity of snow, ever experienced in this region.

The statement concerning the locations of the quarters of the various brigade commanders and other general officers of the patriot army would make a most interesting feature of our story, but these, with few exceptions, it is impossible at present to give. Of the locale of the quarters of General William Irvine, however, during the first months at least of the encampment of Washington's army in Morristown, it is gratifying to be able to speak with some degree of certainty. Standing on the northeasterly corner of what is known as the Bailey Hollow road, about one and a half miles down the Jockey Hollow road from the Morristown Green, there was, in the year 1780, a house owned by Captain Augustine Baily (sometimes spelled Bayles). This house, only the site of which is now (1905) to be seen, was the quarters of Irvine, one of Washington's most trusted officers.

It was probably as commander of the Second Brigade of Pennsylvania troops during the winter of 1779-80 that he established his quarters in the Bailey house on the Jockey Hollow road. A cannon ball, picked up recently on the site of his quarters on the Jockey Hollow road, was on exhibition with other Revolutionary relics in the window of a young Morristown jeweler on the Fourth of July, in the year 1904.

Of the quarters of General Anthony Wayne, mention will in due course be made. Arnold's tavern, in the village of Morristown, was doubtless the temporary home of not a few of the American general officers during the second encampment of the army there, and other officers and soldiers seem to have been quartered in the building on the south side of the Green, known as the "Continental House," then used as a storehouse for government supplies. The quarters of the surgeon-general of Washington's army, Dr. John Cochran, was in the house of Dr. Jabez Campfield, on the road leading toward Whippany, on what is now the corner of Morris street and Oliphant lane. Of this famous house more will be said in due time.

On the arrival of Washington in Morristown, in the

early part of the month of December, in the year 1779, he established his headquarters in what was then known as the "Ford Mansion," situated on the road leading to Whippany, and about a mile eastward of the village Green. The "Ford Mansion" was then owned and occupied by Theodosia, widow of Colonel Jacob Ford, Jr., deceased, since the beginning of the year 1777, and her children. In the issue of The New Jersey Gazette of December 13, a few days only after the arrival of the patriot army in Morristown, there appeared the announcement: "We understand that the Head-Quarters of the American Army is established at Morris-Town, in the Vicinity of which the troops are now hutting."

Washington's body guard, called also his life guard, comprising (at their maximum) about 250 picked men from different regiments of the Continental army, established their camp about 400 feet, approximately, to the southeast of the headquarters of the commander-in-chief, at what is now the fork of Morris and Washington avenues. As early as about the middle of December, after Washington's arrival (on the first), a row of about a dozen huts had been erected for the accommodation of the life guard. Each hut contained about eighteen men, the apparent discrepancy between the number of the life guard and the hut accommodations being explained by the fact that some of the men were always on furlough or in the hospital. To the southeast somewhat and in what is now the beginning of Washington avenue, were probably located the officers' quarters, including those of the officer in command of the life guard, who was Major Caleb Gibbs.

"The Commander-in-Chief's Guard" was organized on the twelfth day of March, in the year 1776, at Cambridge, Massachusetts. The general order, pursuant to which this corps was organized, is here appended:

"Head-Quarters, Cambridge, March 11, 1776.

"The General is desirous of selecting a particular number of men as a guard for himself and baggage. The colonel or commanding officers of each of the established regiments, the artillery and riflemen excepted, will furnish him with four, that the number wanted may be chosen out of them. His Excellency depends upon the colonels for good men, such as they can recommend for their sobriety, honesty and good behavior. He wishes them to be from five feet eight inches to five feet ten inches, handsomely and well made, and, as there is nothing in his eyes more desirable than cleanliness in a soldier, he desires that particular attention may be made in the choice of such men as are clean and spruce. They are all to be at headquarters tomorrow precisely at 12 o'clock at noon, when the number of men wanted will be fixed upon. The General neither wants them with uniforms nor arms, nor does he desire any man to be sent to him that is not perfectly willing or desirous of being of this Guard—they should be drilled men."

Carlos E. Godfrey, M. D., in his valuable work "The Commander-in-Chief's Guards Revolutionary War," says: "The necessity for such a corps was early manifested after Washington had assumed command of the American forces at Cambridge July 3, 1775, by the rapid accumulation of valuable papers and for the safety of his person from the enemies that abounded in and about the camp; and, during the existence of the organization, it was always esteemed a mark of particular distinction by the soldiers to be members of this command."

One of the most interesting features of the above named book is the fac-simile signatures of the officers and men composing "The Commander-in-Chief's Guards."

The last survivor of "Washington's Life Guard" was Sergeant Uzall Knapp, whose remains rest under a handsome brown freestone monument at the foot of the flag-staff at Washington Headquarters, Newburg, New York.

"I have been at my present quarters since the first day of December," wrote Washington from the Ford Mansion on the twenty-second of the following January, to his quartermaster-general, Nathaniel Green, "and have not a kitchen to cook a dinner in; * * * nor is there a place, at this moment, in which a servant can lodge, with the smallest degree of comfort. Eighteen belonging to my family and all Mrs. Ford's are crowded together in her kitchen, and scarce one of them able to speak for the colds they have.'

Silas B. Condict, in Genealogical History of the Ford Family of Morris County, (written in the year 1879), says "Darius Pierson, when a boy, carted wood for General Washington during the winter that he was at the Ford Headquarters in Morristown. Our grandparents have often told us of the extreme cold of the winter that Washington spent when at the Ford mansion then comparatively a new house (the same house now standing on those beautiful grounds), and of the great suffering those noble soldiers endured then encamped on Fort Nonsense. General Washington would often tell Darius to go in the house and warm himself, while he, Washington, would unload the wood."

A log kitchen was soon afterward built at the east end of the house for the accommodation of Washington and his family; and at the west end of the house another log structure was erected for use as a general office. This office was occupied during the day, particularly, by Washington and some of his staff; his sleeping-room was on the second floor of the house. Among the members of his family of eighteen were a portion of the winter at least, Martha Washington, and Colonel Alexander Hamilton, Major Tench Tighlman, several servants, and last, but by no means least, Mrs. Thompson, an Irishwoman, the efficient and resourceful housekeeper. Readers of this story will, without doubt, agree with the writer in speaking of Mrs. Thompson as a resourceful housekeeper, when it is related that at a time of great scarcity of food at headquarters, and throughout the army, for that matter, she remarked one day to Washington:

> "We have nothing but the rations to cook, sir."
>
> "Well, Mrs. Thompson," replied he, "you must cook the rations, for I have not a farthing to give you."
>
> "If you please sir, let one of the gentlemen give me an order for six bushels of salt."
>
> "Six bushels of salt!" exclaimed Washington in manifest astonishment; "what for?"
>
> Fully equal to the occasion, the housekeeper replied: "To preserve the fresh beef, sir."

The order was given, and on the following day there was no scarcity of food at the table of the outgeneraled commander-in-chief. Upon ascertaining the apparent source of the ample food supply, Washington administered a mild rebuke to his housekeeper, in the following words:

> "You have done wrong in expending your money, for I

do not know when I can repay you. I owe you too much already to permit the debt being increased, and our situation is not such as to induce very sanguine hope."

Never did the hopefulness of the womanly nature find more expression than in the ready response of Mrs. Thompson.

"Dear sir," she said, " it is always darkest just be fore the daylight;" and a finer illustration of womanly tact is seldom seen than that exhibited in the closing words of her remark, "I hope your excellency will forgive me for bartering salt for other necessaries now on the table."

Inasmuch as salt, during the period under consideration, was $8 a bushel, the people in the country surrounding Morristown were very willing to exchange their products for it. Some of them, indeed, as we learn from a contemporary newspaper, were willing to "exchange one bushel of salt for seven and a half bushels of flax seed."

Allusion has been made to the scarcity of food in the patriot army during the winter of its second encampment in Morristown, and no better or more convincing evidence of this can be given than the citation of a few extracts from extant letters of Washington. For example on the sixteenth of December, in the year 1779, the commander-in-chief wrote from his log cabin office, west of the Ford mansion to Joseph Read, at Philadelphia:

"The situation of the Army with respect to supplies, is

beyond description, alarming. It has been five or six weeks past on half allowance, and we have not more than three days bread at a third allowance, on hand, nor any where within reach. When this is exhausted, we must depend on the precarious gleanings of the neighboring country. Our magazines are absolutely empty every where, and our commissaries entirely destitute of money or credit to replenish them. We have never experienced a like extremity at any period of the war. * * * This representation is the result of a minute examination of our resources."

Again, on the eighth of the month following, Washington wrote to the magistrates of New Jersey:

"The present situation of the army, with respect to provisions, is the most distressing we have experienced since the beginning of the war. For a fortnight past, the troops, both officers and men, have been almost perishing for want. They have been alternately without bread or meat the whole time, with a very scanty allowance of either, and frequently destitute of both. They have borne their sufferings with a patience that merits the approbation and ought to excite the sympathy of their countrymen. But they are now reduced to an extremity no longer to be supported."

"We have had the virtue and patience of the army put to the severest trial," wrote Washington in a private letter to a friend. "Sometimes it has been five or six days together without bread; at other times as many without meat; and once or twice, two or three days at a time, without either. * * * At one time the soldiers ate every kind of horse food but hay. Buckwheat, common wheat, rye and Indian corn, composed the meal which made their bread."

The subsequent response of the people of New Jersey to the noble appeal of Washington for provisions for his destitute army was so prompt and generous that he was able on the twentieth of January of the same year to write to Dr. John Witherspoon as follows:

"All the counties of this State that I have heard from have attended to my requisition for provisions, with the most cheerful and commendable zeal."

Of the severity of the winter of 1779-80, and the consequent suffering of the patriot army, a better conception cannot be obtained by the reader than from an extract from the military journal of Dr. Thatcher. This extract is under date of the fourteenth of December of the former year, and of January 3, 1780, it says:

"The snow on the ground is about two feet deep and the weather extremely cold; the soldiers are destitute of both tents and blankets, and some of them are actually barefooted and almost naked. * * * But the sufferings of the poor soldiers can scarcely be described; while on duty they are unavoidably exposed to all the inclemency of the storm and severe cold; at night they now have a bed of straw on the ground and a single blanket to each man; they are badly clad and some are destitute of shoes. * * * The snow is now from four to six feet deep. * * * For the last ten days we received but two pounds of meat a man. * * * The consequence is the soldiers are so enfeebled from hunger and cold as to be almost unable to perform military duty or labor in constructing their huts. It is well known that General Washington experiences the greatest solicitude for the sufferings of his army and is sensible that they in general conduct with heroic patience and fortitude."

It is through the courtesy of Henry B. Hoffman, of

Morristown, that the writer is able to present the following letter, the original of which is in the possession of Mrs. James B. Bowman, of Mendham, a descendant of Stephen Day, Esq., to whom said communication was originally addressed:

"Morristown, November 6th, 1780.

"Sir—

"The great demands of the Army for Forage from this county, and the method in which it has been taken proves very distressing. I have therefore at the request of a number of the Magistrates appointed a meeting to-morrow at my office to consult on this important affair and endeavor to alleviate the distress of individuals by a general demand from the whole county. I request your personal attendance at ten o'clock in the forenoon.

"Am respectfully your obedient servant,

"JOS. LEWIS, Com.

"Justice Day."

Joseph Lewis, at the period above mentioned, was Deputy Quartermaster-General of New Jersey. His residence was on what is now Morris Street, next beyond the house occupied by the Rev. Timothy Johnes, (whose daughter he married) and on the same side of the street. His office may have been at his residence. The Justice Day to whom the foregoing letter was written was Justice Stephen Day, of Chatham; he to whom Washington once wrote, asking him to solicit supplies for the Continental Army, which he did. Squire Day headed the list with a beef.

Captain William Tuttle of the New Jersey brigade,

is authority for the statement that "there were paths about the camps on Kimball Hill that were marked with real blood expressed from the cracked and frozen feet of soldiers who had no shoes."

From a poem entitled "Rhoda Farrand," first published in a magazine, Our Continent, edited by Judge Tourgee, several years ago, the following extract is given, which thrillingly relates its own story:

"We are here for the winter in Morristown,
And a sorry sight are our men to-day,
In tatters and rags with no signs of pay.
As we marched to camp, if a man looked back,
By the dropping of blood he could trace our track;
For scarcely a man has a decent shoe,
And there's not a stocking the army through;
So send us stockings as quick as you can,
My company needs them, every man.
And every man is a neighbor's lad;
Tell this to their mothers: They need them bad.
Then, if never before, beat Rhoda's heart,
'Twas time to be doing a woman part,
She turned to her daughters, Hannah and Bet,
Girls, each on your needles a stocking set.
Get my cloak and hood; as for you, son Dan,
Yoke up the steers just as quick as you can;
Put a chair in the wagon, as you're alive,
I will sit and knit while you go and drive,
They started at once on Whippany road,
She knitting away while he held the goad.
At Whippany Village she stopped to call
On the sisters Prudence and Mary Ball.
She would not go in, she sat in her chair,
And read to the girls her letter from there.

That was enough, for their brothers three
Were in Lieutenant Farrand's company.
Then on Rhoda went, stopping here and there,
To rouse the neighbors from her old chair."

The result of the heroic efforts of this patriotic woman, assisted by her not less patriotic daughters and son, was, that the stockings poured into the New Jersey camp down the Jockey Hollow road "in a perfect shower." From S. A. Farrand, one of the headmasters of the Newark (N. J.) Academy, who, the writer is proud to say, is a grandson of the Rhoda Farrand of the poem quoted from, the writer learns that the poem is in the main historically correct. The poem was written by Miss Eleanor A. Hunter, a great-granddaughter of Rhoda Farrand, In reply to the query of the present writer as to how she happened to write this patriotic poem, she says: "It was a story told me by my mother. She related it to me many times, and I never wearied of listening to it. She had heard it as a child from Grandmother Rhoda herself. One evening, after a visit to Morristown, my mother and I were talking about Revolutionary days and she told me the story once more. Suddenly the thought came to me: 'What a good poem that would make.' I retired to my room and put the story in rhyme then and there and brought it out and gave it to my mother." The poem, as already mentioned, was subsequently published.

"Where's the general? Where's the general?" exclaimed a young man visiting at the Ford mansion in the winter of 1779-80, as, in great trepidation, he rushed downstairs and into the spacious hallway on the first floor at midnight of a certain evening.

"Be quiet, young man, be quiet," was Washington's mild rebuke, as with his customary moderation he also descended the stairway from his sleeping-room. The cause of the commotion and its attendant circumstances, occurring at the unseasonable hour suggested, was what proved to be a false alarm of the approach of a British force. These alarms, which were not infrequent occurrences during the winter of Washington's occupancy, as headquarters, of the now famous Ford mansion, were followed by the barricading of the doors by the life guard and the opening of the windows, at each of the latter of which about five of the guard would place themselves, with muskets loaded and cocked, in readiness for repelling attack. On the approach of the American troops dispatched from camp for the defense of the headquarters, the life guard would retire from the positions assumed, and, rejoining their particular command, await further orders. The necessity for their services having ceased the troops would then return leisurely to camp.

"Timothy Ford, a son of Washington's hostess" at the Ford Mansion, was a severe sufferer during the winter spent there by the commander-in-chief, "from the effects of a wound received in a battle the previous fall; and among other pleasing courtesies we are told that every morning Washington knocked at Timothy's door, and asked how the young soldier had passed the night."

How like the living present it causes the past to appear, as one reads in a private letter written from Basking Ridge, on the twenty-second day of December, in the year 1779, that:

> "I rode out today on purpose to take a view of our encampments. I found it excessively cold; but was glad to see most of our poor soldiers were under good roofs. The encampments are exceedingly neat; the huts are all of a size, and placed in more exact order than Philadelphia; you would be surprised to see how well they are built without nails. Headquarters is at Morristown, and the army extends from thence along the hills nearly to this place."

Martha Washington ("a small, plump, elegantly formed woman") reached the Ford mansion by way of Trenton, where Virginia troops were paraded in her honor, on the twenty-eighth of December, in the year 1779, while the great snow storm mentioned by Dr. Thatcher was raging. That she was a worthy companion of her distinguished husband, the following authentic incident will demonstrate. During the winter of her sojourn at the Ford mansion she was honored by a call from several representative Hanover ladies. As one of these ladies afterward remarked, "We were dressed in our most elegant silks and ruffles, and so were introduced to her ladyship. And don't you think we found her with a speckled homespun apron on, and engaged in knitting a stocking! She received us very handsomely. and then resumed her knitting. In the course of her conversation she said very kindly to us, whilst she made her needles fly, that 'American ladies should be patterns of industry to their countrywomen. * * * We must become independent of England by doing without those articles which we can make ourselves. Whilst our husbands and brothers are examples of patriotism, we must be examples of industry.'

"'I do declare,' said one of these visitors, 'I never felt so shame and rebuked in my life.'"

There was evidently pressing need of industry, and of economy also, on the part of the good women of Morris County, for during the winter of 1779-80 their "husbands and brothers" were paying for first-quality hay 100 pounds per ton; for wheat, $50 per bushel; for corn, $30 per bushel, and for other necessaries in proportion. If a carriage ride were indulged in, the bill was, for one horse, twenty-four hours, $6, or twenty-five cents per hour.

The value of slaves in New Jersey at the time may be inferred from such advertisements as the following: "One Thousand Dollars Reward for the recovery of my negro man, Toney." One dollar in specie was equivalent to forty in paper money; and the poor soldiers of the patriot army were paid in paper money. That Washington was not left with but a mere "corporal's guard" to continue the struggle for national independence, was due to the inborn and unquenchable love of freedom, which brightly burned in the hearts of the patriot soldiery composing his army.

CHAPTER XVII

"True fortitude is seen in great exploits
That justice warrants, and that wisdom guides;
All else is tow'ring frenzy and distraction."

HE winter of the years 1779-80 witnessed one of the most important gatherings ever held in Morristown, if not, indeed, in America. It was convened in Dickerson's tavern, then kept by Robert Norris, on what is now the corner of Water and Spring streets. Important in itself, because of the object and the personnel of the gathering, it was important also when the consequencs to its central figure and to the American colonies are carefully considered.

The central figure of this momentous gathering in Morristown was none other than Benedict Arnold, hitherto by common consent one of the bravest and most efficient officers in the Continental army; the object, his court-martial; the consequences, as will be seen, the making of a traitor to the cause of freedom, the loss to the patriot army of a splendid officer and the widespread alarm of Freedom's steadfast friends, which found expression in the sad exclamation of Washington, when irresistible evidence of Arnold's treason was presented to him: "Whom can we trust now?"

Benedict Arnold was born in Norwich, Connecticut, in the year 1740. On the breaking out of the Revolution he eagerly espoused the cause of the colonies. In the month of May, in the year 1775, he ably assisted Colonel Ethan Allen in the capture of Ticonderoga and Crown Point. In conjunction with General Montgomery, Arnold, in the month of December, in the year 1775, after a tedious and hazardous march through the State of Maine, and with but a mere handful of the troops with which he had started, besieged Quebec for a period of three weeks. At the end of this time an unsuccessful assault was made on the enemy's works, in which he exhibited indomitable courage. In this assault, Arnold received a severe wound and was carried from the field. In harassing the retreating British troops under General Tryon, from Danbury, Connecticut, Arnold bore honorable part with Generals Wooster and Silliman, the former of whom was slain.

On hearing of the volunteered approach of Arnold with his ample force of patriot troops, the Indians fled in great haste from before besieged Fort Schuyler, in consequence of which the siege was suddenly abandoned by the enemy. In the battle of Saratoga, resulting in Burgoyne's surrender, Arnold specially distinguished himself, receiving a second wound in the right leg. After the evacuation of Philadelphia by the British, because, in part, of his disabled condition, General Arnold was placed in command of that city, and there occurred the unfortunate events which led to his court-martial. This, in brief, is Arnold's military record prior to the year 1780.

The terse summons to the gathering in Dickerson's tavern, was as follows: "Headquarters, Morristown, December 22, 1779. The court-martial, whereof Major-General Howe is president, to sit to-morrow, 10 o'clock, at Norris's tavern." From this order it appears that the necessary arrangements for the trial had already been made. In accordance with the order from the commander-in-chief, issued from the Ford mansion the following officers, constituting, by appointment of Washington, the court-martial, convened at the Dickerson Tavern on Thursday morning, December 23: Major-General Robert Howe, president; Brigadier-General Henry Knox, Brigadier-General William Maxwell, Brigadier-General Mordecai Gist (sometimes spelled Gest) and eight colonels, and before this body Benedict Arnold was summoned for trial.

The court-martial, which convened on the morning of December 23, was resumed on four subsequent days, and on the last, December 30, it was adjourned, to afford Arnold opportunity to procure additional evidence. On Wednesdey, the nineteenth day of January following, and on four consecutive days thereafter, the court-martial continued its session, adjourning at last until the twenty-sixth day of the same month. At this latter session the decision of the court-martial was rendered.

The writer has been informed, and reliably, as he conceives, that the particular room in Dickerson's tavern in which the court was convened was that situated on the right as one entered the front door of this famous hostelry. This is said to have been the barroom and the bar seems to have run across the easterly end of it. Down a few steps, at the southwest end of the room alluded to, was a large, old-fashioned stone bake oven, the form of which could be seen on the exterior of the building.

The charges brought against Arnold were, briefly stated: permitting a Tory vessel (while he was in command at Philadelphia, in the year 1778) to enter port without acquainting the commander-in-chief or the State officials of the fact; closing stores and shops, thus preventing purchases by the people of the "Quaker City," but making purchases for his personal advantage; the imposition upon the local militia of what were considered menial services; the purchase, at an inadequate price, of a prize-ship captured and brought into port by a State privateer; granting to an unworthy person a pass to enter the enemy's lines; the transportation of the private property of Tories in wagons belonging to the State; an indecent and disrespectful refusal to explain to the Council of Pennsylvania the reasons for using the State wagons for the benefit of

Tories, and lastly, partiality exhibited toward the adherents of the King of Great Britain and the neglectful treatment of the patriot authorities of Philadelphia.

These charges, as originally and fully stated, had been brought to the attention of Arnold in the spring of the year 1779, by the supreme executive council of Pennsylvania, and he personally demanded of Washington a court-martial, and requested a speedy investigation of the crimes alleged. May first of the year 1779, was the first date designated by the commander-in-chief for Arnold's trial, but more time for the gathering of evidence being requested by the State officials preferring the charges, the trial was postponed one month. By this time the military campaign of 1779 was in progress, and a court-martial was highly impracticable. The cessation of active hostilities, and the retirement of the patriot army into winter quarters at Morristown in the month of December, of the year 1779, afforded the opportunity of formally and particularly investigating the criminal charges brought against General Arnold. What must, in the opinion of the writer, have proved a most disagreeable task, that of prosecuting the charges against General Arnold, inevitably fell to Lieutenant-Colonel John Lawrence, the judge advocate.

Not only the recollection of Arnold's previous brilliant and invaluable services in the cause of freedom, but his personal appearance upon the occasion, and its vivid reminder to all present of those services, must, as it seems, have rendered the discharge of the duty assigned to Colonel Lawrence merely perfunctory. Indeed, there is evidence that such was the case. Not now to emphasize the facts that the officer arraigned before the court at Dickerson's tavern, had not at the time, reached the fortieth year of his age; that he wore the insignia of a major-general of the patriot army, and that his unprecedented bravery on not, by any means, a single field of battle, was evidenced by the sword knots fastened about his waist, the gift of his illustrious commander-in-chief; he bore in his maimed and crippled body the badges of two severe wounds, the marked evidences of which were sufficient to have disarmed prejudice and rancor, and favorably disposed the observer toward the distinguished prisoner. Explicitly stated, Arnold's right leg had been broken between the knee and hip joint at Quebec, and at Saratoga the same leg had again been broken, this time between the knee and foot. The result was a short and mis-shapen leg, and lameness which necessitated the constant use of a cane in walking.

Arnold, leaning upon his cane, acted as his own counsel in this famous trial. As evidence in his favor he laid before the court numerous letters and documents, including complimentary letters from the commander-in-chief and commendatory resolutions of Congress. Following the presentation of his evidence, Arnold addressed the court at considerable length. From his address, carefully recorded by the clerk of the body before whom he was being tried, the following suggestive extracts are given:

> "When one is charged with practices which his soul abhors, and which conscious innocence tells him he has never committed, an honest indignation will draw from him expressions in his own favor which on other occasions might be ascribed to an ostentatious turn of mind. My time, my fortune and my person have been devoted to my country in this war. * * *"

Referring to the charge that he had made private purchases to his own advantage, he said:

> "If this be true, I stand confessed in the presence of this honorable court the vilest of men; I stand stigmatized with indellible disgrace. Where is the evidence of this accusation? I call upon my accusers to produce it. On the honor of a gentleman and a soldier I declare to gentlemen and soldiers, it is false. If I made considerable purchases, considerable sales must have been made to me by some persons in Philadelphia. Why are not these persons produced?"

After the close of Arnold's address the court was adjourned to the twenty-six day of January, when the judge advocate arrayed all available evidence against the young officer on trial. This was supplemented by a careful summing up by the prosecutor. As an indication of the general expectancy of the acquittal of Arnold in which he himself shared, it may be said that an officer in Stark's brigade, encamped on the Basking Ridge road, wrote to a friend: "It is expected he will be acquitted with honors." While the verdict of the court-martial was, technically speaking, neither a conviction nor an acquitaal, the closing paragraph amounted to a suggestion that Arnold receive from the commander-in-chief a reprimand for his alleged misconduct. This reprimand Washington subsequently administered privately and in the most delicate manner consistent with the court's suggestion. The exact words of Washington's reprimand were:

> "The Commander in Chief would have been much happier in an occasion of Bestowing commendations on an officer who has rendered such Distinguished services to his country as Major General Arnold, but in the present case, a sense of Duty & a Regard to candour oblige him to declare that he Considers his conduct in the instance of the Permit as peculiarly Reprehensible, both in a Civil & Military view & in the affair of the Waggons as imprudent & Improper."

At the finding of the court Arnold was disappointed and indignant, and, stung by the verdict and the reprimand, he resolved to quit the service and retire to private life. From this course the magnanimous commander-in-chief succeeded in dissuading him, and he was appointed by Washington to the command at West Point, one of the most important in the service, which Arnold accepted. No more convincing proof of Washington's confidence in Arnold's loyalty could be adduced than this important assignment. If only Arnold had clearly understood, what was generally conceded by those conversant with the facts to have been the case, that the verdict of the court-martial convened at Dickerson's tavern, was intended as a mere sop to the prejudices of the Council of Pennsylvania, and that the mild reprimand of his military chief partook largely of the nature of a perfunctory service, he would have been saved from the rash step which has ever since linked his otherwise honorable name with infamy, and the American arms would have retained his invaluable services to the close of the struggle for freedom.

A letter from Arnold, during the winter following his trial, to Washington, requesting "leave of absence from the army during the ensuing summer," on account of impaired health, can only be construed as an indication that the commander at West Point was still brooding over what he considered a gross wrong perpetrated upon him as the result of the generally trivial charges brought against him by the Pennsylvania Council. To Arnold's request Washington replied: "You have my permission, though it is my expectation and wish to see you in the field." The story of Arnold's attempt at the betrayal of his country, is too familiar to readers of history to necessitate rehearsal. The saddest commentary upon his treason is the fact, that after his removal to England, he lived in obscurity, and was detested and avoided by the people whose cause he had rashly espoused. Whose was the greater responsibility for his treasonous conduct—Arnold's, or that of his virtually self-confessed persecutors—does not yet appear. Coupled with this expression of opinion, by the writer, however, is the conviction, that no apology should be made for the overt act of treason against one's country, whatever be the provocation, since the Infinite Creator hath "ordained thy will by nature free, not overruled by fate inextricable, or strict necessity."

In "Appendix A," of the "Proceedings of the M. W. Grand Lodge of Free and Accepted Masons, of the State of New Jersey," for the year 1900, may be found the following: "Note—The following memoranda referring to the Masonic Convention at Morristown, N. J., during the Revolutionary War, at which Brother George Washington was personally present, is a transcript of the rough notes which were found among the manuscripts left by the late Edmund D. Halsey, Esq., of Morristown. Mr. Halsey did not live to complete his account of the Convention, but it is thought that the notes following are well worthy of preservation in the archives of New Jersey Masonry:

"One of the most interesting events which took place in Morristown during the war for independence was the meeting of the Military Union Lodge of Free and Accepted Masons, to celebrate the feast of St. John the Evangelist, in December, 1779, in the old Arnold Tavern. The presence of Washington, the patriotic character of the resolutions adopted, and the number of distinguished officers who took part, made it peculiarly noteworthy. It was probably the first meeting of the Order in the town, and we can imagine with what curiosity the gathering at the inn, and the stately procession from thence across the public square to the old church, was witnessed by the people, and what an assemblage of citizens and soldiers filled the sacred building to hear the 'polite discourse' of Dr. Baldwin. No newspaper was then printed in the county from which a report of the proceedings can be gathered, and the letters which have been preserved of that period are silent on this subject.

"The revival of interest in matters of this period has brought to light many of the circumstances attending this meeting, including its minutes which were found in the records of the Brotherhood in Connecticut and which for many years were supposed to have been lost.

"In February, 1776, Richard Gridley, Deputy Grand Master of St. John's Grand Lodge, in Massachusetts, granted a warrant to 'American Union Lodge, whose members belonged to the Connecticut troops and were then engaged in the military service of the Colonies about Boston. After the evacuation of Boston, and when the army had moved to the vicinity of New York, a confirmation of this charter was applied for from the Masonic authorities of New York. This was denied, but a new warrant was authorized under the name of 'Military Union Lodge, No. 1.' This latter name was distasteful to the members, and they never used it when it could be avoided, but continued to call themselves by their more original and patriotic title.

"The Lodge kept up its meetings when the army was not on the march, and members were received from time to time from regiments of different States. In December, 1778, General Washington was present at the celebration of St. John's Day in Philadelphia, leading the procession to Christ's Church, where a Masonic sermon was delivered by Rev. Dr. William Smith, Grand Secretary of the Grand Lodge of Pennsylvania. The name of Washington became a Masonic toast and first in order at Masonic festivals.

"The Continental Army arrived in Morristown about the first of December, 1779, and proceeded to build their huts on the Kemble and Wick Farms, between that town and Baskingridge. Washington took up his residence at the Ford mansion, and the officers of his staff were quartered in various houses about the village. Almost immediately, on the fifteenth, the Masonic brethren came together and held a meeting at 'Colonel Gray's quarters' to elect officers and to prepare for the coming festival of St. John,the evangelist.

The Minutes of this meeting, as of that which followed, are found in the 'History of Free and Accepted Masons in New York,' by Charles T. McClenachan, Historian of the Grand Lodge, a work from which I am kindly permitted to make extracts at pleasure. The originel minutes are in possession of the Grand Lodge of Connecticut. Captain-Lieutenant Jonathan Heart, of the Third Connecticut Regiment, was chosen Worshipful Master; Lieutenant and Paymaster Richard Sill, of the Eighth Regiment, Senior Warden; Captain Robert Warner, of Colonel Wyllis' Regiment, Junior Warden; Captain William Richards, of Starr's Regiment, Treasurer; Surgeon John R. Watrous, of Wyllis' Regiment, Secretary: Lieutenant-Colonel Thomas Grosvenor, Senior Deacon; Captain Henry Champion, of the First Connecticut, Junior Deacon; Privates Joseph Lorain and Thomas Binns, of Captain Pond's Company, Sixth Connecticut Regiment, Tylers.

"Worshipful Master Jonathan Heart was appointed 'a committee from the different lines in the army at Morristown to take into consideration some matters respecting the good of Masonry' (probably to arrange for the coming festival). In preparation for this, Captain Thomas Kinney and Major Jeremiah Bruen, of Morristown, went to Newark and borrowed from St. John's Lodge, No. 1, which had been established there in 1761, the necessary paraphernalia. In the old minute-book of this Lodge, under date of December 24th, 1779, is found the following receipt for this property. 'An acct. of sundrie articles taken out of the Lodge Chest of Newark St. John's Lodge, No. 1, by consent of Bro. John Robinson, Bro. Lewis Ogden, Brother Moses Ogden and lent unto Brother Thomas Kinney and Bro. Jerry Brewin to carry as far as Morristown, said Brothers Kinney and Brewin promising on the word of Brothers to return the same articles as p's Inventory below unto our Bro. John Robinson, present Secretary when called-for witness our hands Brothers as below:—

'24 Aprons, besides one that was bound and fring'd which Bro. Kinney claims as his own.

'2Ebony Truntchions tipt with silver, the other they are to get if to be found.

'3Large Candlesticks.

'3 Large Candlemolds.

'1 Silk Pedestal Cloth Bound with Silver Lace.

'1 Damask Cutchion.

'1 Silver Key with a blue Ribbon stripped with black.

'1 Silver Levell with a blue Ribbon stripped with black.

'1 " Square " " " " " " "

'1 " Plumb " " " " " " "

'Newark, Dec'r 24, 1779.

'(Signed) Thomas Kinney
Jerh. Bruen.'

* * * * * * *

"The meeting for which these preparations were made was held in the Arnold (formerly Kinney's) Tavern, on the north side of the Green, which had been Washington's headquarters in the winter of 1777, after the battle of Princeton. It was one of the principal hotels in the place, and was frequented by all the army officers. The 'dancing assembly,' for which $13,000 in Continental scrip was raised, was held here. * * * "At this time (of the celebration of the festival of St. John, the Evangelist) the general court martial for the trial of General Arnold was holding its sessions at the Dickerson Tavern, corner of Water and Spring streets, kept, while its owner was in the service, by Robert Norris. The entry in its minutes, December 27th, shows that the court met only to adjourn, for six of its members and the Judge Advocate were of the Masonic fraternity, and had more agreeable business on hand that day.

"In Mr. McClenachan's book is a full account of this meeting. The minutes read:

'Morristown, December 27th, 1779.
An Entered Apprentices' Lodge was held this day, for the celebration of the festival of St. John the Evangelist.

'Officers present—Brothers Jonathan Heart, Worshipful Master; Richard Sill, Senior Warden; Robert Warner, Junior Warden; William Richards, Treasurer; John R. Watrous, Secretary; Thomas Grosvenor, Senior Deacon; Brother Little, Junior Deacon, and Lorain and Binns, Tylers.

"Members present—Brothers Stillwell, Higgins, Worthington, Curtis, Barker, Gray, Sherman, Craig, Wilson, Bush, Judd, Heath, S. Richards, S. Wyllis, Parsons, Huntington, Smith, Judson, Clark, Hosmer, J. Wyllis, Fitch, Pierce, Sergeant, Graham, Fitch, Whiting.'

* * * * * * *

"Nearly all the members of the Lodge present were from the Connecticut line. This State had a division of two brigades at Morristown. The First Brigade consisted of the First Regiment, Col. Starr; the Third Regiment, Col. Wyllis; the Fifth Regiment, Col. Bradley, and the Seventh Regiment, Col. Swift. The Second Brigade consisted of the Second Regiment, Col. Butler; the Fourth Regiment, Col. Durkee; the Sixth Regiment, Col. Meigs; and the Eighth Regiment, Col. Sherman. An additional regiment, commanded by Col. Samuel B. Webb, was afterward added to this Brigade.

* * * * * * *

"Next in the minutes are the names of sixty-eight visiting brethren. First of all comes Washington, and with him was Major Caleb Gibbs, of Rhode Island, the commander of his life guard, until succeeded by his Lieutenant, William Colfax, of New Jersey. He was wounded in the foot in the assault on the enemy's redoubt at Yorktown. He was dispatched in May, 1780, by Washington to meet Lafayette, who had just arrived in Boston, to escort him to the Head Quarters, at Morristown, where Washington writes 'a bed is prepared for him.'" * * * Following is the list of the "visiting brethren:" Colonel Alexander Hamilton, Robert Erskine, General John Lawrence, General Mordecai Gist, General Otto Williams, General William Maxwell, General Elias Dayton, General Anthony W. White, Colonel Henry Jackson, Colonel John Brooks, Colonel Richard Butler, Lieutenant-Colonel Morgan Conner, Colonel Henry Sherburne, Captain Thomas Hughes, Lieutenant John Hubbart, Ensign Jeremiah Greenman, Colonel Thomas Kinney, Colonel Jacob Arnold, Major Jeremiah Bruen, Dr. Jabez Campfield, John Armstrong, Lieutenant Jeremiah Van Renselear, Dr. Nicholas Schuyler, Lieutenant Samuel Lewis, Lieutenant Gilbert R. Livingston, Lieutenant Philip Connine, Captain Leonard Bleecker, Lieutenant and Paymaster John Stagg, Adjutant Peter Ellsworth, Lieutenant Thomas Hunt, Lieutenant Francis Hamner, Colonel Thomas Proctor, Captain Thomas Machin, Captain James Maclure, Captain-Lieutenant John Waldron, Lieutenant Isaac Guion, Captain Elisha Harvey, Lieutenant Peter Woodward, Captain-Lieutenant Thomas Thompson, Chaplain Andrew Hunter, Captain John Sandford, Captain Daniel Piatt, Captain Isaac Craig, Major Thomas Church, Captain-Lieutenant Thomas Campbell, Captain John Savidge, Captain Nathaniel Van Sant, Surgeon Charles McCarter, Lieutenant Peter Summers, Lieutenant Wilder Bevins, Lieutenant-Colonel Francis Mentges, Chaplain William Rogers, Lieutenant Edward Spears, Surgeon Noah Coleman, Dr. Abraham Baldwin, Captain Henry Ten Eyck, Captain Joseph Fox, Lieutenant James Bruff, Paymaster-General Hezekiah Wetmore, Captain Wilhelmus Ryckman, Captain Samuel Shaw, Thomas Edwards, Lieutenant Benjamin L. Peckman, Durfee.

"The Lodge was opened, and after the usual ceremonies had been performed, the brethren formed a procession in the following order:

"1. Bro. Binns, to clear the way.

"2. The Band of Music.
"3. Brother Lorain, with a Drawn Sword.
"4. The Deacons, with their Rods.
"5. The Brethren, by Juniority.
"6. The Passed Masters.
"7. The Secretary and Treasurer.
"8. The Wardens, with their Wands.
"9. The Worshipful Master.

"The Brethren then proceeded to the Meeting-house, where a very 'polite' discourse, adapted to the occasion, was delivered by the Rev. Doct. Baldwin, of the Connecticut Line. After service, the Brethren returned by the same order to the Lodge-room, where a collation was served, &c., &c., which being over, the following business was transacted.

"Voted unanimously, that the thanks of the Lodge be presented to the Rev. Dr. Baldwin, for the polite address delivered by him this day in public.

"Voted unanimously, that the Secretary wait on the Rev. Dr. Baldwin, with a copy of the minutes, and a request that he will favor the Lodge with a copy of the address, and permission to have it published.

"A petition was read, representing the present state of Freemasonry to the several Deputy Grand Masters in the United States of America, desiring them to adopt some measures for appointing a Grand Master over said States, of which the following is a copy:

PETITION.

"To the Most Worshipful, the present Provincial Grand Masters in each of the respective United States of America:

"The petitioners, Ancient, Free and Accepted Masons in the several Lines of the Army of these United States, assembled on the Festival of St. John the Evangelist, at Morristown, Dec. 27th., 1779, to you, as the patrons and safeguard of the Craft of America beg leave to prefer their humble address.

"With sincere regret we contemplate the misfortunes of war, which have unhappily separated us from the Grand Lodge in Europe, and deprived us from the benefits arising therefrom, so essentially necessary for the well-being of Masonry, and which has, in many instances, been subversive of the very institution of the Order. At the same time we lament that political disputes and national quarrels should influence the exercise of charity and benevolence, and their several virtues, so necessary for our present and future happiness. Yet, considering the present situation of our Lodges and Masonry in general, the necessity, for the honor of the Craft, and the importance of enjoying the benefits of so valuable an institution, that some exertions are made for checking the present irregularities, restoring peace and harmony to the Lodges, for opening a way to the enjoyment of the fruits of benevolence, charity and brotherly love, and for the re-establishment of the Order on the ancient respectable foundation; which we conceive can never be done more effectually than by the appointment of a Grand Master in and over the United States of America.

"We therefore most earnestly request that the present Provincial Grand Masters in the respective said United States would take some measure for the appointment of a Grand Master in and over the said Thirteen United States of America, either by nominating a person proper for that office, whose abilities and rank in life shall answer the importance of that conspicuous and elevated station, and transmit such nomination to our Mother Lodge in Britain, that the appointment may be made, or in such other manner as shall to them appear most eligible. And we further beg leave to express our wishes that the several provincial Grand Masters in these States would, in the intermediate time, enter into unanimous and vigorous measures for checking the growing irregularities in the Society, cementing the different branches, erasing the distinction between Ancient and Modern in these States, that the Craft may be established in unanimity, the established principles of its institution more universally extended, and that our conduct may not only be the admiration of men in this world, but receive the final applause of the Grand Architect of the Universe in the other, where there is nothing but light and love.

"Voted, That the foregoing petition be circulated through the different Lines in the Army.

"Voted, That a committee be appointed from the different Lodges in the Army, from each Line, and from the Staff of the Army, to convene on the first Monday of February next, at Morristown, to take the foregoing petition into consideration.

"Voted, That when the dividend of the expense of this day shall be paid, each brother will put into the hands of the Treasurer or Secretary what he shall see fit, for the use of the poor of this town.

"Voted, That the money so collected be transmitted to Bro. Kinney, to appropriate to the necessities, first of the widows and orphans of Masons, next to soldiers' wives and children in distressed circumstances; if any shall remain, he will apply it to those poor persons in this town whom he shall judge stand most in need thereof.

"Lodge closed till called together by the Master's order.'

"Dr. Abraham Baldwin, who delivered the 'polite discourse,' was Abraham Baldwin, who was born in Guilford, Conn., Nov. 6th., 1754, graduated at Yale in 1772 and was tutor there until after the beginning of the War. At the time of the meeting he was Brigade Chaplain in the Connecticut Line.

* * * * * * *

"The meeting-house in which this address was delivered was that of the First Presbyterian Congregation, a frame building erected at least twenty years before, and to which a steeple had been added in 1763. It stood back of and to the east of the present church, and was a plain, square building, covered, like the Old Court House, with shingles. In

March, 1796,after the erection of the present structure, it was ordered to be taken down at the expense of the congregation, but was, in fact, moved to the west of the church property, was turned into a distillery, and became one of the seventeen which Dr. Barnes alleged to have been in the bounds of the parish in his day."

From the following letter, written by Washington to General William Irvine, on the ninth day of January, in the year 1780, it may be reasonably inferred that the expedition under the command of Lord Stirling (to which our story will soon refer), had, previous to the date above mentioned, either been suggested to the commander-in-chief by some officer of the patriot army, or independently contemplated by him:

"Circumstanced as things are—men half starved—imperfectly clothed—riotous—and robbing the country people of their subsistence from sheer necessity, I think it scarcely possible to embrace any moment, however favorable in other respects, for visiting the enemy on Staten Island, and yet if this frost should have made a firm and solid bridge between them and us I should be unwilling—indeed I cannot relinquish the idea of attempting it."

With whomsoever the idea of an expedition to Staten Island originated, it was decided upon by Washington, as the following second communication to General Irvine proves:

"Monday, January 10, 1780. I have determined in case the present condition of the ice and prospect of its continuance will warrant the enterprise, to make an attempt upon the enemy's quarters and posts on Staten Island."

It was on the fifteenth day of January, five days later, in the year 1780, that Quartermaster Joseph Lewis, as we learn from one of his letters, received orders from General Greene "to procure three hundred sleds or sleighs to parade Friday morning at this post and at Mr. Kimble's."

"I did not fail to exert myself on the occasion," wrote Lewis, "and the magistrates gained deserved applause. About five hundred sleds or sleighs were collected, the majority of which were loaded with troops, artillery and so forth. These sleds and as many more are to return loaded with stores from the British magazines, on Staten Island, except some few that are to be loaded with wounded British prisoners. About 3,000 troops are gone, under the command of Lord Stirling, with a determination to remove all Staten Island, bag and baggage, to Morristown!"

This expedition, of which Quartermaster Lewis thus half-humorously writes, and which set out from Morristown probably about the seventeenth day of January, of the year 1780, was a failure, so far as the accomplishment of the intended object was concerned, for the enemy having in some way received warning of the movement, they were fully prepared to meet the American force, and thwart their designs. In the following extract, cited from the New Jersey Gazette, of January 19, we have a fine specimen of the patriotism which is determined to put the best construction upon even the misfortunes of war:

It will "show the British mercenaries with what zeal and alacrity the Americans will embrace every opportunity, even in a very inclement season, to promote the interests of the country by harassing the enemies to their freedom and independence."

Three days later, Quartermaster Lewis, in a somewhat more serious frame of mind, and yet with an apparent tinge of humor, wrote from Morristown:

"I suppose you have heard of the sucess of our late expedition to Staten Island. It was expensive, but answered no valuable purpose. It showed the inclination of our inhabitants to plunder."

That this expedition was not only expensive, and so far as the accomplishment of the main design was concerned, fruitless, but disastrous, also, may be inferred from the circumstance, that of the 3,000 troops dispatched to Staten Island, about 500 returned to camp on "Kimble's Hill," with frozen feet. By way of retaliation for the raid into their lines, a detachment of British troops in command of Lieutenant-Colonel Bushkirk, between the hours of 11 and 12 o'clock, on the night of January 25, landed quietly at Elizabethtown. The force consisted of three or four hundred infantry and one hundred dragoons. They burned the meeting-house, townhouse and another building, plundered some of the inhabitants, took several prisoners and retired without the loss of a man. The view taken by Washington of the above-mentioned British descent upon Elizabethtown may be learned from the following order issued from the Ford mansion to General St. Clair, on the twenty-seventh day of the same month and year:

"You will be pleased to repair to our lines and investigate the causes of the late misfortune and disgrace at Elizabethtown, and report your opinion thereupon, as soon as inquiry is made."

On the twenty-ninth day of February, in the year 1780, Washington wrote to Joseph Reed, of Philadelphia:

"We have opened an assembly at camp. From this apparent ease, I suppose it is thought we must be in happy circumstances. I wish it was so, but, alas, it is not. Our provisions are in a manner, gone. We have not a ton of hay at command, nor magazine to draw from. Money is extremely scarce, and worth little when we get it. We have been so poor in camp for a fortnight, that we could not forward the public dispatches, for want of cash to support the expresses."

Of the subscription paper of the "assembly" mentioned by Washington, in the foregoing letter, the original of which is now in the possession of the Biddle family, on the Delaware, the following is a correct transcript: "The subscribers agree to pay the sums annexed to their respective names, and an equal quota of any further expense which may be incurred in the promotion and support of a dancing assembly to be held in Morristown, the present winter of 1780. Subscription Moneys to be paid into the hands of a Treasurer to be appointed."

Nath. Greene ....400 dolls paid
H. Knox ....400 ditto paid
John Lawrence ....400 dolls paid
J. Wilkinson ....400 dolls paid
Clement Biddle ....400 dolls paid

Robt. H. Harrison ....400 dolls paid
R. K. Meade ....400 dolls paid
Alex. Hamilton ....400 dolls paid
Tench Tighlman ....400 dolls paid
C. Gibbs ....400 dolls paid
Jno. Pierce ....400 dolls paid
The Baron de Kalb ....400 dolls paid
Jno. Moylan ....400 dolls paid
Le Ch Dulingsley ....400 dolls paid
Geo. Washington ....paid F. D. ($400)
R. Clairborne ....paid 400 dolls
Lord Stirling ....paid 400 dolls
Col. Hazen ....paid 400 dolls
Asa Worthington ....paid 400 dolls
Benj. Brown ....paid 400 dolls
Major Stagg ....paid 400 dolls
James Thompson ....paid 400 dolls
H. Jackson ....paid 400 dolls
Col. Thomas Proctor ....paid 400 dolls
J. B. Cutting ....paid 400 dolls
Edward Hand ....paid 400 dolls
William Little ....paid 400 dolls
Thos. Woodford ....paid 400 dolls
Geo. Olney ....400 dolls paid
Jas. Abeel ....400 dolls paid
Robert Erskine ....400 dolls paid
Jno. Cochran ....400 dolls paid
Geo. Draper ....400 dolls paid
J. Burnet ....400 dolls paid

The Rev. Joseph F. Tuttle, D. D., L. L. D., in speaking of the "dancing assembly," held in Morristown, during the winter of 1780, says: "I will frankly confess this subscription paper produced an unpleasant sensation in my mind, and no reasoning have, as yet, entirely removed the sense of unfitness in the contrast of dancing assemblies * * * and the sufferings of the barefooted, naked, starving soldiers in the camp only four miles off. Just think of what one of those men, who did not attend the assembly balls, related. It was Capt. Wm. Tuttle who said, 'there was a path which lead from the Wicke house down to the Jersey camp and I have often seen that path marked with blood, which had been squeezed from the cracked and naked feet of our soldiers, who had gone up to the house to ask an alms!' How they suffered there, with the snow piled about them, with insufficient clothing and very scanty and poor food; and yet there was dancing at * * * But it is not my object to criticise this contract; for dancing and dying, feasting and starvation, plenty wreathed with flowers, and gaunt famine barefoot and wreathed in rags, are contrasted facts in other places than at Morristown, and at other times than 'this present winter of 1870.' My object in mentioning this subscription paper is to throw light on the currency of the day. Here were thirteen thousand six hundred dollars subscribed to pay the dancing master and tavern keeper for a few nights entertainment. Nominally it is up to the extravagance of the modern Fifth Avenue; but the entire sum subscribed in 1780 by those thirty-four gentlemen, for assembly balls, was not worth more than three hundred silver dollars. * * * Let us rather admire than condemn these brave men, at Morristown, who were striving to invest the stern severities of that winter with something of the gayer and more frivolous courtesies of fashionable life."

The assembly dances, to which reference has been made were held in the Arnold tavern hall, and in the large room on the second floor of the "Continental Store."

A more realistic bit of pictorial reference to the sojourn of Washington's army in Morristown, has not come to the attention of the writer, than the following, quoted from "The Story of an Old Farm," by Andrew D. Melick, Jr.: "There was constant going and coming between the different posts, and the highways and byways were alive with soldiers. Farmer-lads on their way to mill with sacks of corn athwart their horses' backs, rode 'cheek by joul' with spurred and booted troopers, and listened with open-eyed wonder to their warlike tales. The rattle of farm wagons was supplemented by the heavy roll of artillery trains, and squads of infantry were met at every hand."

The time for the removal of the American army from its winter quarters in Morristown and vicinity, and its active participation in another campaign, was approaching. The well authenticated incident about to be related (the popular version is here given), will serve as an illustration of the methods resorted to in the endeavor to procure horses for the transportation of army stores, and for use in the cavalry battalions.

On the right of the road leading westward toward Mendham, and a short distance from the intersection of the Jockey Hollow road with the former road, stood a house, of the New England style of architecture. It was the residence of Henry Wick, the owner of a considerable portion of the land on which the camps of the patriot army were pitched. His daughter, Temperance, familiarly called "Tempe," was an expert horsewoman, and was the owner of a young horse to which she was strongly attached. Perhaps her fondness for this noble animal may have been in a measure owing to the imbibition, on her part, of the sentiment of the poet, who says:

> "Let cavillers deny
> That brutes have reason; sure 'tis something more,
> 'Tis heaven directs, and stratgems inspires
> Beyond the short extent of human thought."

A mile, it may have been, below the Wick house, on the road to Mendham, lived Dr. William Leddell, a brother-in-law of "Temple Wick." On a certain day in the spring of the year 1780, while preparations for the removal of the patriot army were in progress, Temple Wick saddled and bridled her horse, and rode down to Dr. Leddell's for a social call. The call ended she mounted her horse to return home. Nearly in front of the residence of her brother-in-law, she was accosted by several American soldiers, who commanded her to dismount, and let them have her horse. One of the soldiers had rudely seized the bridle reins. Appearing to be submissive to the loss of her horse, meanwhile entreating the soldiers not to take her favorite, she was formulating in her active brain the ruse which, as we shall see outwitted them.

"I am sorry," she coolly remarked, "to part with my horse, but if you are resolved upon taking him from me, let me ask of you two favors, first, that you return him to me, if possible, and second, whether you return him or not, to treat him well."

Completely thrown off their guard by the seeming acquiescence of the gentle rider in the loss of her horse, the reins were released by the soldier who had held them. "Temple" immediately touched the animal with her whip, and like an arrow shot by a strong arm from the bow he sped up the hill toward home. As she rode away at full speed, one or more of the soldiers discharged their muskets in the direction of the bold rider; not, however, with the intention of hitting her, but probably as a means of frightening her into stopping in her rapid flight.

Onward sped horse and rider, up the long hill leading to the Wick house, on reaching which the horse was taken round to the north side, into the kitchen, from thence into the parlor, and through the parlor into the spare bed chamber at the northwest corner of the building. The single wooden window shutter was at once closed, and the horse, after a caress or two from its rider, was left in the darkened room. The soldiers, unwilling to be baffled in their endeavor to procure the horse, hastened on foot up the hill to the Wick house, and after searching the premises in vain for the coveted prize, they departed crestfallen. "Tempe's" favorite horse was kept for three weeks in the spare bed chamber, by the expiration of which time the American troops had taken their departure from the vicinity. The prints of the horse's hoofs upon the floor of the bed chamber in the Wick house were visible for many years after the occurrence of the incident related. They disappeared when, a few years since, a new floor was laid in the room.

The writer has conversed with several persons, each of whom "with my own eyes" saw the hoof prints of "Tempe" Wick's favorite saddle horse in the spare bed chamber. The single window in the room mentioned may be seen in the picture accompanying the present chapter; it is on the first floor and farthest from the front of the famous house. Interesting to relate, the exterior and interior of the Wick house, still (1905) standing, is practically the same as in Revolutionary times. The rooms, so far as dimensions and relative positions are concerned, are exactly as they were in the year 1780. "Leddell's Mill" is still in operation grinding the grain as it did 125 years ago. The stone house—"Dr. Leddell's"—still greets the visitor as he approaches the spot where a woman's tact and bravery outwitted a squad of soldiers greedy for a good horse.

CHAPTER XVIII

"A clatter of hoofs on the road! a shout!
Bring General Wayne to his feet, in a flash
He mounts his steed, for the troops are out!
And now Mad Anthony makes a dash
To turn them back."

Ballads of New Jersey in the Revolution.

ROM several reliable contemporary witnesses it is learned that during his sojourns in Morristown Washington was seldom heard to laugh aloud; and in view of the grave responsibilities which continuously weighed upon the mind and heart of the commander-in-chief of the patriot army, this circumstance should not, and doubtless will not, cause surprise. That Washington's customary seriousness, in the face of the exigencies that confronted him, especially during his two sojourns at the county seat of Morris, did not result in moroseness, is evidenced by the well authenticated fact that a placid smile upon his noble countenance was a frequent and noticeable occurrence.

A few instances, however, have been recorded of a hearty laugh indulged in by the ordinary sedate and dignified commander-in-chief. One of these has come to us through General John Doughty, whose acquaintance with his chief was intimate, and who became a resident of Morristown after the close of the Revolution. It seems that Washington had purchased a young and spirited horse, whose breaking to the saddle he had committed to a man in Morristown, who had made loud professions of efficiency in that particular line. The process of breaking, which took place in a large yard south of the Morristown Green, was eagerly witnessed by the commander-in-chief and some of his friends. It was not without several characteristic flourishes that the professed expert leaped to the horse's back, but scarcely was he seated when the young animal threw his head downward and his heels upward in consequence of which sudden movements the over-confident rider was precipitately hurled to the ground. Fortunately, the man received no injury save a little internal shaking up and a few slight bruises. As the dismounted rider lay on the ground, dazed but uninjured, Washington burst into hearty laughter, which is said to have brought tears to his eyes. Who afterward successfully broke the young horse for the commander-in-chief the writer is unable at present to say.

General John Doughty, whose name has been mentioned, was a man of so great importance as to be deserving of more than a mere passing allusion. From a writer (J. D. O.), who has carefully prepared a life-sketch of this illustrious soldier, the following extract is quoted:

"John Doughty, the son of Thomas, a gentleman of Scottish descent, and of Gertrude Leroux the descendant of a Huguenot family, was born about the middle of the last (the eighteenth) century. In 1770 he graduated at King's (now Columbia) college in the city of New York, and in 1776, when the war broke out between Great Britain and the colonies, he began his military career as 'Captain Leftenant in a company of artellery of the State of New Jersey,' as expressed in the commission which is in my possession. The next year he was promoted to the service of the Continental, or regular army, and as Captain or Mayor of Artillery, he served during the entire war with Washington, Knox, Steuben, Lafayette, Hamilton and others.

On the conclusion of peace, he was ordered to our Western territory, to establish forts or block houses on the Ohio river and elsewhere, and to select sites for our future cities. It is melancholy to find that even in those early days of the Republic, there existed corrupt and designing men, who dared to insult a public officer by offering money and other inducements to select their lands for these sites. The integrity and sagacity of Major Doughty have been fully proved by subsequent events, and particuarly by the city of Cincinnati; where he established a fort and garrison. Many years ago I met in Virginia an enthusiastic citizen of Cincinnati, who assured me that the name of John Doughty was still remembered and venerated in that great Capital.

In the course of this Western expedition Major Doughty had occasion to survey the Tennessee river, and while in a barge manned by sixteen United States soldiers, he was surrounded and attacked by a large force of Indians in canoes. Seated in the stern of his boat he kept up a continuous fire against the enemy. the muskets or rifles being reloaded and handed to him by his men. When eleven out of the sixteen soldiers had been killed or disabled, matters began to look serious, and the Major thought the only thing to be done was to put an end to the Indian chief. Standing up, he 'took a aim' (to use his own words) as cool and deliberate as if he had been shooting a robin. The shot happily was successful, the chieftain fell and the Indians fled. With his diminishing crew it was impossible to make any headway against the current of the rivers, and he floated down the Tennessee, Ohio and Mississippi, until he reached the Spanish post in Louisiana. He threw himself upon the hospitality of the commandant of the garrison, by whom he was kindly entertained, and furnished with an escort to his own country. His protracted absence had caused the greatest anxiety to his relatives and friends, as well as to the Government. The letter addressed to him by Gen. Knox, Secretary of War, congratulating him on his safe and unexpected return, attests the high estimation in which he was held by the Department at Washington. A short time after, he was appointed by General Washington, Colonel commandant of a new regiment of infantry, to consist of three battalions, 'in consideration,' as General Knox writes, 'of his long and valuable services.' This position he did not long hold, but in those piping times of peace, preferred, like Cincinnatus, to retire to his own country home. But he was not long permitted to remain inactive. The Government having received alarming accounts of the encroachments of the British on our northern frontier, whereby the people on the border were greatly excited and a collision between the two countries. was to be apprehended, entrusted Colonel Doughty with the delicate and confidential mission of ascertaining the truth of these reports. The story of the alleged encroachments was found to be false or exaggerated and the reports were pronounced frivolous and unfounded.

Together with Washington, Schuyler, Knox and other officers of the army of the Revolution, Colonel Doughty was one of the founders of the honorable Society of the Cincinnati. * * * The remaining portion of his life was spent in agricultural pursuits, in the cultivation of literature, and in the exercise of a generous and elegant hospitality. * * * The property of General Doughty consisted of about four hundred acres of land lying on each side of the Basking Ridge road, beginning at Morristown and extending nearly a mile to the Southwest."

On the eighteenth day of April, in the year 1780, two distinguished foreigners arrived in Morristown; they were the French Minister, Chevalier de la Luzerne, and Don Juan de Miralles, a Spanish gentleman the latter of whom was a representative of the Spanish Court before the American Congress. A review of four of the more presentable battalions of the patriot army, in honor of these foreign diplomats, having been decided upon by the commander-in-chief, Baron Steuben, the thorough disciplinarian of the army, was instructed to make the necessary preparations for the event. This review, or parade, which occurred on the twenty-fourth of April, took place on the grand parade, on the Jockey Hollow road. The large platform erected in the field as a reviewing stand, was filled with ladies and gentlemen of distinction, from various portions of the States, among whom were Governor Livingston and Mrs. Livingston, of New Jersey, and officers of the American army encamped in Morristown and vicinity. The evolutions performed by the four carefully selected "crack" battalions were of a character to afford satisfaction to the commander-in-chief;

and received, also, the expressed approbation of Chevalier de la Luzerne, who occupied a special seat on the reviewing stand. Don Juan de Miralles, as will in due course be seen, was not present upon this interesting occasion.

In the evening a ball was given by the chief officers of the American army, probably in the hall on the second floor of the "Continental House," at which Washington and Luzerne were present, as well, also, as not a few ladies and gentlemen of more or less distinction. From the camp ground of Knox's artillery brigade on the Mendham road, a display of fireworks, including cannon firing, sky rockets, and other curious pyrotechnics, was given for the entertainment of those who, for several reasons, did not attend the "grand ball." As the ballroom was lighted by means of tallow candles, requiring frequent "snuffings," numerous non-attendants doubtless enjoyed a larger measure of illumination than those who, to the music of the times, "tripped the light fantastic toe."

While the four battalions of the patriot army were performing their military maneuvers on the parade ground, and while other "crack" battalions, owing to lack of shoes and stockings and presentable clothing, were unable to participate in "mock war" for the gratification of distinguished visitors, Don Juan de Miralles was tossing with death fever on his bed at Short Hills, whither, on the day after his arrival in Morristown, he had gone on a visit to friends. On the twenty-sixth or twenty-seventh of the month of April he succumbed (in Morristown, according to one account, at least) to the disease with which he had been stricken, and on the twenty-ninth was buried with the honors due to his official station at Morristown.

The style in which he was buried is said to have surpassed in magnificence that of any other burial ever occurring at the county seat of Morris. His coffin was covered on the outside with rich black velvet, and lined with fine cambric. For burial, he wore a scarlet suit, embroidered with gold lace, a gold-laced hat, a wig carefully cued, white silk stockings and diamond shoe and knee buckles. On his fingers appeared a profusion of diamond rings, and suspended from a superb gold watch were several seals richly set with diamonds. The honorary pallbearers were six field officers, and on the shoulders of four artillery officers in full uniform, the actual pallbearers, he was borne to the grave. The chief mourners were Washington and other officers of high rank, and several members of the American Congress. A procession extending over a mile, composed of army officers and representative Morristown citizens, followed the remains to the grave, while minute guns were fired by the artillery. A Spanish priest performed the last rites at the grave, employing the impressive form of the Roman Catholic church. To prevent the disturbing of the buried remains for "filthy lucre's" sake, a guard of soldiers was placed at the grave of the Spanish Minister in the Presbyterian church cemetery.

Mention has not a few times been made of the

"Continental House," a famous structure, the history of which is briefly as follows: During the encampment of the American army in and near Morristown in the year 1777, Moore Freeman, deputy quartermaster-general of New Jersey at the time, applied to the trustees of the Presbyterian church for leave to erect a storehouse for the Continental army on "the parsonage lot," as the lands belonging to the church were sometimes called. Consent being given, the building was erected. It stood on the present site of the national bank, and next to a house which had been built by a "Mr. Huntington, deceased." This Mr. Huntington may have been Simon Huntington, who died July 17, 1770, in the seventy-fourth year of his age. The Huntington house seems to have stood somewhat to the southeast of the Continental House.

The "Continental House," as its name partially indicates, was used for a few years after its erection as a storage place for army supplies of various kinds. To this storehouse Colonel Benoni Hathaway seems to have brought some of the "merchantable powder," manufactured at Ford's powder mill, on the Whippanong River. In this building some of the officers and soldiers of Washington's army were quartered, a portion of the latter, no doubt, as guards, during the winters of 1777, 1779 and 1780.

Here were brought several cannon captured by American troops in a British sloop, which was grounded in Elizabethtown Creek. The names of some of the Morris County soldiers who assisted in bringing these guns to the county seat are: Captain William Day, Ephraim Sayre, James Brookfield, Samuel Day, Ellis Cook, Caleb Horton (son of the first pastor of Madison) Joseph Bruen, Benjamin Harris and Benjamin Bonnell. During Washington's second sojourn in Morristown, in the winter of 1779-80, the upper part of the Continental House was used for several assembly balls. It was not, however, used as a tavern until after the close of the seven years' struggle for independence. It was burned in the year 1846 when the palatial New Jersey Hotel, which it adjoined, was destroyed by fire.

A very pretty incident is related as having occurred in the spring of the year 1780, at the Dr. Jabez Campfield residence, situated on what is now Morris street, a picture of which appears in this volume. This house was the quarters of the surgeon-general of the American army, Dr. John Cochran. Mrs. Cochran was the only sister of General Philip Schuyler, whose daughter Elizabeth, a charming girl of twenty-two years of age, spent several months as a visitor at her aunt's in the early part of the year last mentioned. At the quarters of the surgeon-general, Colonel Alexander Hamilton, one of Washington's aides, and a resident at the Ford mansion, was a frequent visitor during Miss Schuyler's sojourn at the former place. It was said that the presence of Miss Schuyler at the Cochran home was the chief attraction to Colonel Hamilton, and it is popularly believed that the courtship which resulted in the subsequent marriage of this interesting couple had its beginning at the quarters of Dr. John Cochran.

In the month of September, of the year 1848, Lossing, the entertaining writer of history, visited Morristown. He was the guest over the one night he spent at the county seat of Morris, of the Hon. Gabriel H. Ford, son of Colonel Jacob Ford, Jr., at the Ford Mansion. In the account of his flying visit to Morristown, as given in "Field Book of the American Revolution," he says:

"I have said I spent an evening at Morristown with Judge Ford, the proprietor of the headquarters of Washington. I look back upon the conversation of that evening with much pleasure, for the venerable octogenarian entertained me until a late hour with many pleasing anecdotes illustrative of the social condition of the army, and of the private character of the commander-in-chief.

"As an example of Washington's careful attention to small matters, and his sense of justice he mentioned the fact that, when he took up his residence with his mother, he made an inventory of all articles which were appropriated to his use during the winter. When he withdrew in the spring, he inquired of Mrs. Ford whether everything had been returned to her. 'All but one silver tablespoon,' she answered. He took note of it, and not long afterward she received from him a spoon hearing his initials—'G. W.' That spoon is preserved as a precious relic in the family. * * * Mr. Ford, then a lad, was a favorite with Hamilton, and, by permission of the chief, the colonel would give him the countersign, so as to allow him to play at the village after the sentinels were posted for the night. On one occasion he was returning home about nine o'clock in the evening, and had passed the sentinel, when he recognized the voice of Hamilton in a reply to the soldier's demand of 'Who comes there?' He stepped aside, and waited for the colonel to accompany him to the house. Hamilton came up to the point of the presented bayonet of the sentinel to give the countersign, but he had quite forgotten it. 'He had spent the evening' said Judge Ford, who related the anecdote to me, 'with Miss Schuyler, and thoughts of her undoubtedly expelled the countersign from his head.' The soldier lover was embarrassed, and the sentinel, who knew him well, was stern in the performance of his duty. Hamilton pressed his hand upon his forehead, and tried hard to summon the cabalistic words from their hiding place, but, like the faithful sentinel, they were immovable. Just then he recognized young Ford in the gloom. 'Ay, Master Ford, is that you?' he said in an undertone; and stepping aside, he called the lad to him, drew his ear to his mouth, and whispered, 'Give me the countersign.' He did so, and Hamilton stepping in front of the soldier, delivered it. The sentinel, seeing the movement, and believing that his superior was testing his fidelity, kept his bayonet unmoved. 'I have given you the countersign; why do you not shoulder your musket?' asked Hamilton. 'Will that do, colonel?' asked the soldier in reply. 'It will do, for this time,' said Hamilton; 'let me pass.' The soldier reluctantly obeyed the illegal command, and Hamilton and his young companion reached headquarters without further difficulty. Colonel Hamilton afterward married Miss Schuyler."

From "Publications of the Pennsylvania Society of the Colonial Dames of America, No. 1, Edited by the Committee on Research," the following valuable extract is given:

"(Captain John Steele, son of Captain William and Rachel Carr Steele, was born in Lancaster County, Pennsylvania, in the year 1761. At the age of seventeen he ran away from college to enter the army, and was soon made captain of a company of veterans from Cumberland Valley. He was nineteen years old when the following letter was written. Wounded at Brandywine, he followed Washington through his campaigns until the surrender of Cornwallis, when Captain Steele was officer of the day. Immediately after the war he married Abigail Bailey, of Lancaster County. He frequently represented his district in the Senate and House of Representatives of Pennsylvania. In 1809 he was appointed Collector of the Port of Philadelphia, which office he held until shortly before his death in 1827. He was one of the original members of the Cincinnati. He is buried in the old Pine Street Presbyterian churchyard, Philadelphia.)"

"Dear Will: I have omitted several opportunities of writing, with a daily expectation of seeing you and my brother Jake, which I now cease to hope for, as we have taken the field for several days in consequence of a sudden and unexpected excursion of the enemy, from Staten Island and Jersey, who have, (as usual) committed the most cruel and wanton depredations by burning and destroying the houses and property of many peaceable and defenceless inhabitants;

but the most striking instance of their barbarity was in taking the life of a most amiable lady, wife of Parson Caldwell of Springfield, who left nine small children. the youngest eight months old which sat in its Mamma's lap a witness to the cruel murder, though insensible of its loss, nor did their barbarity end there, for after several skirmishes (in which it is thought we killed at least 150 and a proportionate number wounded, together with several officers, one of which was General Stirling) they retired to Elizabeth Town Point, where they remained fortifying and possessing themselves of parts of the town; and 'tis said that two nights ago they made an indiscriminate sacrifice of all the females in the place:—a cruel slaughter indeed! Yesterday a Captain from the British army deserted to us, the cause to me unknown, but he is beyond doubt a damned rascal, but it all conspires to make glorious the once dreaded (though now ignominious) arms of Britain.

"I am at present enjoying myself incomparably well in the family of Mrs. Washington, whose guard I have had the honour to command, since the absence of the General and the rest of the family, which is now six or seven days. I am happy in the importance of my charge as well as in the presence of the most amiable woman upon earth, whose character should I attempt to describe I could not do justice to, but will only say I think it unexceptionable: the first and second nights after I came it was expected that a body of the enemy's horse would pay us a visit, but I was well prepared to receive them, for I had not only a good detachment of well disciplined troops under my command, but four members of Congress who came volunteers with their musquets, bayonets and ammunition. I assure you they have disposed of a greater share of Spirits than you have ever seen in that body or perhaps ever will see as long as they exist. I leave you to judge whether there is not considerable mint due their commander. I only wish I had a company of them to command for a campaign! and if you would not see an alteration in the constitution of our army against the next, I would suffer to lose my ears and never command a Congressman again. The rations they have consumed considerably overbalance all their service done as volunteers, for they have dined with us every day almost, and drank as much wine as they would earn in six months. Make my best love to my dear sister Betsey, parents, brothers and sisters, as well as to all my good neighbors; but in a most particular manner to somebody I can't write to for fear of miscarriage.

"I am your affectionate Brother,

JACK STEELE,

"Headquarters, Morristown, June 14th, '80."

Washington, with the greater portion of the patriot army, left Morristown in the early part of the month of June, in the year 1780. By the twenty-first of the month he was on his way toward West Point, on the Hudson. Two brigades of the army, however, in command of General Greene, were left in the vicinity of Springfield, about ten miles southeast of the county seat of Morris. Landing at Elizabethtown Point on the night of June 5, with 5,000 men, including the famous Coldstream Guards, Lieutenant-General Knyphausen, the British commander, made an attempt on the following day to reach Morristown. At Connecticut Farms he was met by an American force in command of General Maxwell, and Colonel Dayton. The patriot army was, however, pushed back toward Springfield, where, on the twenty-third of June, a battle was fought, resulting in the hasty retreat of the British force. Among the participants in the actions at Connecticut Farms and Springfield was Lieutenant-Colonel Benoni Hathaway, of Morristown. At the former place, Colonel Hathaway received a severe wound in the neck, from a British sentinel, whose repeated challenge he deliberately failed to answer. At the battle of Springfield, in which Colonel Hathaway exhibited great bravery, there occurred a disagreement between him and General Heard, an efficient officer, whom Hathaway accused of unnecessarily leaving the field with his command. On his return to Morristown Colonel Hathaway preferred charges against his superior officer, his communication to Governor Livingston being as follows:

Morristown, 15 July, 1780.

"To his Exelency the Governor. I send you in Closed Severel charges which I Charg B D Haird with while he commanded the Militare Sum Time in jun Last at Elizabeth Town farms which I pray His Exilency would Call a Court of inquiry on these Charges if his Exilency thinkes it worth notising from your Hum Ser Benonoi Hathaway Lut Coll." To exilency the Governor.

"This is the Charges that I bring against General Haird While he Commanded the Milita at Elizabethtown farms sum Time in June last 1780.

"1—Charg is for leaving his post and Marching the Trups of their post without order and Leaving that Pass without aney gard between the Enemy and our armey without giving aney notis that pass was open Between three and fore Ours.

"2—Charg is Retreating in Disorder Before the Enemy without ordering aney Rear gard or flanks out leading of the Retreat Him Self.

"3—Charg is for marching the Trups of from advantiges peace of ground wheare we mit Noyed them much and Lickley prevented thear gaining the Bridg at Fox Hall had not the Trups Bin ordered of which prevented our giving our armey aney assistence in a Time of great Destris.

"4—Charg is for marching the Trups of a Bout one mile from aney part of the Enemy and taken them upon an Hy mountan and kept them thear till the Enemy had gained Springfeald Bridge.

"List of Evidence

Coll Van Cortland
Wm Skank the Brigad Major
Capt Benjman Cartur
Capt Nathaniel Horton
Adjt Kiten King
Major Samuel Hays
Leutnant Backover."

Morristown was of too great importance, strategically, to be entirely abandoned by the American forces, hence, on his departure in the early part of June, in the year 1780, Washington had left there about 2,000 Pennsylvania troops, which, with the local militia, were considered adequate to the protection of the county seat of Morris. These Pennsylvania troops were at the time encamped on the grounds at the southeast corner of the Jockey Hollow and Mendham roads, the position formerly occupied by Hand's brigade. Between these troops and their officers there was a difference of opinion concerning the term of service for which they had enlisted; the rank and file contending that it was for three years only, while the latter were equally as earnest in their contention that it was for the war, regardless of how long it might continue.

If this had been the only cause of dissatisfaction on the part of the troops encamped on the Jockey Hollow road, the trouble of which we are about to speak might not have ocurred; but these soldiers had received no pay for twelve months and they were also without necessary food and clothing.

"Though the Pennsylvania troops (we now quote from Thatcher in his Military Journal, written while the Revolution was in progress) have been subjected to all the discouragements and difficulties felt by the rest of the army, some particular circumstances peculiar to themselves have contributed to produce the revolt. When the soldiers first enlisted, the recruiting officers were provided with enlisting rolls for the term of three years, or during the continuance of the war, and as the officers indulged the opinion that the war would not continue more than three years, they were perhaps indifferent in which column the soldier's name was inserted, leaving it liable to an ambiguity of construction. It is clear, however, that a part, enlisted for three years, and others for the more indefinite term 'during the war.' The soldiers now contend that they enlisted for three years at furthest, and were to have been discharged sooner, in case the war terminated before the expiration of this term. The war being protracted beyond the time expected, and the officers knowing the value of soldiers who have been trained by three years' service, are accused of putting a different construction on the original agreement, and claiming their services during the war. The soldiers, even those who actually listed for the war, having received very small bounties, complain of imposition and deception, and their case is extremely aggravated by the fact, that three half Joes have now been offered as a bounty to others, who will enlist for th remainder of the war, when these veteran soldiers hav served three years for a mere shadow of compensation! I was scarcely necessary to add to their trying circumstances a total want of pay for twelve months, and a state of naked ness and famine, to excite in a soldier the spirit of insurrec tion. The officers themselves, also feeling aggrieved, an in a destitution, relaxed in their system of camp disciplin and the soldiers occasionally overheard their murmurs an complaints."

Continued brooding through the autumn of the yea 1780, over the situation, resulted in the decision to re volt. In accordance, therefore, with preconceive plans, the entire force of Pennsylvania troops, with th exception of portions of three regiments, marche under arms to the magazine (or storehouse) wher they supplied themselves with provisions and ammu nition. This was on the first day of January, in th year 1781. They seized six field pieces, and from th stables of General Wayne took the required comple ment of horses to move them.

By some writers of local history it is stated that th magazine from which these revolters procured thei supplies was the one located on the south side of th Morristown Green, known as the "Continenta House," subsequently transformed into a tavern an kept by one O'Hara. The more reasonable theory however, as the present writer conceives (and a theory indeed, which has substantial support in extant dcou mentary evidence), is that from the magazine estab lished by General Wayne, after his arrival in Morris town late in the year 1780,just to the east of the Wick house, the revolters procured provisions and ammunition. From the "Continental House," near the Morristown Green, the mutineers are by some said to have procured the field pieces, as this magazine was the repository of cannon while in use as a storehouse of government supplies, but it is far more likely that the field pieces were found nearer camp. Indeed, it is practically certain that they were taken from the summit of Fort Hill, to the rear of the camp ground, where cannon had previously been planted for defense against attack by the enemy. The mutineers are said to have been in command of a sergeant-major, by them appointed, whom they called "major-general."

Of the fragments of the brigade which had not at first joined in the revolt, some of the line officers took command, and with them attempted to restore order. There is a local tradition to the effect that the revolters, in their resistance to this attempt, fired and killed Captain Adam Bettin, of the Tenth Pennsylvania Regiment, and wounded several other officers. It is said that on either side several were killed. Of the wounding and killing of several of the officers and soldiers there is little doubt; but the popular theory concerning the manner of Bettin's death should in view of the facts in the case, be abandoned. The facts, as extant records indicate, are as follows: Some of the mutineers were in pursuit of an officer who had attempted to use force in quelling the mutiny. As the pursuers turned a corner of one of the camp streets they suddenly encountered Captain Bettin. In their excited state of mind, mistaking Bettin for the officer they were pursuing, the mutineers fired, and killed him on the spot; his killing was, therefore, surely accidental.

The threat of the mutineers to bayonet their opposers if they did not instantly join in the revolt produced the desired effect, and the rank and file of the entire brigade were soon involved in the mutiny, which is now one of the interesting incidents of local history.

General Anthony Wayne, who was in command of the Pennsylvania troops in Morristown at the period under consideration, was quartered at the residence of Peter Kemble, on the Basking Ridge road, about a mile southeast from camp. Hearing, on the morning of January first, of the mutiny of his troops, Wayne mounted his horse, and, in company with some of his staff officers, sped westward toward the camp, in the hope of being able to restore order. In a field on the opposite side of the road from camp where some of the mutineers were gathered, Wayne addressed his soldiers, endeavoring to persuade them to return to duty. After listening for some time to their beloved commander, the soldiers became restless; and one of their number discharged his musket over Wayne's head. Wayne, supposing the musket had been discharged at him, immediately threw back his outer clothing, thus baring his breast, and exclaimed: "Shoot me, if you will!" But no further shots being fired the brave officer was convinced that there was no murderous intent on the part of his troops. After further vain attempts to restore order General Wayne returned to his quarters at Peter Kemble's.

Toward evening, with the sergeant-major at their head, the mutineers marched down the Fort Hill road on their way, in accordance with mutual resolution, toward Philadelphia. As the mutineers came in sight, Wayne went out from his quarters to ascertain the occasion of the strange spectacle which greeted his eyes. He intercepted the resolute mutineers at a point a little to the southeast of the crossing of the Basking Ridge road by the road from Fort Hill. The locality is indicated by a picture accompanying the present volume. Upon ascertaining the intent of his troops, he endeavored, first by expostulation, and then by threats, to dissuade them from their purpose.

Cocking his pistol and pointing it toward some of the leaders of the revolt, Wayne threatened to shoot them if they did not, with the body of troops, return at once to their camp on Kemble Hill, and then and there was enacted a scene which might well engage the artist's skill in depicting upon canvas what occurred. Wayne's threat had scarcely escaped his lips when scores of bayonets were at his breast.

> "General," sternly spoke one of the revolters, "we respect and love you; often have you led us into battle, but we are no longer under your command; we warn you to be on your guard; if you fire your pistol or attempt to enforce your commands, we shall put you instantly to death."

Suddenly impressed, as the writer conceives, with

the justness of the cause which could impel men to open revolt against their superior officer, Wayne resolved to join his brave soldiers in their endeavor to secure an adjustment of the grievances they had so long and so patiently borne for freedom's sake. The brigade quartermaster was at once ordered by General Wayne to furnish the revolters with a supply of provisions. No finer evidence of the popularity of Wayne could be adduced than the fact that even after the occurrence just mentioned, the revolters, acting upon the advice of their beloved general, concluded to march to Princeton by way of the Basking Ridge road. Led by their former commander, General Wayne, accompanied by other officers, the Pennsylvania troops reached Princeton, where they laid their grievances before a committee of Congress, appointed for the purpose. Ever will it stand to the credit of the intelligent manhood of these troops that the justice of their cause was recognized, and their demands satisfied.

Sir Henry Clinton, on being informed of the mutiny of the Pennsylvania troops, sent a sergeant of the British army, and a Jersey Tory by the name of Ogden, to offer them the protection of the British Government; holding out flattering inducements by way of persuading them to this desertion of the cause of freedom. The offer was not only indignantly spurned, but the two British emissaries were delivered over to General Wayne, who had them tried as spies. They were convicted, and promptly executed.

"See! comrades," said one of the leaders of the mutineers, "he takes us for traitors. Let us show him that the American army can furnish but one Arnold, and that America has no truer friends than we."

As a well deserved tribute to the patriotism and efficiency of the Pennsylvania troops, an account of whose mutiny has been given, the following extracts from two letters of General Wayne, written, one of them, at least, to Washington, but a few weeks previously, are here appended:

"I forgot to mention to your excellency, that the 1st and 2nd Brigade (Pennsylvania) marched at a moment's warning, leaving our tents standing, guards and detachments out, pushed with rapidity to secure this pass, where it would be in our power to dispute the ground inch by inch, or to proceed to West Point as occasion might require, which was effected in as little time as ever so long a march was performed in. * * * The 1st Pennsylvania Brigade moved immediately, and on the arrival of the 2d express I was speedily followed by our gallant friend, Gen'l Irvine, with the 2nd Brigade. Our march of sixteen miles was performed in four hours, during a dark night, without a single halt, or man left behind. When our approach was announced to the General, he thought it fabulous, but when assured of his 10th Legion being near him, he expressed great satisfaction and pleasure."

General Anthony Wayne, or "Mad Anthony," as he had already come to be known, is a unique figure in the annals of the Revolution. His father, or grandfather, it is not clear which, was a native of the Emerald Isle. Chester County, Pa., was the birthplace of Anthony. The year of his birth was 1745 or 1746;

hence at the time of the mutiny among his troops, he was but about thirty-six years of age. At the outbreak of the Revolution he organized in his native State a volunteer corps. In the year 1776 Congress appointed him to the command of a regiment. He participated in the operations in Canada. At Ticonderoga he was in command of the patriot army. Later he was commissioned a brigadier-general by Congress. At Germantown, Wayne commanded a division of Washington's army; and at the battle of Monmouth he greatly distinguished himself. By one of the most brilliant assaults of history he recaptured Stony Point from the British, receiving a wound during the assault. A vote of thanks and a gold medal were bestowed upon Wayne for his famous act at Stony Point. In the campaign resulting in the surrender of the British at Yorktown he was again wounded.

General Wayne was with the patriot army during its first encampment at Morristown and vicinity in the winter of the year 1777. He was quartered in the house of Deacon Ephraim Sayre, at Bottle Hill, now Madison. His body-guard were quartered in the kitchen in the rear of the main house. General Wayne occupied a room, known as "the front room," situated on the northerly end of the Sayre house. He was accompanied by a small mulatto servant, whose martial spirit was stimulated by the carriage of a wooden sword, with edges finely sharpened. Wayne did not accompany the American army to Morristown in the winter of the year 1779-80. On the way from his post to Pennsylvania late in the year 1779, however, he passed through Morristown. He may have rejoined the patriot army at Nyack, in the summer of the year 1780, and late in the same year he came to Morristown, and established his quarters at the Kemble house on the Basking Ridge road. Of his connection with the mutiny of his troops we have already spoken at sufficient length for present purposes.

Consideration for fondly cherished local tradition, on the part of the present writer, is responsible for the version of the "Tempe" Wicke episode previously given in these pages. There is, however, another version which seems to be more in accord with reason, and which is not without a good basis in extant documentary evidence; this version of the episode is as follows: During the mutiny of the Pennsylvania troops down the Jockey Hollow road, which, as our readers have seen, ocurred on the opening day of the year 1781, the mutineers had in some way found access to a liberal supply of alcoholic drinks; whether rum or applejack, the writer is unable to say. Judging from the evidence furnished by fragmentary records of the mutiny, there was, to employ a modern phrase, "a hot time," in the vicinity of the Wicke house, on the first day of January, in the year 1781. The intoxication, and consequent rioting, were continued for several days after the departure of the main body of General Wayne's troops for Princeton, by detachments of soldiers left behind to guard the camp equipage and officers' baggage. Doubtless there were, also, not a few stragglers, who had, without orders, remained in the vicinity of their former encampment.

Mrs. Wicke, who was in poor health at the time of the mutiny of Wayne's troops, was greatly annoyed by the noises attending the unbridled carousals of the drunken soldiers. "For on January 1st, 1781, there came the mutiny in General Wayne's command so near his (Mr. Wicke's) home that the sounds of the shots that killed Captain Bettin must have reached the ears of its inmates;" such is the statement to be found in No. 111, of "A Branch of the Woodruff Stock," by our talented townsman, Francis E. Woodruff. Mr. Wicke—again we quote from the above named authority—"was Captain of a company of Morris County cavalry that did good service in the war and engaged in at least one sharp fight, though frequently detailed as guard for Governor Livingston"—was absent from home, and Mrs. Wicke and her daughter, "Tempe," seem to have been the only adult occupants of the house. During the day, Mrs. Wicke had an ill turn, induced, perhaps, by the excitement incident to the unusual occurrences about the place. The immediate attendance of a physician became necessary. Upon "Tempe" Wicke, therefore, devolved the duty of going for Dr. William Leddell, the family physician, who lived about a mile to the westward. As a means of insuring more completely the safety of her mother during her absence, "Tempe" carried her into the cellar. Saddling and bridling and mounting her favorite horse, the devoted daughter sped away down the hill toward Dr. Leddell's. Her errand accomplished, she again mounted her horse for a hasty return home. In front of the Leddell house she encountered two or three intoxicated soldiers—some of the mutineers, perhaps, but more likely some of the stragglers alluded to, whose too free use of intoxicants (procured, possibly, from the officers' baggage) had made them reckless. Rudely seizing the horse's bridle, they commanded "Tempe" to dismount, and allow them to take the animal. Mr. Francis E. Woodruff says, in one of his carefully compiled pamphlets. "It was nearly in front of Dr. Leddell's that she ('Tempe' Wicke) refused to give up her pet (saddle horse) to our disorderly soldiers and galloped away from them." On reaching home "Tempe" hastily dismounted from her foaming horse, led him through the kitchen and front room into the spare bed chamber, secured him and closed the wooden window shutter. Here he was kept three of four days; by the end of which time the mutineers had entirely disappeared from the neighborhood.

In a communication to the writer, written while the series of articles on "History of Moristown, N. J. The Story of its First Century," were running in the Saturday issues of The Newark Evening News, a well informed local historian, said: "I read your horse story the same evening. It is very well told. Would advise your shading two or three points. (1) Some report '3 days,' not '3 weeks.' One possible, the other incredible; mutineers did not hang about so long. (2) Not

1780, but 1781. Discipline good in 1780, except for fowls. Farmers' round robin, end of 1780, made much complaint of fowls, fence rails, and bad manners, none about horses. * * * No order to draft horses. (Drafting of horses always orderly and serious business, anyhow). (3) If mutineer fired, he certainly fired wild to scare girl. They were not murderous."

In reply to the query—"Did you ever hear of a ring in the room where the horse ("Tempe" Wicke's) was kept, to which the horse was tied?" recently submitted in writing to Miss Mary E. Leddell, by the writer, she says: "I have heard of a hole in a timber in which a ring-bolt was inserted for the tie-strap." Miss Leddell was the former owner and is the present occupant of the historic Dr. William Leddell place. Of Dr. Leddell she is a lineal descendant.

In view of the frequent references in these pages to the "Wicke house" and the "Dr. Leddell house," it will doubtless be interesting to readers to learn something of their history, in addition to what has already been said in these pages concerning them. "The Wicke Tract was purchased in 1746. Our first record of Henry Wicke as of Morris County, was in 1748. We suppose the house was built in 1747"—such was the reply of Miss Mary E. Leddell, to the query. "Do you know when, or by whom, the Wicke house was built?" submitted to her by the writer in the month of July, of the present year. To the query, "Did you ever hear where the 'magazine' of General Wayne was situated; how far to the east of the Wicke house?" she replied: "In the orchard half-way between the house and the Jockey Hollow road." While the following query and reply are not strictly Apropos, their importance will, it is thought, justify their introduction here. "Did you ever hear whether the oak tree now standing at the head of Captain Bettin's grave was there when he was buried?" Reply: "I have never heard that it was standing. I suppose it was, as oaks are of slow growth, and that is a large tree."

It may have been in the latter part of the month of June, of the present year, that a letter of inquiry concerning the appearance and history of the Dr. William Leddell house, was mailed to Miss Leddell; her reply is of such great interest to lovers of local annals, that it should not be permitted to fall into "the swallowing gulf of dark forgetfulness and deep oblivion." It is, therefore, given verbatim:

"Basking Ridge,
Somerset County, New Jersey,
July 5th, 1905.

"Rev. Andrew M. Sherman,
Morristown, N. J.

Dear Sir:—"My knowledge of the Revolutionary home of Dr. Wm. Leddell is limited. I never heard it accurately described, but know that it was a frame building which covered a good deal of ground. The kitchen and sitting room were at the western end of the dwelling; kitchen at the back with its outer door opening near the well. Beneath these rooms a basement room was used as a store, in which a thriving business was conducted by furnishing various articles to the soldiers.

"Tradition states that the grounds about Dr. Leddell's dwelling were the most tastefully arranged and neatly kept premises in the vicinity. The terraces which Dr. Leddell had constructed, and on which he located his botanical and kitchen gardens, may be seen today.

"Tradition states that the soldiers located themselves on the mountain east of the Leddell home one afternoon of the last week of November, 1779.

"Dr. Leddell was not at home when they arrived and lighted their first line of camp fires. When the Doctor returned, he saw that these fires were too near his buildings for safety, and sent his body servant—one of his slaves, named 'Sam'—to bid the officers of the company to come to his house. When they came, the Doctor requested them to have the camp-fires extinguished, and other fires lighted, at a safe distance from the buildings. The officers complied with this request and the buildings saved from harm.

"In a memorandum book of Doctor Leddell's we find a note telling of a journey, made July, 1781, when he visited Colonel Pickering, who was Quartermaster and located at New Windsor, on the Hudson. The colonel appointed a committee to adjudge the damage wrought by the army while camping on the Leddell and Wick lands. As both estates were stripped of wood and timber, the loss was heavy. We have no record of this government debt being paid, and it is a pleasure to the members of the present generation to know that their ancestors had the privilege and ability to make admirable sacrifice on the altar of Liberty.

Yours respectfully,

(Miss) MARY E. LEDDELL."

Replying to the inquiry as to the date of the burning of the dwelling of Dr. William Leddell of the Revolutionary period, Miss Leddell said:

"After making inquiry I find no date of the time when Dr. Leddell's dwelling was burned, but my knowledge of some circumstances leads me to think it was burned prior to 1818. The fire was caused by flames from the oven-flue. The Dutch oven in the kitchen was being heated, preparatory to baking. The soot in the flue taking fire, blazed above the chimney top, and sparks falling on the dry roof caused it to ignite."

Reference has been made to the encampment, in the late fall of the year 1779, of a portion of Washington's army on grounds to the east of the Dr. Leddell house. Having been informed that John W. Melick, of Morristown, had, when a boy, seen some of the traces of the camping grounds alluded to by Dr. Leddell in his memorandum book, the writer procured from the former the following written statement:

"In the summer of the year 1877, the First Presbyterian Church Sunday School, of Mendham, held a picnic in the woods on the Leddell farm. The grounds were reached by leaving the main road and taking a by-road that passed between the saw mill and the stone house. We then skirted the lake, and, passing into the woods at the right, reached the grove which had been cleared of underbrush. This grove was situated about half a mile northeast of the stone house (Dr. Leddell's), and about midway between the house and an open field, which was said to have been one of the parade grounds of the Revolutionary soldiers (one of the Pennsylvania brigades). After we had eaten our dinners, my father climbed the hill at the south which at that time was heavily wooded, and, at a distance of about one-fourth of a mile from the picnic grounds, discovered some of the stone fire-places, which we concluded had been used by soldiers in the Revolution. After removing the leaves and some of the dirt, traces of the ashes could be seen. I was only 14 years of age that time, but it was a very interesting experience for us, and especially for the older members of the Sunday School, to see those reminders of our country's struggle for liberty.

"Very respectfully yours,

JOHN W. MELICK.

"Morristown, N. J.,
October 2, 1905."

"Sun of the moral world! effulgent source
Of man's best wisdom and his steadiest force,
Soul searching Freedom! here assume the stand
And radiate hence to every distant land."

CHAPTER XIX

F the mutiny of "Mad Anthony" Wayne's Pennsylvania troops down the Jockey Hollow road, a concise account of which has been given in a previous chapter, may be spoken of as an "ill wind," then there may very appropriately be quoted, at this point of our story the familiar and significant lines:

> "Except wind stands as it never stood,
> It is an ill wind turns none to good."

In consequence of this mutiny, and that of the New Jersey troops encamped near Pompton, which occurred on the twenty-seventh day of the same month, and year, the American Congress so far awoke to the gravity of the situation and to the recognition of the justice of the claims of the patriot soldiers, as to move that national body to the prompt employment of measures for the relief of the long-suffering American army. By means of taxation, and by other measures adopted by the National Legislature, money was soon raised for the prosecution of the war for independence. The establishment of the Bank of North America, upon the recommendation of Robert Morris, the masterful financier of this critical period of our national history, proved an invaluable aid in conducting the Revolution to a successful issue.

The complete rout of the British troops under Tarleton, and the capture of more than five hundred prisoners, at the Cowpens, on the seventeenth day of January, in the year 1781, by the American force, commanded by Morgan; the virtual defeat of Cornwallis at Guilford Courthouse, on the fifteenth day of the following March, by the combined forces of Morgan and Greene; the retreat of the patriot forces under Greene from Hobkirk's Hill, on the twenty-fifth day of April of the same year, after a severe engagement; and the drawn battle of Eutaw Springs, on the eighth day of September, in the year 1781, in which Greene captured 500 prisoners, closed the campaign in the Carolinas.

Passing over a few of the minor operations of the two armies, conducted mainly in Virginia, it may be said that in the month of August, in the year 1781, we find Cornwallis concentrating his forces at Yorktown, where he threw up strong fortifications. With a large land force Washington invested Yorktown, while the York and James rivers were effectively blockaded by a French fleet in command of Count de Grasse. A cannonade commenced by the American forces on October 9, 1781, and continued until the nineteenth day of the same month, resulted in the unconditional surrender of Cornwallis, with 7,000 soldiers, to Washington.

Among the participants in this last and decisive battle of the Revolution, it should be said, was the Jersey Brigade, then in command of Colonel Elias Dayton. The three regiments composing the brigade of Jersey troops, having been employed in all the labor incident to the siege, were present at the surrender of Cornwallis.

The surrender of the British army at Yorktown was the death blow to British hopes in America. A preliminary treaty signed at Paris on November 30, 1782, was followed by a proclaimed cessation of hostilities on April 19, 1783. On September 3, the same year, a final and definite treaty of peace was signed at Paris, by the terms of which Great Britain acknowledged the independence of the United States. After a seven-years struggle the American people were politically free, and "The greatest glory of a free-born people, is to transmit that freedom to their children."

Less than a decade ago, there were discovered in the State Library, at Trenton, some papers, so old and musty as to render the deciphering of them somewhat difficult. To J. Frank Lindsley, then editor of the Morris County Chronicle, belongs, in part, at least, the credit of this discovery; and in the newspaper edited by him, copies of the papers discovered were published.

"A Copie of the Inventories of such Property as has been damaged or destroyed by the Continental Army & Militia in the County of Morris, together with the Appraisements thereof done agreeable to an Act of the General Assembly of the State of New Jersey passed at Trenton, December 20, 1781." Such is the heading of old and musty papers, a few extracts from which are here presented:

"No. 20.

Inventory of sundry Articles taken from Ellis Cook by the Continental Army, (Viz.)

1780 1 Ox Chain		£0	15
Dec'r. 1 Narrow Ax			7
3 Sheep, at 10s		1	10
20 Fowls, 9d			15
10 Bushels Potatoes, 2s. 6d.		1	5
	4	12	6

ELLIS COOK.

"No. 23.

Inventory of sundry Articles taken from Uzal Kitchel by the Continental Army (Viz)

1777 3 Hives Bees, 20s.	£3	0	0
Feb'r. 2 Hogs (12 months) 30s.	3	0	0
1 Sheep		10	
Keeping Cattle on hay 7 1-2 months	3	15	
	10	15	

UZAL KITCHEL.

"No. 28.

Inventory of sundry Articles taken from Joshua Guren by soldiers of the Continental Army (Viz)

1779 Sheep 20s.; 1 Calf 5 months old 25s.	£2	5	0
Decem'r 1 Great Coat (Blanketing)		15	

	£	s.	d.
1 Linen Peticoat (new)		15	
2 Good Shifts (half worn)		10	
1780 2 Bushels Rye 4s.	0	8	
Aug. 2 Sheep 20s.; 2 Narrow Axes 5s......	1	15	
6 Bushels Potatoes 2s.		12	
	£7		

JOSHUA GUREN.

"No. 29.

Inventory of sundry Articles taken from Phinehas Fairchild by the Continental Army (Viz)

	£	s.	d.
1777 1 Hive Bees 20s.; 1 Beever Hat, new 45s.;	£3	5	
Jan. 4 pr. woolen Stockings 5s.; 1 pr. worsted Do. 7s.		12	
1779 3 Sheep & six Lambs 90s.; 2 bus Wheat 12s.	5	2	
Dec'r 1 Bag & 19 Fowls 18s. 1d.; pewter quart & pint	1	5	7
	10	4	7

PHINEHAS FAIRCHILD.

"No. 30.

Inventory of sundry Articles taken from Joseph Lindsley by the Continental Army (Viz)

	£	s.	d.
1777 1 Vest Broad Cloath	£1	5	
Jan. 1 pr. Striped Cotton Trowsers		10	
1 fine Shirt		15	
3 Linen Aprons	1	2	6
1779 1 Woolen Cover lid	1		
Dec. 3 Hives Bees 20s.	3		
3 Geese 2s.		6	
1780 1 woolen Cover lid	1		

Dec. 4 Sheep 10s.	2		
1782 6 Bushel Potatoes 2s. 6d.		15	
June 1 Calf 3 (Months old)	1	2	6
	£13	0	0

JOSEPH LINDSLEY.

"No. 31.

Inventory of sundry Articles taken from Ebenezer Stiles by the Continental Army (Viz)

1783			
Sept. 26 Pasture furnished a Brigade of Teams Appraised	£1	10	
1780 2 1-2 days cutting wood 4s.		10	
Feb. 4 2 Ox Chains 15s.	1	10	
7 Fowls 7s.; 1 pr pinchers 2s. 6d.		6	6
1 Shoemakers Hammer		1	6
2 Axes 15s.; 1 Hive Bees 20s.	1	15	
Pasturing 6 Cattle 1 day		5	
Quartering at his house Lighthorsemen 20 days	1		
	7	9	0

EBENEZER STILES.

"No. 32.

Inventory of sundry Articles taken from Joseph Beach (Viz)

1777			
May 25 1 Horse	£20	0	0
1 Worsted Coat & Vest	2		
1 Flannel Vest		5	
1780 1 Linen Do.		9	6
March 1 Lindsey Peticoat		15	
1 pewter porringer		2	
1 Japan'd qt. Mug		4	

	£	s.	d.
1 Diaper Table Cloth		10	
1 Window Curtain		12	
100 Fowls	3	15	
	28	12	6

JOSEPH BEACH.

"No. 34.

Inventory of sundry Articles taken from James Miller by the Continental Army (Viz)

	£	s.	d.
1778 1 Cover lid	£1		
Dec'r.			
1779 2 Hive Bees	2		
Dec'r.			
Jan. 1 pr. Small Steelyards		7	6
1 Bridle (good)		6	
1782 1 Calf 18s.; 1 Cow Bell 7s.	1	5	
June 2 Calves (3 months) 40s.; 1 Tuky (Turkey) 2s. 6d.	2	2	6
6 Sheep 60; 1 Pillow 7s. 6d.	3	7	6
10 Bushel Potatoes 2s.	1		
	11	8	6

JAMES MILLER.

"No. 35.

	£	s.	d.
Daniel Freeman had a Horse impressed in the service of the United States & kept three Years	£5	0	0

DANIEL FREEMAN.

"No. 38.

Inventory of Articles taken from Joseph Peirson Jun'r by the Continental Army (Viz)

	£	s.	d.
1780 1 Calf	£0	18	0
Dec'r 1 Do.		18	

Oct. '83 1 Heifer (3 y'r old)...............	4		
Nov. 1 Barrel Cyder		7	6
	6	3	6

JOSEPH PIERSON JUN'R.

"No. 39.

Inventory of sundry Articles taken from John Day (Viz)

1779 6 Bushels Wheat	£1	16
Dec'r 1 Bushel Corn		4
1 Bag		4
	2	4

JOHN DAY.

From the Morris County Chronicle, of the year 1899, the following extract is presented:

"The old, musty papers * * * are records of more than a hundred years ago. Apart from their historic value, they are instructive as giving glimpses of the mode of life of those who preceded us by many generations in the march of life. They afford ideas of the values of articles used in every day life. The names of those who are now with us enjoying our respect and confidence, will be found here, and among them will be recognized some who are remembered with respect and veneration."

Soon after the commencement of the Revolution, there removed to Morristown a man who subsequently became prominent in county, State and national affairs, and who, in the struggle for freedom, rendered most excellent service. John Cleves Symmes was his name. So remarkable was the career of this man, that the following sketch, based upon data gathered from what are probably reliable sources of information, is presented: He was born in the town of Riverhead, Suffolk County, New York, on the twenty-first day of July, of the year 1742. In early life he engaged in school teaching and surveying. For his first wife he married Miss —— Tuttle, a daughter of Mr. and Mrs. Daniel Tuttle, of Southold, in the county and State above mentioned. About the year 1770, Mr. Symmes removed with his young bride to Sussex County, New Jersey. They seem to have settled in Flatbrook; and here, on the twenty-fifth day of July of the year 1775, a daughter was born to them, whom the parents named Anna. As previously stated, Mr. Symmes removed to Morristown soon after the commencement of the Revolution—it may have been in the spring of the year 1776. On his removal to the county seat of Morris he selected as his home what has since been known as "Solitude," situated on the left of the road now called Sussex Avenue, about a mile and a half north from the Morristown Green, as one goes toward Mt. Freedom. Whether the house occupied by Mr. Symmes was built prior to his removal to Morristown, or erected by him after his settlement here, the writer is unable at present to say. The situation of his residence was called "Solitude" partly, no doubt, because of its remoteness from the Morristown village, but chiefly because of its thickly wooded environment.

When the infant daughter, Anna Symmes, was about one year of age, her mother died—this was probably in the latter part of the month of July, of the year 1776; while the parents were living at "Solitude."

In his "Washington in Morris County, New Jersey," the Rev. Dr. Joseph F. Tuttle, says, that in the first battle of Springfield, fought as our readers have seen, on the fourteenth day of December, of the year 1776, "the celebrated John Cleves Symmes * * * participated, with a detachment of militia from Sussex County." In "Officers and Men of New Jersey in the Revolutionary War," by William S. Stryker, Adjutant-General, which is unquestioned authority, as far at least as it goes, may be seen the following record concerning Mr. Symmes: "Colonel, Third Battalion, Sussex, resigned May 23d, 1777, to accept appointment as Justice of the Supreme Court of New Jersey." From this statement it may reasonably be inferred, that in the first battle of Springfield, Mr. Symmes was a colonel in command of the "detachment of militia from Sussex County." By another apparently reliable author the statement is made that "as colonel of a New Jersey regiment he participated in many important battles." It is said, also, in "Ohio Historical Collections," by Howe, that Mr. Symmes participated in the battle of Saratoga, which occurred on the seventh day of October, of the year 1777. But in view of the official statement that he resigned his colonelcy on the twenty-third day of May, of the same year as that above mentioned, to accept a civil appointment, it is quite improbable that Colonel Symmes was a participant in the battle of Saratoga. There is owever, a possibility that in the interval between his esignation from the militia service, and the assump-ion of his duties as a justice of the New Jersey Su-reme Court, he may have in some capacity taken part 1 the battle specified.

It was while Mr. Symmes was a Justice of the Su-reme Court of New Jersey, that the trial of "Parson 'aldwell's" murderer occurred; and the writer has een the statement that during this famous trial, Jus-ce Symmes presided over the court.

For his second wife, Mr. Symmes married a daugh-er of Governor Livingston, of New Jersey; this may ave been about the year 1778. The marriage cere-10ny was probably performed at "Solitude;" and 1ere are some glimmerings of evidence in favor of 1e spacious front hallway of this interesting house aving been the place where he gave a practical exem-lification of his belief in the teaching of the eminent 'nglish philosopher, who says: Were a man not to 1arry a second time, it might be concluded that his rst wife had given him a disgust to marriage; but by 1king a second wife, he pays the highest compliment) the first, by showing that she made him so happy s a married man, that he wishes to be so a second me." Governor Livingston was probably present at 1e marriage of his daughter to Justice Symmes; and is said he was afterward a frequent visitor at "Soli-1de." The capture of both Governor Livingston and 1stice Symmes was devoutly wished by the British 1thorities and during a visit of the Governor to Mr.

Symmes, a party of Tories are said to have secreted themselves in a swamp near the house, intending in the night time to carry them away as prisoners into the enemies lines. For some reason, however, now unknown, the plot miscarried.

When Anna Symmes was four years of age it was concluded to place her in the home of her grandparents, Mr. and Mrs. Tuttle, at Southold, New York. To reach Southold, more than a hundred miles distant from Morristown, it was of course, necessary to pass through the enemy's lines. Disguising himself, therefore, as a British officer, Mr. Symmes boldly set out on horseback for Southold. Anna sat on the saddle in front of her father. They reached the home of Mr. and Mrs. Tuttle, and little Anna was left there, Mr. Symmes returning to Morristown.

Justice Symmes and his daughter did not meet again until the year 1783. Anna, who was then about eight years of age, was soon afterward placed in a young ladies' seminary.

During the year 1785 Mr. Symmes served the State as a member of the Council, the members of this body then being elected annually. In the years 1785-86 he was a member of the Continental Congress. It was in the year 1787 that an ordinance was passed by Congress, making provision for the establishment of a territorial government northwest of the Ohio River. In anticipation of this action of Congress (in which anticipation Mr. Symmes, by reason of his service in that body the two previous years, doubtless shared) lands in that region were sold by the general government.

An association called the "Ohio Company," purchased 5,000,000 acres of land lying between the Muskingum and Scioto rivers, fronting on the Ohio River. About this time, the exact date of which seems to be unascertainable, Mr. Symmes and a few others purchased 2,000,000 acres of land in the rich and beautiful region on the Ohio River, between the Great and Little Miami rivers. His purchase included the site of the present city of Cincinnati. Mr. Symmes' associates in this extensive purchase were chiefly composed of the officers of the New Jersey line who had served in the Revolution; among whom were General Jonathan Dayton and Rev. Elias Boudinot, D. D. It could not have been long after his extensive land purchase in Ohio, that Mr. Symmes removed from New Jersey to the West: which was thereafter his home. On the twenty-third day of October, of the year 1787, he was appointed a Judge of the Supreme Court of Ohio. He settled, with his family, at the North Bend of the Ohio River, and there he proposed to found the capital of the future State. This was frustrated by the choice of the site of Cincinnati for a blockhouse around whose protecting cannon emigrants to the wilderness preferred to settle. There Fort Washington was afterward built;" and in the year 1795 Captain William Henry Harrison was stationed in command of the garrison. Judge Symmes erected a blockhouse and a commodious dwelling at NorthBend. It was during the year 1795, that Anna Symmes, then about twenty years of age, once more became a member of the household. She was "a remarkably beautiful girl," and "traces of that beauty lingered in her face at the time of her death, when she was almost ninety years of age."

At Lexington, Kentucky, in the home of Mrs. Peyton Short, Anna Symmes' older sister, Anna, is said to have first met Captain William Henry Harrison. An acquaintance was then and there begun which culminated into mutual and life-long attachment. After a brief courtship the two became engaged. Judge Symmes gave his consent to the marriage; but when certain slanderous reports against Captain Harrison reached him, he withdrew his consent. Anna, however, had confidence in the young captain, and resolved to marry him.

"On the morning of the day fixed for that event Judge Symmes rode to Cincinnati, unsuspicious of any such doings. He was offended. He did not meet Harrison until several weeks afterward, when he met him at a dinner-party given by General Wilkinson, at Fort Washington. 'Well, sir,' said the Judge sternly to Captain Harrison, 'I understand you have married Anna.' 'Yes, sir,' answered the Captain. 'How do you expect to support her?' inquired the father. 'By my sword and my right arm,' quickly answered the young officer. The Judge was pleased with the spirit of the reply, and he became at once reconciled. He lived to be proud of his son-in-law."

John Cleves Symmes died on the twenty-sixth day of February, of the year 1814, at Cincinnati. "About 30 rods (we quote from 'Ohio Historical Collections,' by Howe) in a westerly direction from the tomb of Harrison (9th President

U. S.) on an adjacent hill, in a family cemetery, is the grave of Judge Symmes. * * * On it is the following inscription: 'Here rest the remains of John Cleves Symmes, who, at the foot of these hills, made the first settlement between the Miami rivers. Born on Long Island, State of New York, July 21st, A. D. 1772. Died at Cincinnati, February 26, A. D. 1814.'"

Apparently, about the year 1781, there removed to Morristown one Walter Mould and his family. He seems to have come from New York City, where, it is said, he was engaged in business at No. 23 William street. Mould, who is spoken of as a man "of standing and responsibility," is said to have been an Englishman, and to have been employed as an artisan in some of the shops of Birmingham, one of the great manufacturing towns of his native country. It is even recorded that Mr. Mould brought across the Atlantic with him the tools and implements of his trade, which seems to have been that of a machinist.

At the close of the Revolution, coin of any sort was very scarce; of copper coin this was especially true. Under the articles of confederation the United States could exercise no power over the currency, nor supply in any way the existing deficiency; hence, no national mint had been established. By legislative authority a few of the States established State mints. At Rupert, Vermont; at New Haven, Connecticut; in Massachusetts and in New Jersey such mints were established, and coin was issued by them for the transaction of reviving business.

The mint at Rupert, Vermont, was in operation as early as the year 1785, and the copper cents issued by this mint bore on one side a plow, and a sun rising from behind hills; and on the other side a radiated eye surrounded by thirteen stars. A small supply of half cents were also issued by the mint at Rupert. The Connecticut coins had on one side the figure of a human head and on the other that of a young woman holding an olive branch. The mint at New Haven, established also in the year 1785, continued in operation for a period of about three years. In the year 1786 a mint (or mints, for there seems to have been two in the State) was established in New Jersey. The history of its origin was as follows:

After his removal to Morristown, Walter Mould, knowing of the scarcity of coin, and doubtless of the establishment of mints in other States, suggested to some of the residents of the county seat of Morris, among them the Hon. Silas Condict, "his next door neighbor," that he understood the art of coinage, and that he was willing to engage in the business, provided legislative permission was granted him. Mr. Condict was at the time a member of the State Legislature, and, acting upon his advice, Mould applied to the Legislature, then in session, for authority to coin copper pennies. This was in the year 1786. On the first day of June, of the year last mentioned, an Act was passed by the Legislature of New Jersey authorizing Walter Mould, Thomas Goadsby and Albian Cox, whom the former had associated with him, to coin copper pennies to the value of £10,000. These men were required to give bonds in the sum of £10,000, with sufficient security, that they would faithfully and honestly perform their contract. This they did.

The coinage of copper cents was soon after commenced, according to local tradition, at "Solitude," in a room set apart for the purpose. It is said that Mould with his family, occupied "Solitude" as a residence. Another mint seems to have been later established at Elizabethtown, perhaps by Robert Ogden, Jr., but under the auspices, however, of Colonel Matthias Ogden. Mould may have been connected in some capacity with the Elizabethtown mint.

The coins minted at Morristown bore upon one side, the representation of a heart-shaped shield, with stripes running perpendicularly, with the inscription "E Pluribus Unum," and on the other side a plow, above which was the representation of a horse's head (a substitute for the head of Queen Anne of English contemporaneous pennies), with the inscription, "Nova Caesarea," and the date of issue. These coin are now known as the "horse-head" pennies. They were coined for three successive years only—1786, 1787 and 1788. A national mint was established in the year 1792. From a well known Northern New Jersey antiquarian the writer learns, that he has within a few years past, paid as high as $1.00 each for some of the famous "horsehead pennies."

"Solitude," subsequent to its occupancy by Walter Mould, was an inn and tavern, and for many years was kept by Captain Benjamin Holloway, grandfather of Morristown's efficient chief of police, J. Frank Holloway. The traffic between Sussex and Warren counties and the markets below was so great that the "Wheatsheaf Inn," as Captain Holloway's famous tavern came to be known, carried on a thriving business. In illustration of this statement it may be said that frequently so crowded was this hospitable inn that it was necessary for the "youngsters" of the household to sleep on the hay in the adjacent barn.

The "Wheatsheaf Tavern" as the writer is informed by a life-long Morristonian, was a two-story frame structure. At the western end of the building was a stone L, which was used as the kitchen; and underneath the kitchen was a basement. The bar of this hostelry was in the front right-hand corner of the spacious hallway, running from front to rear of the building. The partition shutting off the barroom from the hallway was semi-circular in form, the lower part of it being of paneled boards, and the upper part of lattice work, running perpendicularly, and painted a light green color. The drinks were passed out to patrons through a small semi-circular opening, similar to that used by the teller in a commercial bank of the present day. A portion at least of the partition swung on hinges, thus constituting the means of ingress and egress to and from the barroom.

In front of the tavern were several large black cherry trees, which not a few grown-up boys recollect with keen pleasure. At the left of the entrance to the premises from the main road, there stood for many years a harness shop; and here quite a business was carried on in the manufacture of saddles, the leather used being made from pig skins furnished by Mr. Holloway from his stock yard.

"Solitude," including many acres, is now the property of Gustav E. Kissell, a New York banker. He is now having constructed on another and more desirable promontory of his farm a new house, which, when completed, will rank with Morristown's most elegant residences.

Mr. Kissell's valuable property has been most appropriately named "Wheatsheaf Farm." In his possession is the interesting three-by-four-feet sign, which for many years swung in front of "Wheatsheaf Inn," after which, presumably, the farm of Mr. Kissell was named. Near the top of this old sign is a painted representation of a sheaf of wheat, and below is the name of the proprietor—"B. Holloway." Captain Holloway derived his title from service in the State militia after the Revolution.

Not only as the residence of Chief Justice Symmes, and as the locale of the mint where the famous "horsehead pennies" were coined, is "Solitude," now "Wheatsheaf Farm," noted, but it is said that a silver mine was once worked on this property. The late Hon. Augustus W. Cutler stated to persons now living that he had a silver shoe buckle made from silver mined on the "Symmes" land. It is a peculiarly significant fact in this connection that John Dickerson, the Morristown silversmith or jeweler of Revolutionary days, of whom mention was made in a previous chapter, once advertised the theft of fifty ounces of silver from his shop, as well also as "buckles just cast." This seems to be corroborative of the statement of our late townsman, Mr. Cutler, whose interest in and knowledge of Morristown, traditional and historical, are well known.

"The Morristown Ghost; An account of the Beginning, Transactions and Discovery of Ransford Rogers who seduced many by pretended Hobgoblins and Apparitions, and thereby extorted money from their pockets. In the County of Morris and State of New Jersey, in the year 1788. Printed for every purchaser —1792."

Such was the title page of a 16mo pamphlet which made its appearance in New Jersey soon after the close of the Revolution; 1792 was the year. By some, it was thought to have been written by the Ransford Rogers named on its title page, as a means of pecuniary profit to himself; and as a method, also, of punishing the people of Morristown for the treatment he claimed to have received at their hands. To a printer in Elizabethtown, Sheppard Kollock by name, the publication of the pamphlet was at the time, by many persons attributed. So far as possible, the first edition of this remarkable pamphlet, which contained the names of many prominent persons in Morristown and vicinity, from whose pockets money was alleged to have been extorted by the "Morristown Ghost," is said to have been bought up and destroyed.

From two or three sources, however, the writer of this history has received communications during the few months past, suggestively offering him "an original copy of the 'Morristown Ghost,'" from which it is safe to infer that, notwithstanding the strenuous iconoclastic efforts of the fathers, alleged to have been duped by the Yankee schoolmaster, clad in ghostly apparel, at least "just one" copy of the obnoxious pamphlet has survived. It may be that the several correspondents who have generously placed at his command "an original copy" of the devoutly-wished-for original "Morristown Ghost," have done so as a means of retaliation upon the Yankee preacher, for the alleged depredations of the Yankee pedagogue of "long ago" upon the county seat worthies who now lie in honored graves, of which the English poet so quaintly speaks in the lines:

"Here may thy storme-beth vessell safely ryde
This is the port of rest from troublous toyle,
The worlde's sweet inn from paine and wearisome turmoyle."

But these epistolary offers of an "original copy" of the "Morristown Ghost" are not by any means the only attempts which have been made to "get even" with the Yankee preacher, who is "now writing books," which have added to his amusing experiences while writing the story of Morristown's first and famous century, as the following incident will illustrate:

Accosted one day not long since by a well-known typo, whose perennial (we speak hyperbolically) perambulations among the printing establishments of northern New Jersey are proverbial (hyperbole again), the writer patiently listened while said typo remarked, in tones of ghostly accent not dissimilar, as said writer imagines, to those of the Yankee pedagogue when clad in the habiliments of the departed: "Mr. Sherman, Mr. So- and-So has 'an original copy' (can it be possible there has been a retaliatory collusion on foot between correspondents and typo?) of the 'Morristown Ghost;' it is the only one in existence, all the other copies having been destroyed. So-and-So wouldn't take a thousand dollars for it (no, the writer is certain he would not, since for nothing, nothing can be received); it was presented to him by an old gentleman, who assured him it was the 'last of the Mohicans.'"

"Of course, you will write up the 'Morristown Ghost,' Mr. Sherman, in connection with your admirable story of Morristown's first century. Now, I can procure this 'original copy' for you, containing 'all the names,' on condition you will show it to no one, since if others saw it they might have a reprint made of it, with all the names of Rogers's dupes, and realize a fortune from the sale of the rare edition. This I propose doing myself soon, as I am now negotiating for the purchase of the facilities for a reprint; for I am certain 'there is money in it.' "

The promise, on the part of the writer, to preserve inviolate, so far as showing it to a third party was concerned, the "only copy of the 'Morristown Ghost" extant, was the work of a moment only; and the promise would have been sacredly kept had "the goods been delivered, since, to quote from an English author: "To tell our own secrets is generally folly, but that folly is without guilt; to communicate those with which we are entrusted is always treachery, and treachery for the most part combined with folly." But "the goods were never delivered," notwithstanding a several times repeated asseveration, on the part of the "perambulating typo," to leave them at the residence of the Yankee preacher. Is it to be inferred, or would the present writer so state, that said typo is wholly unlike George Washington, with "his little hatchet," who, as the story runs, could not tell a lie? Emphatically no! Or is it the case that the said typo could tell a lie but would not? or would he and couldn't he? Perhaps the following sequel to our little story will furnish the facts from which the reader may draw his own inference:

A few days after the aforementioned conversation between the "Yankee preacher-author" and the "perennial perambulating typo," the latter delivered to the writer a copy of a comparatively recent reprint of "The Morristown Ghost," made by local publishers, who, if gossip is to be relied upon, thought they saw "bar'ls of money" in it. By this publishing establishment the typo has not a few times been employed, and between the parties of the first part and the parties of the second part there still exists, it is sincerely to be hoped, a friendly feeling not of the common sort. Now, since the delivery of the wrong goods to the writer, by the aforesaid typo, the latter, as the former imagines, has frequently awoke from his slumbers only to see the immense pile of the reprint of "The Morristown Ghost," which has for several years encumbered the sagging shelves of said publishers, disappearing like autumn leaves before the equinoctial at $1 or less per copy, in consequence of the extensive advertisement given it by the writer in his story of Morristown's first century.

"The year previous to the publication of the book," 'The Morristown Ghost' (the writer now quotes from a very interesting letter recently received from Edwin A. Ely, a genuine Jersey antiquarian), "there appeared in the New Jersey Journal, Elizabethtown, October 19, 1797, the following advertisement:

"'Friday evening next, at the Academy in this Town, will be presented,

"'A Dramatic Piece, called
"'The
"'Morris-Town Ghost;
"'Or, The
"'Force of Credulity;
"'To which will be added,
"'Chrononhotonthologos.

"'Tickets at three shillings each, to be had at Mr. Shute's.

Doors to be opened at five o'clock, and the entertainment to begin precisely at six.

"'Elizabeth-Town, October 19, 1791.'"

"This play (which is said to have been written by a son of Rev. James Richards, D. D., a former Morristown pastor) was repeated January 27, 1792, but I find no other play announced at the Academy in looking over the New Jersey Journal for several years. The drama was probably written for the occasion and I find no trace of its having been printed. (The actors were probably all bought up, and destroyed, the present writer may be pardoned for injecting).

From the circumstance of the "dramatic piece" enacted by those "bad boys" at Elizabeth-Town, in the year 1791, the year previous to the publication of the "Morristown Ghost" in the form of a 16mo pamphlet, it is very evident the story of the ghostly depredations of Rogers and his accomplices in Morristown and vicinity, was "in the air" before it was "in a book;" which is presumptively, at least, in favor of the authenticity of the story as graphically related in the volume, of which every copy, so far as possible, was "bought up and destroyed," after its publication. Byron says:

Words are things; and a small drop of ink,
Falling like dew upon a thought, produces
That which makes thousands, perhaps millions, think."

This is especially true of written words; and of this truth we have a practical illustration in the following circumstance: David Young, whose name, nearly four-score years ago, adorned the title pages of many of the almanacs of the period suggested, "accidentally," as we are informed, found a copy of the original "Morristown Ghost" at Elizabeth, and, doubtless aware that this was the "only copy" in existence, and devoutly wishing to confer upon his fellowmen the benefits of a new edition, there soon appeared in New Jersey a little book bearing the following title: "The Wonderful History of the Morristown Ghost; thoroughly and carefully revised. By David Young, Newark. Published by Benjamin Olds, for the author. J. C. Totten, Printer." This was in the year 1826. Whether David Young, mathematician and almanac compiler, made "bar'ls o' money" from his reprint, the writer is unable to say. The reprint produced by the enterprising Morristown publishers, already mentioned, was, of course, of more recent date.

Notwithstanding the delivery, by the "perennial perambulating (hyperbole continued) typo," to the "Yankee preacher-author" of the "wrong goods," the latter has for some time been in possession of what constitutes "the heart" of the "Morristown Ghost," to wit, the full name of the county seat worthies from whose none-too-deep pockets (the Revolution had impoverished some, at least, of them) money is alleged to have been extorted by Ransford Rogers and his accomplices, and he now proceeds to—publish these names? Not yet; not yet, dear reader. Speaking of the names of the fathers duped by Rogers and his auxilliary ghosts, recalls the recent receipt of a letter by the writer from a gentleman residing many miles from Morristown. After expressing the pleasure with which he had been reading the story of Morristown's first century, as puglished serially in the Saturday issues of the Newark Evening News, he continues:

"When you come to deal with the 'Morristown Ghost,' a copy of the early account of which (perhaps Young's) I have, please let me know if you learn the names of the persons who were duped. The names, I think, were once published, and afterward the prints suppressed. I am curious to know the names of the victims."

In the present writer's reply to the very interesting letter above mentioned he made an honest confession of having in his possession "the names" of all the fathers duped by the Morristown ghost and his auxiliaries; but added, that for the sake of the living descendants of those duped fathers, he did not consider it kind to publish them in the story of Morristown's first century.

"Why not?" have several friends in manifest astonishment inquired of the writer, when he has expressed his disinclination to do so; "why not; it is matter of history, is it not?"

Matter of history it most assuredly is, but this kind of argument is a two-edged sword that cleaves two ways. Because it is history, and not myth or legend, is a most potent reason, as the writer conceives why he should not publish the names of our worthy sires, the victims of superstition, and of the misfortunes of war by which some of them were impoverished, and hence made hyper-sensitive to the glitter of gold. How about the superstitions of the twentieth century? Would not our time be more profitably employed in "showing them up?"

Since the amusing experiences of the writer previously mentioned, it has been his rare pleasure to see with his own eyes, and handle with his own hands, a genuine copy of the original edition of "The Morristown Ghost." A careful comparison of the typography of this book with that of "The Prompter; or a Commentary on Common Sayings & Subjects," printed at Newark, New Jersey, in the year 1793, by John Woods, proves, to the satisfaction of the writer, that both books were printed at the same office.

CHAPTER XX.

"Glendower.—I can call spirits from the vasty deep.
Hotspur.—Why so can I, or so can any man,
But will they come when you do call for them?"

T was once the prevailing belief among the people of Morris County that during the Revolution large sums of money had been buried in the earth by Tories and others, and that these buried treasures were zealously guarded by spirits. A single instance, only, of the "others" will be cited, that of Elihu Bond, the father of Mrs. Martha Doremus Pruden, widow of Cyrus Pruden, recently deceased at Morristown. Mr. Bond, the father of Mrs. Pruden, served as a private in the New Jersey line in the Revolutionary army. "During the war he buried a small chest containing silverware and money; and when, at the close of the war, he went to recover his buried treasure, he found it undisturbed and intact. This chest, together with the several silver spoons and a few coins that

were hidden in it, are now in possession of the Washington Association, and on exhibition in Headquarters at Morristown."

The knowledge of the art of dispelling the guardian spirits was considered indispensable to the obtainment of the coveted buried treasures. Schooley's Mountain, situated about twenty miles west of Morristown, was supposed to be the locality chiefly selected for the burial of these treasures, which was done, in the case of Tories, partly as a means of protection against confiscation by the State. Not a few of these Tories, after burying their treasures, had left home, and never returned, having either been slain in the service of the King, whose cause they had espoused, or, if they had survived the war, had been compelled to leave the State and seek a new home in some other country.

It was in the summer of the year 1788 that two Morris County men were traveling through New York State, where, at a place known as Smith's Clove, in Orange County, they formed the acquaintance of a Yankee schoolmaster, one Ransford Rogers by name, hailing from the Nutmeg State. Smith's Clove lies back of Haverstraw, between it and Stony Point. For some time these two enterprising men had been in search of a person who could locate and recover the buried treasures at Schooley's Mountain in their native county. The Yankee schoolmaster, by reason, as he claimed, of his thorough knowledge of chemistry ("chymistry" he called it) and other sciences, possessed the power not only to raise the spirits, good and evil, but likewise to dispel them. At last these two Morris County worthies had discovered "their man," and he was therefore urged to accompany them to Morristown, where he could give a practical demonstration of his skill in "chymistry." To say that these Jersey travelers had suddenly become wealthy, prospectively, would only be to say that they were under the complete sway of the superstition of the times.

Rogers was too shrewd a man to at once accept the invitation to accompany them to their native heath; not unlike the adept at mock modesty of more recent times, he at first declined the proposal, but the promise of a school in the vicinity of the county seat of Morris induced an oral consent which had been mentally preexistent. About three miles to the westward of Morristown, on the road leading toward Mendham, and on a hill near the modern residence of Samuel F. Pierson, stood, at the close of the Revolution, a schoolhouse. Over this school Rogers was installed as teacher through the influence of his personally and mercenarily interested admirers, who hoped he would bring them "much gain by soothsaying."

It was early in the month of August, in the year 1788, that the Yankee pedagogue assumed the grave responsibilities of his suburban appointment. In their undue haste to receive a demonstration of Rogers's occult skill, the treasure-seekers eagerly importuned him to give an exhibition of his art. Realizing that Jerseymen were not, after all, such stupid specimens of humanity as he had at first imagined, the imperative need of an accomplice in the practise of his black art dawned upon the mind of Rogers, and, late in the month of August, therefore, he made a hurried trip to New England to select from among his fellow-"chymists" an assistant in his mystic work. He seems to have experienced no difficulty in finding a "kindred spirit," for early in the month of September, Rogers returned to Morristown with an accomplice, with whom he must have been thoroughly satisfied, since the man's name was Goodenough.

Evidently impressed with the desirability of expedition of movement, a secret meeting was held soon after Rogers's return to Morristown, with his imported accomplice, at which some eight or ten selected participants were present, and as an indispensable preliminary to active operations, these persons were solemnly assured by the imported pedagogue, of the presence at Schooley's Mountain of the commonly reported buried treasures. The prevailing belief that this treasure was vigilantly guarded by spirits, and that these must be raised and carefully consulted before it could be utilized by the living, was shrewdly emphasized by Rogers at this initial meeting of the elect. The Yankee schoolmaster gave another rare exhibition of his proverbial modesty by the assurance on his part, at the meeting above mentioned, of his ability to entice the spirits from their resting places, situated somewhere in the earth's bowels, and of his thorough acquaintance with the language of these denizens of darkness, which constituted a sympathetic mutual bond which would insure the impartation from the spirits, to him, of the last remnant of occult knowledge required for the discovery and actual possession in hand of the treasures interred by Tories and semi-Tories in the days of the Revolution. No finer illustration of the shrewdness of Rogers was exhibited than his solemn admonition to the elect, administered at the close of their initial meeting, held apparently at the residence of Mr. ———, situated at a secluded spot on the Mendham road, known as "Solitude." This admonition was to refrain from all immorality, on the ground that indulgence therein would offend the denizens of darkness and prevent the yielding up by them of the buried treasures.

The original number of the elect did not long continue, since the dazzle of prospective gold and the irresistible impulse to communicate to others the "hope of gain" soon increased the coterie of gold seekers to forty. Rogers's pretended meetings with the guardian spirits became frequent. As a means of bolstering up the credulity of the elect, he utilized his knowledge of "chymistry" by compounding various chemical ingredients, which, thrown into the air, exploded, causing a variety of appearances mysterious and extraordinary, to the active superstition of the people involved. These appearances and other phenomena attending Rogers's chemical experiments were supposed by his victims to be of a supernatural origin and character. The skill of the Yankee schoolmaster was still further displayed, and the credulity of the elect (elect in the sense of having been carefully selected by Rogers as easy victims), still further stimulated by occasional and dreadful subterranean explosions caused by "timed" explosives placed in the earth, and which, occurring according to careful planning in the night, were a source of great terror to the elect people. Such was the terror occasioned by these phenomena that it was with great reluctance the victims ventured out after dark. But another effect of the "chymical" experiments alluded to was the growing impatience of the elect to take active measures toward the discovery of the buried treasures.

So importunate did they become that a general meeting was called, and notwithstanding the severe storm prevailing not a single treasure seeker was absent. Some, it is said, rode a distance of twelve miles to be present at this spirit conventicle. Between the call for the general meeting, and its occurrence, Rogers had thoroughly instructed his accomplice; everything was "cut and dried." To the assembled and wonder-stricken coterie the spirit appeared, and informed them that on a certain night in the near future they must again meet in a field situated half a mile from human habitation, where they would be required to form certain specified angles and circles, to get outside of which would result in their immediate extirpation.

At about half-past 10 o'clock on the night appointed, the elect gathered and marched round and round in solemn procession. A terrible subterranean explosion occurring in the near vicinity so thoroughly "jarred" them that their teeth must have chattered. Impressed by the supernatural character of these phenomena—"noises," the writer presumes the victims called them—the elect were suitably predisposed to catch the faintest whisper of the guardian spirits; hence, when with hideous groans they made their appearance to Rogers, and he, in the presence of the subdued throng, conversed with them, the elect were fully prepared to accept with avidity their communications, which were, that in order to obtain the buried treasures, each of them (there may have been half a hundred of the elect by this time) must deliver £12 (about $30) to them (the spirits), as an acknowledgment. At the same time the spirits manifested their extreme fondness for Rogers by enjoining the elect to fail not to acknowledge him as their mundane leader in future operations. It is said the spirits on the occasion mentioned wore machines over their mouths to prevent their voices "giving them away."

November, in the year 1788, was the time of the manifestations thus related. At several subsequent meetings the manifestations of ghostly presence consisted of hidous groans, mysterious rappings, suggestive and tantalizing jingling of gold and silver coin; and, by way of encouragement in their unworldly enterprise, the elect were exhorted by the spirits to "Press forward!" There is one feature of the ghostly transactions under review which cannot fail to particularly impress the reader, which is this: The guardian spirits were willing—so willing, indeed, that it was a part of their considerate requisition—to receive gold and silver coin rather than the "loan paper" then current in New Jersey, in the way of acknowledgment by the elect.

The spirits were willing to be burdened with metallic money, and to permit the elect to enjoy the convenience of a form of money of lighter weight and more evanescent character also. And another interesting feature of the ghost story is the fact that the elect were not at all reluctant to retain for their own use the "loan paper" money, and deliver over to the spirits the hard coin as "an acknowledgment," whatever that meant in the nomenclature of the spirit land. The reader is cautioned, however, not to regard this transaction, so far as the elect were concerned, as purely unselfish; for local tradition informs us that they expected speedy reimbursement in coin from the well-stocked underground bank. It is said that by the month of March of the following year (1789), the spirits had received from the elect the full amount of the required acknowledgment, and all in coin, be it remembered. How their shroud pockets must have sagged! By this time the spirits had assumed such familiar relations with their cash contributors, that some of the more responsible of them were not a few times aroused from their midnight slumbers in order to have imparted to them by their spirit friends the better course of procedure in obtaining the earth-emboweled treasures.

At several private meetings, at which the manifestations were various, the elect were informed by the disinterested spirits that in the month of May following, they would receive returns for their hard cash, and then did the words of the immortal Bard of Avon come true in the case of each of this batch of happy promisees:

> "I am giddy; expectation whirls me 'round.
> The imaginary relish is so sweet
> That it enchants my sense."

The month of May was not long in arriving, and upon its arrival the entire company of the elect were assembled in an open field, where the prescribed circle was formed, and the appearance of the spirits awaited in breathless suspense. When they did appear it was to assume a position at a prudent distance from the circle; and then followed a scene that beggars description. Symptoms of intense irascibility, attended by the most horrible groans, were exhibited by the spirits, and in their effort to give expression to their irascibility they twisted themselves into postures of the most ghastly sort, which, amid the encompassing darkness, were hideous in the extreme. If the affrighted spectators had been able to summon up the power of speech each would have cried out:

> I feel my sinews slacken'd with the fright
> And a cold sweet thrills down all o'er my limbs,
> As if I were dissolving into water.

In speechless horror, however, the elect listened to the severe upbraidings of the spirits, for the alleged irregularity of their procedure, for their faithlessness, and for their incapacity to "keep a secret," and, worst of all, the spirits indignantly declared that, owing to their inconsistent deportment, the elect would be debarred from receiving, for the present, the coveted treasures. So enraged did the spirits become, and so overwhelmed by fright were their victims, that the thought of money vanished entirely from their minds, and in their extremity they looked to Rogers for protection. But it was horror added to horror for the elect to discover, that the imported schoolmaster was, apparently, as much frightened as they. Indeed, his efforts to appease the enraged spirits seemed at first almost futile. He did, however, succeed, after recourse to a variety of incantations, in dispelling the ghostly visitants, and once more tranquillity reigned within the circle.

The elect soon dispersed, and, strange to say, their credulity still survived, and their confidence in the Yankee schoolmaster was in no measure abated. They still looked forward expectantly to the possession of the long coveted treasures, lying somewhere in old mother earth.

Rogers might have been perennially and pleasantly remembered by his friends, the elect, as an expert "chymist," fully qualified to raise even the devil himself, had he been satisfied to drop the matter where it was. But a wise man has said: "We may recover out of the darkness of ignorance, but never out of that of presumption." Rogers had become presumptuous. He soon removed to Morristown village, having given up his school on the Mendham road; he evidently "didn't have to" teach any more.

Two other Yankees who had recently removed to the county seat of Morris, and who had heard of Rogers's "chymical" operations, expressed a feverish desire to become members of the expectant circle of treasure seekers. To this proposition Rogers demurred; but he was at length persuaded by them to engage in a second enterprise of a similar character. The nucleus of this second venture, consisting of five pieces of new and raw material, soon held their initial meeting. In addition to the groans and noises hitherto composing the spirit manifestations to the elect, each member of the new circle, including the three Yankees, took from a prepared pile a piece of paper, wrapped it around his wrist, and thrust the hand out of the door into the darkness, and patiently waited for the spirits to write upon the paper. Withdrawing the hands and the papers and huddling the latter together, they were anxiously examined, when lo! upon one of them, there were found written the mention of a time and place for meeting the spirits and receiving from them instructions concerning the discovery and obtainment of the buried treasures. The writer trusts that no reader will for a moment suppose the spirit message above mentioned was written by either of the Yankee schoolmasters , for that would be to attribute to them cuteness of the highest order; cuteness bordering on genius.

The spirit-suggested meeting was held at the house of Ransford Rogers, in the village of Morristown. He was evidently growing very religious, for at this meeting the exercises were opened with prayer. A sheet of paper was then taken by each member of the new enterprise, whereupon they all proceeded in orderly fashion to a nearby field, where a circle was drawn. With one arm elevated they all fell "with awful reverence prone," engaging, with closed eyes, in prayer, and in supplication that the spirit would be pleased to enter the circle and on the paper write his message from ———. On returning to Rogers's house the papers were shuffled together, and lo! on one the spirit-message was written, in penmanship so elegant that it became a marvel to the amazed coterie.

"The membership of this company must be increased to eleven. Each of the augmented membership must pay to the spirit (as an acknowledgment,' the writer imagines), twelve pounds in gold (specie payment still required)." Such may have been, in substance, the spirit message aforesaid. Rogers evidently "knew" his men. They were identified with the village church, and were presumably, at least, of a pious turn of mind. Hence, the Yankee from Smith's Clove, Orange County, New York, resolved that the gold-seeking enterprise should be conducted on strictly Christian principles, and having so resolved, he (as the "Morristown Ghost") inaugurated a systematic visitation of church members, representing himself as "the spirit of a just man," made perfect, and piously exhorted them to enter the charmed circle. Result? He persuaded thirty-seven persons, mostly members of Parson Johne's church, to cast their lot in with the gold-seekers. It was not long before some of the more susceptible of these new members began to receive nocturnal visits, and were exhorted by the spirits to "pray without ceasing," "look to God," and in other ways conduct themselves as good men should.

To inflame their credulity to white heat various tricks were now and then performed by the spirit (the "Morristown Ghost," is meant) for the benefit of the treasure-seekers. 'As a token of spirit approbation each member was presented by Rogers with a parcel. which they were informed by the "chymical" expert contained the burned and powdered bones of the spirit's bodies. This gift had been preceded, however, by the payment (as "a retainer," perhaps) of a portion of the required twelve pounds gold. The powdered bones were to be carefully guarded, but the parcel was not to be opened. The next requirement to be mentiond may not have been particularly difficult, nor onerous, for the treasure-seekers to comply with; it was none else than to drink freely of "Apple jack;" as a result of which compliance, future meetings became somewhat convivial, as well as religious, and on their return home, it was not always easy for the treasure-seekers to find the door latch. But then they were church members, and hence excusable for their little irregularities.

Rogers seems, also, in addition to his knowledge of "chymistry," to have been something of a therapeutist, for it is said he compounded pills, and prescribed one to be taken by each member of the company of treasure-seekers, said pill to be supplemented by liberal potions of "Apple jack," to prevent deleterious effects. These instructions having been dictated by the spirits, the Yankee schoolmaster (retired) should not be held altogether responsible for the effects of his erratic therapeutical practises.

"And thus the whirligig of time brings in his revenges," is a saying which was strikingly illustrated in the sequel to the operations of the spirits of the year 1788-89 in Morristown. Among the coterie of spirit-guided treasure-seekers was a man well advanced in years. On leaving home for a few days, he so far forgot the sacredness of his promise, as to leave behind his parcel of burned bones. Finding, and out of womanly curiosity breaking open the mysterious parcel, his wife, on discovering its contents, feared to touch the powder. She, too, was a victim of the superstition of the times, and apprehending that the powder was in some way connected with witchcraft, she went at once to her pastor for advice in the matter. Learning, upon his return home, of what had occurred during his absence, the husband, whose name was—but this story is not to divulge names—declared he was ruined. Ruined only in the realm of distorted imagination, and ruined in this sense only until he disclosed to his wife the secret spirit operations with which he and his neighbors had so long been identified, for she was the Moses who guided him out of the Egypt of darkness. She at once pronounced the whole thing the work of the devil, and declared her intention to make the matter public. Alarmed at the resolution of this good woman, Rogers and his accomplices pursued their spirit visitations with renewed vigor, and with the performance of freshly conceived tricks to overcome the scruples of the superstitious. These efforts might have succeeded in postponing a little longer, at least, the day of retribution, had not Rogers, having imbibed too freely of Apple jack, made several blunders while conversing one night, as a spirit (the Morristown Ghost) with a resident of the county seat. It was the man's wife, however, who detected the inconsistency of spirit conduct which led to Rogers's exposure. Finding next morning where the spirit visitant of the previous night had been, the tracks of a man, the husband followed them to a nearby fence, where he discovered a horse had been tied. The man's eyes were now wide open, and so were those of others. The spell was broken. The bubble had burst. Rogers was arrected, and confined in the jail on the Green. But, protesting his innocence, he was bailed out of jail. He attempted surreptitiously to leave the State. Again he was arrested, this time making a confession.

Such was the enslaving power of credulity that

many of Rogers's followers remained for no little time steadfast in their delusions. At last, however, the confession of the leader resulted in their recovery from the delusion which had so long enchained them. Rogers escaped from the jail and left the State, never to return. Is it possible his now mortified and crestfallen victims connived at his escape and assisted him in his effort to flee the scenes of his "chymical" depredations?

Rogers is said to have realized about $1,500 from his practise, in Morristown and vicinity, by the art of "chymistry." In his operations he had "interested" and successfully duped a brave Revolutionary officer; an esteemed disciple of Blackstone; a Morristown justice of the peace; two local physicians in good practice; a local miller, not of the "Dee" but of the Whippanong; a Whippanong resident of substance, and had tried, but in vain, to "interest" two other residents of the latter place, one of them a subsequent member of Congress. A Dover justice of the peace was induced, but reluctantly and "without faith," to join the enterprise, but it is said he was shrewd enough to come out of it in improved condition, financially. And thus endi eth the story of the "Morristown Ghost," which has been related by the writer, not because of any pleasure experienced on his part, but being a phase of local history, it must needs be told.

Many of the American colonists found themselves in an impoverished condition at the close of the seven years' struggle for national independence. The people of Morris County, however, were in some respects more fortunate than those of other sections of the country, for their fields had not been devastated nor their dwellings destroyed by the enemy. Because of the prompt and energetic utilization of the resources of the county, its growth was rapid in population and in wealth. Nothing contributed more fully to this growth than the iron industry, for the development of which numerous forges were either rebuilt or built anew in various sections of the county. The log cabins of pre-Revolutionary and even Revolutionary times were superseded by more comfortable and, in not a few instances, by more pretentious houses. Better roads were made. The acreage of arable land was much increased and a new impetus given to agricultural pursuits. Additional schools were established throughout the county, including at the county seat a school for the fitting of young men for college. Several newspapers were also established.

In the year 1791 a new and more commodious meeting-house was completed by the Presbyterians. A picture of this meeting-house may be seen in this volume. It will be noticed that there was in this structure of 1791 but a single front entrance. A few years later, a large window was substituted for this central entrance; and two entrances, one on either side of the window, were made; as may be seen in other extant pictures of the building. It is through the courtesy of Harriet A. Freeman, a life-long resident of Morristown, and a member of the First Presbyterian Church, that we are able to offer to our readers this interesting picture of the old First Church edifice.

From the text: "I have fought a good fight, I have finished my course, I have kept the faith." Rev. Timothy Johnes, D. D., preached, in the year 1793 his half century sermon to a great congregation.

"In 1791, (the words of Rev. Rufus S. Green, D. D., appearing in 'History of Morris County,' are here quoted) he fractured his thigh bone by a fall, which confined him for months to his bed, and made him a cripple for the remainder of his life. After more than a year's confinement he was able to attend public worship. Aided by one or two of his elders he reached the desk, where, seated on a high cushioned chair, he would occasionally address the people. In this condition he preached in 1793 his half-century sermon to a crowded assembly, who came from all quarters to hear it. * * * In the delivery of that discourse he manifested unusual animation, and in the closing prayer he seemed to breathe out his whole soul in fervent petition for the peace, prosperity and salvation of his people. The service was closed by singing the 71st Psalm—'God of my childhood and my youth,' etc. In reading the first verse, said an eye-witness, 'his voice began to falter and became tremulous. He proceeded with much emotion, while the tears trickled over his venerable cheeks, and before he could utter the last line his voice seemed to die away amidst the sobs and tears of the whole assembly.'

"Seldom did he address his people after this. In the following winter, as he was riding to church on Sabbath morning, his sleigh was upset a short distance from his house, which broke his other thigh bone. He was carried to his home, and never left it till he was removed by the hands of others to the grave yard. He died September 15th, 1794, in the 78th year of his age, the 52nd of his pastorate and 54th of his ministry.

"His tombstone bears the following inscription: 'As a Christion few ever discovered more piety—as a minister few labored longer, more zealously or more successfully than did this minister of Jesus Christ.'

"During his pastorate of over half a century he received into the church 600 members and 572 half-way members, officiated at 2,827 baptisms, and 948 marriages, and disciplined 170 members."

From a manual of the First Presbyterian Church of Morristown, prepared by the Rev. Albert Barnes, D. D., in the year 1828, the following tribute to the Rev. Timothy Johnes, D. D., is quoted: "Few men have ever been more successful as ministers of the gospel than Dr. Johnes. To have been the instrument of founding a large and flourishing church; to have been regarded as its affectionate father and guide; to have established the ordinances of the gospel, and formed the people to respect its institutions; to have produced that outward order and morality and love of good institutions now observable in this congregation, was itself worthy of the toils of his life. In being permitted to regard himself as, under God, the originator of habits and good institutions which are to run into coming generations, he could not but look upon his toils as amply recompensed.

But he was permitted also to see higher fruit of the labor of his ministry. It pleased a gracious God, not only to grant a gradual increase of the church, but also at two different times to visit the congregation with a special revival of religion. The first occurred in 1764. * * * The second revival commenced in 1774. * * * In 1790 there was another season of unusual excitement on the subject of religion. * * *

In "History of Morris County," the Rev. Dr. Green further says: "Rev. Aaron C. Collins was settled January 6th, 1791, as colleague pastor of Dr. Johnes. He was dismissed after a brief and unpleasant pastorate, September 2d, 1793.

Rev. James Richards, D. D., was settled May 1st, 1795, and dismissed April 26th, 1809. * * * On the 21st of July, 1794, a call from this church was made and put into his hands, in which he was offered $440 salary in quarterly payments, the use of the parsonage and firewood. This was in due time accepted by him, and on the 1st of May, 1795 he was ordained and installed pastor of the church by the Presbytery of New York. * * * In November, 1795, the old church was taken down, vacated and sold in lots. A good part of it was converted into a distillery and cider-mill on Water Street. So great, so it was said, was the attachment of many of the members for it that they could not refrain from using it in its new location. On November 26th, 1795, Mr. Richards preached the first sermon in the new and present (1880) house. The old plan of rating and collecting was now discontinued; and in its place the pews were sold and assessed. The number purchasing or renting pews was 158, and sum paid was $533.35. The expenses for 1797, according to an old memorandum, were: Salary, $440; sweeping the church, $15; sexton, $15; cake for wood cutters, $19; printing, $2; 'Cyder,' $5.62. Total, 496.62. Cake and cider formed it would appear no inconsiderable part of the sum total of expenses. The minister was promised so much salary, parsonage and firewood. The 'wood-frolick,' as it was called, was a great event in the parish. It brought together the greater part of the congregation, the ladies preparing supper at the parsonage, which was heartily enjoyed by those who were busy during the day in bringing together the year's supply of fuel for their minister, which averaged about 40 cords. We find the amounts expended by the parish for these frolics in 1797, as seen above, to be for cake and cider, $24.62; in 1798, bread and beef, $18.94; in 1799, 1 cwt. of flour and 200 lbs. of beef, $10.83.

The spinning visit was similar in character, though we do not find that it was attended with expense to the parish. By this means there were collected together various amounts of linen thread, yard and cloth, proportioned to the 'gude' wife's ability or generosity. The thread was woven into cloth for the use and comfort of the pastor and his family, and as it was not always of the same texture and size it sometimes puzzled the weaver to make the cloth and finish it alike..

The meagerness of Mr. Richard's salary was a source of great perplexity to him as the expenses of his growing family increased, and finally led to his accepting a call from the First Presbyterian Church of Newark, N. J. During his pastorate of fourteen years he admitted to the Church on examination, 214, and on certificate 29. He baptized 444, and solemnized 251 marriages. At the time of his dismission the church numbered 298 members in full communion."

Rev. Reune Runyon, pastor of the Baptist church from 1771 to 1780, was succeeded by Rev. David Luffbury. "The year previous to his settlement, on the 27th of September, 1786, a considerable number of members residing in the neighborhood of Schooley's Mountain were dismissed to form an independent church, which was constituted under the name of Schooley's Mountain Church.

"Rev. David Jayne supplied the church once a month during the year 1791. In August of this year it was voted to join the New York Association, and send delegates to the convention of churches to meet in that city for the purpose of forming said association. From its organization to the present time (1880) the church has been united with the Philadelphia connection.

"Rev. William Vanhorne, was pastor of the Baptist

church of Morristown, from 1792 to 1807. Mr. Vanhorne, however, like his predecesors, supplied the pulpit only once a month, being during the time the pastor of the Scotch Plains church."

To the late Hon. Edmund D. Halsey, lovers of Morristown annals are indebted for the roll of a local militia company organized about the year 1791, which follows:

"A List of Capt. Joseph Halsey's Company Militia..

Morristown, 7 June, 1791.

Capt. Jos. Halsey, Lieut. William Johnes, Ens'n Dan'l Lindsly, Serg'ts. Jesse Cutler, Seth Gregory, Abijah Sherman, Zenas Lindsly, Corp'ls John Kirkpatrick, Isaac Hathaway, Timothy Fairchild, (Privates), Silas D. Hayward, William Marsh, Timothy Force, Sims Condict, David Humphrevil, Ebenezer Humphrevil, Samuel Ford, George F. Fenery, Silvanus Tuttle, Josiah Hathaway, Silas Baldwin, Samuel Ayers, Absalom Trowbridge, John Hathaway, David Trowbridge, Abraham Beers, John (2) Hathaway, Joseph Trowbridge, John Woodruff, Daniel Mills, Jobe Mills, Jacob Meeker, Isaac Walker, Shadrack Hayward, Timothy Extill, Daniel Coleman, David Mills, Jabez Guiness, Dave D. Budd, Thadeus Mills, James Vance, William Burnet, Matthias Crane, Uzal Pierson, Joseph Coleman, Isaac Woolley, Abraham Rutan, George Oharrow, Trune Goble, William Marshel, Hezekiah Mitchell, David G. Wheeler, Daniel Spenser, John Bollen, Elijah Holleway, Henry Feter, Joshua Gorden, John McDaniels, George Mills, Michael Conner, Silas Hathaway, Ichabod Crane, John Still, George Marsh, Thomas Jean."

The following statement concerning the origin of the famous Morris Academy is from "History of Morris County:

"The Morris Academy was organized November 28th, 1791. This was done by 24 gentlemen, who subscribed each one share of £25 for the purpose. The subscribers were Caleb Russell, Israel Canfield, Daniel Phoenix, Jr., Alexander Carmichael, Gabriel H. Ford, Timothy Johnes, Jr., Moses Estey, Jabez Campfield, William Campfield, (Rev.) Aaron C. Collins, Jonathan Hathaway, John Jacob Faesch, Richard Johnson, John Kinney, Abraham Kinney, Isaac Canfield, George Tucker, David Ford, Nathan Ford, Theodorus Tuthill, John Mills, Joseph Lewis, Jacob Arnold, Chilson Ford.

"The first board of proprietors consisted of Jabez Campfield, president; Caleb Russell, first director; Gabriel H. Ford, second director; Nathan Ford, third director; Daniel Phoenix, Jr., treasurer; and Joseph Lewis, clerk. Mr. Campfield resigned at the expiration of one month, and was succeeded by Mr. Russell.

"The contract for building the academy was let to Caleb Russell for $520. The lot was purchased from the First Presbyterian Church, as appears from the trustees' book: 'At a meeting of the trustees at the house of Caleb Russell, Esq., 5th day of September, 1792, the president, Mr. Lindsley, Mr. Ford, Mr. Mills, Mr. Johnson and Mr. Ogden being met, a deed being made out for one hundred feet of land in front and one hundred and thirty feet deep on the hill opposite the Conners land, agreeable to a vote of the parish requesting the trustees to act discretionary on this affair, the 22nd Feb. 1792—the said deed was then signed, conveying twenty-nine hundredths of an acre of land to the proprietors of the intended academy for the sum of thirty pounds Jersey money. Caleb Russell, Esq., gave his obligation for said sum.'

"After the building was completed Caleb Russell, although he was clerk of the county and had a variety of other business to attend to, consented to take charge of the academy as principal. On the 5th of November, 1792, the school opened, with 35 scholars as follows: Elias Riggs, Stephen Thompson,

Anthony Day, Henry P. Russell, Henry Axtell, David Bates, Munson Day, Charles Russell, Ezra Halsey, Richard B. Faesch, Jacob Stiles, Jacob Lewis, Timothy J. Lewis, James Wood, Nancy Lewis, Betsey Estey, David Estey, Phoebe, daughter of Jeduthan Day, Sally Conklin, Hannah Hathaway, Eleazer Hathaway, George W. Cook, Thomas Kinney, Henry Mills, David Stites William Beach, John P. Johnes, Alexander Phoenix, Silas Day, Robert M. Russell, Eliza P. Russell, Charles Freeman, Chilion Stiles.

"Mr. Russell continued in full charge of the school until the close of 1795, and in partial charge until August 1797. He graduated in 1770 at Princeton College, and studied law with Judge Robert Morris, of New Brunswick. He was appointed clerk of Morris county four terms of five years each. He died in office June 8, 1805, aged 56 years. Under him the academy took a very high rank, attracting scholars from New York, Philadelphia, Trenton, New Brunswick, Amboy, Charleston, S. C., and many other places. From November 5th 1792 to April 1795, he had a total of 269 scholars. In the eighth volume of the Proceedings of the New Jersey Historical Society the names of these students, together with those of their parents, are given in full. Among them will be found many who afterward distinguished themselves in Church and State.

"Mr. Russell was assisted by Elias Riggs, Henry Axtell and John Ball, who were among his first pupils, and also by John Woodruff.

"The prices of tuition were: For languages, mathematics and surveying, 25s. per quarter; for French, 30s. and 40s. per quarter; for English studies, 12s., 15s., and 16s. per quarter.

"Mr. Russell was succeeded in August 1797 by Rev. Samuel Whelpley, who continued in charge until 1805."

From the same authority we learn that "the first library in Morris County was established in 1792. On the 21st of

September of that year 11 inhabitants of the county seat met at the house of Benjamin Freeman, at Morristown, and 'advised and consulted' upon the propriety of organizing a society which should be called 'The Morris County Society for the Promotion of Agriculture and Domestic Manufactures.'

"Captain Peter Layton (a relic of the Revolution) was chosen chairman, and Colonel Russell, clerk. The constitution presented was rather defective. A committee was appointed to revise it. The meeting then adjourned to meet at Mr. Freeman's house on September 25th, 1792.

"One hundred people were present at this meeting. Samuel Tuthill was installed chairman with Colonel Russell again clerk. The constitution was read as revised, and was adopted. From it we take (Art. VIII) the following: 'Upon the application of any member of the society for a book he shall deliver him one, and at the same time take a promissory note for the same, to be returned in one (1) month from the time, on paying one shilling for every week overtime.' On October 7th, 1793, this was amended and the librarian was only to keep an account of the book taken. Article XI informs us that the dues were one dollar a year, 'to be paid on the first Monday in October of each year,' and that the stock was transferable. Ninety-seven of those present then signed the constitution, and a good portion of these paid several dollars over the dues for the sake of encouragement. The total receipts were $227.

"On October 1st, 1792, the election of officers came off. Samuel Tuthill was elected president; Joseph Lewis, vice-president; Dr. William Campfield, secretary; W. Campfield, librarian; Israel Canfield, treasurer. Six gentlemen were then elected a committee of correspondence.

"It was resolved that the society purchase three books, and a stamp for marking all books. 'They then adjourned.' The next meeting was April 1st, 1795, at which the by-laws were read and adopted, from which we learn that the librarian was to be at the library to deliver books on all days, Sundays excepted, 'from 6 A., M., to 9 P. M.,' and 'that he shall collect all dues in specie.' The society started with 96 volumes. At the end of the year the treasurer reported $35.47 on hand, and an addition of 20 volumes to the library."

The extracts following, unless otherwise stated, are from "History of Morris County":

"On the 24th of May 1797 the first number of the first newspaper of Morristown was issued. Caleb Russell was the prime mover in this enterprise, having purchased a printing press and secured the services of Elijah Cooper, a practical printer, to attend to the details of the business. The name of the paper was the Morris County Gazette, and it was issued by E. Cooper & Co. Cooper remained until November of the same year, when he left, and Mr. Russell continued sole editor. Early in 1798 he invited Jacob Mann, who had learned the printing business of Sheppard Kollock in Elizabethtown, to come to Morristown and take charge of the paper. The Morris County Gazette was continued until the 15th of May, 1798, when the name was changed to the Genius of Liberty. This paper was edited by Jacob Mann until May 14th, 1801.

"Morristown has had but few postmasters. The first was Frederick King, commissioned early in 1782 by Postmaster General Ebenezer Hazard. Henry King, his son, succeeded him on the 14th of June, 1792, receiving his commission from Postmaster General Timothy Pickering. He held the office 42 years."

"The first fire association of Morristown was organized July 26th, 1797. Its officers were: Samuel Tuthill, moderator; Joseph Lewis, clerk; Alexander Carmichael, Caleb Russell, Colonel Benoni Hathaway, Moses Estey, Captain David Ford and Dr. William Campfield, executive committee. How efficient this association proved and how long it continued we are unable to state."

"Among the attractions and advantages of Morristown as a place of residence its excellent and abundant water supply is not the least important.

"On November 16th, 1799 a charter of incorporation was granted to the following 'proprietors of the Morris Aqueduct': John Doughty, Wm. Campfield, James Richards, David Ford, Aaron Pierson, John Halsey, Wm. Johnes, Gabriel H. Ford, Henry King, Caleb Russell, Daniel Phoenix, Jr., Israel Canfield, Benjamin Freeman, David Mills, George O'Hara, Rodolphus Kent, Joseph Lewis, Lewis Condict, Abraham Canfield, Samuel Ogden, Elijah Holloway, Edward Mills, Wm. Tuttle, Matthias Crane, Jonathan Dickerson and Daniel Lindsley.

"From an editorial in the Genius of Liberty, November 21st, 1799, we condense the following: 'An aqueduct, four miles in length including its various branches, has been laid and completed in this town since the 20th of June last. The fountain is 100 feet above the town, on the north side of a small mountain covered with wood. The pipe has been laid 3 feet under ground, at an expense of between $2,000 and $3,000. The work was executed by Pelatiah Ashley, of West Springfield, Mass.

"This 'fountain' was on the 'Jockey Hollow' road (about one mile from town), where one of the reservoirs is now (1880) situated. The water was conducted from there to the town through brick tile. How many years this was continued we cannot say, but are informed that for many years the aqueduct was a dry one, and Morristown was again left dependent on wells, and so continued until the chartered right was purchased by James Wood, who repaired it and laid chestnut logs of two inches bore as the aqueduct, and had a small distributing 'reservoir'—a wooden cistern, capable of holding one hundred barrels of water—in town, on the Jockey Hollow road, now Western Avenue." "The younger generation knows little or nothing of the pleasures of stage coaches and bad roads. Previous to 1838 Morristonians reached the outside world only by this luxurious method of travel.

"Benjamin Freeman claims the honor of running the first stage from this place to Powles Hook (Jersey City). This was in 1798, or possibly 1797. For $1.25 the traveler could start from here at 6 A. M., on Tuesday or Friday, and be drawn by four horses through Bottle Hill (Madison), and thence to Chatham, where 'if he felt disposed he could take breakfast,' thence to Springfield, Newark, reaching Powles (also spelled Paulus) Hook sometime the same day according to circumstances. On Wednesday or Saturday he could return by the same route, and at the same price.

"John Halsey soon entered into partnership with this primitive Jehu. The profits of the enterprise must have been considerable, for the following year, 1799, Matthias Crane started a rival stage. We doubt however whether the rivalry of Matthias gave the original firm much anxiety, as he could only muster two horses. But other competitors arose. The columns of the papers of those early days abound with flaming advertisements of these rival concerns, not omitting descriptions of the beauties of their various routes. The majority of them ran to Powles Hook, but some only to Newark, from which places the passengers were transported by boat to New York."

"Previous to 1855 the Presbyterians interred their dead in the graveyard in the rear of the First Church, the Baptists theirs in the rear of their church, the Episcopalians in the graveyard of St. Peter's, and the

Methodists in a graveyard on the Basking Ridge road. A list of burials in the two yards first named was kept between the years 1768 and 1806, and published in a quaint old book called the 'Bill of Mortality,' of which the following is the title page:

'Bill of Mortality.

'Being a Register of all the Deaths which have occurred in the Presbyterian and Baptist congregations of Morristown, New Jersey, for the Thirty-Eight years past.—Containing (with but few exceptions) the cause of every decease.—This register, for the first twenty-two years, was kept by the Rev. Doctor Johnes, since which time by William Cherry, the present sexton of the Presbyterian Church of Morris Town.—'Time brushes off our lives with sweeping wings.'—Hervey. Morris Town, Printed by Jacob Mann, 1806.

'Note.—Those marked thus * were Church Members—thus † Baptists—thus * † Baptist Church Members.'

"A supplement was afterward added bringing the list down to 1812. * * * "The 'Bill of Mortality' contains a mournful list of 1,675 burials between the years 1768 and 1806.

* * * "The oldest of our cemeteries is that in the rear of the First Presbyterian Church. The pastor of that church has an incomplete list of over 4,000 burials in it. Large numbers of soldiers were buried in it during the Revolutionary war, of whom he has no knowledge. Large trenches were dug, and the dead

laid in them in rows. Old military buttons have been dug up in quantitites. The same is true of the Baptist yard."

George W. Fleury, a native and life-long resident of Morristown, informs the writer that when, in the year 1871, the remains of those buried in the old Baptist burying grounds in the rear of the church were disinterred for removal, William Beam found a calf-skin pocket book, home-made, containing an English razor, several English brass buttons, and four copper pennies with the inscription: 'St. George, Rex.' The pocket book was about 4x6 inches, and opened once. Mr. Fleury has one of the four pennies mentioned.

The oldest stone in the cemetery (that of the First Presbyterian Church) has the following inscription: 'Here Lyes ye Body of Martha, Wife of Abraham Parson Aged About 23 Years Decd Janry 2d 1731.' After a visit, a quarter century ago, to the burial grounds in the rear of the First Presbyterian Church, of Morristown, the visitor, in a very interesting account of the same, said: "The oldest date that I could discover upon a tombstone was 1722, but a friend informed me that he found a stone dated 1713, so it appears that this ground was used as a burial-place more than half a century before the time of the Revolutionary War."

"My pen is at the bottom of a page,
Which being finished, here the story ends;
'Tis to be wish'd it had been sooner done,
But stories somehow lengthen when begun."